Samuel Toombs

New Jersey Troops in the Gettysburg Campaign from June 5 to July 31, 1863

Samuel Toombs

**New Jersey Troops in the Gettysburg Campaign from June 5 to July 31, 1863**

ISBN/EAN: 9783337425272

Printed in Europe, USA, Canada, Australia, Japan

Cover: Foto ©ninafisch / pixelio.de

More available books at **www.hansebooks.com**

IN THE

# GETTYSBURG CAMPAIGN

## FROM JUNE 5 TO JULY 31, 1863.

— BY —

## SAMUEL TOOMBS,

AUTHOR OF "REMINISCENCES OF THE WAR," AND HISTORIAN OF THE
VETERAN ASSOCIATION, THIRTEENTH NEW JERSEY VOLUNTEERS.

---

### ILLUSTRATED

*By Specially Drawn Maps of the Battle-Field, the Monuments Erected by the State of New Jersey, and Portraits of Brigade and Regimental Commanders.*

ORANGE, N. J.:
THE EVENING MAIL PUBLISHING HOUSE.
1888.

Entered according to act of Congress, in the year 1887, by
SAMUEL TOOMBS,
In the office of the Librarian of Congress, at Washington, D. C.

PRINTED AND BOUND AT
THE ADVERTISER PRINTING HOUSE,
NEWARK, N. J.

TO THE MEMORY OF

THE GALLANT JERSEYMEN WHO SACRIFICED THEIR LIVES

AT THE BATTLE OF GETTYSBURG

FOR THE MAINTENANCE OF THE UNION THIS BOOK

IS REVERENTLY DEDICATED.

# INTRODUCTORY.

A GREAT deal has already been written about Gettysburg. The controversies which have arisen are confusing to those who wish to ascertain the exact truth, while they afford little that is interesting to the general public. Personal reminiscences of the events which there occurred have appeared in print in great number, and if it be true that "few events worth recording befell any man below the rank of major," the reader of this book will find relief in the fact that the writer has no wonderful or remarkable personal adventures to chronicle.

In its main features the battle of Gettysburg is treated very much the same by all the noted participants in that struggle who have written about it, varying only in details which are colored by the writer's own views as to their importance. In preparing for the work of recording the services of New Jersey troops, not only on the battlefield but throughout the whole campaign, beginning with the reconnoissance across the Rappahannock river on June 5, 1863, the best works on Gettysburg have been consulted and the official records of the battle have been examined and studied carefully, with the view of ascertaining just what services the soldiers of New Jersey did perform; and in thus bringing to the surface the experiences of the bivouac, the march, and the battle itself, as they were participated in by the men who represented the State of New Jersey in the Union Army, many interesting and valuable matters have been brought to light which otherwise might have perished.

While, therefore, the author has placed a certain limit upon the scope of this work, by which the valuable services rendered, the heroic achievements performed, and the personal sacrifices made by the patriotic sons of his native State on Gettysburg Heights are to be brought more particularly into prominence, the narrative will embrace the movements of the whole Army of the Potomac and record its priceless services to the Nation on the ground hallowed by the blood of thousands who met death as brave men wish to die.

The instances of personal bravery were more numerous at Gettysburg than in any other battle of the war. Both sides contributed their heroes, and the tragic manner in which the brave Southern General, Armistead, met his death, and the heroic Lieutenant Cushing fell at the post of duty, have already become immortalized as the two prominent instances of self-immolation during the struggle. There is a pathetic side to the death of Armistead, and there are those who believe he really courted it. When the news of the fall of Sumter reached the Pacific slope, the late Confederate General Albert Sidney Johnston was in command of that department. Generals Hancock, Armistead, Garnett and Pickett, were subordinate officers in the Regular Army, then stationed there, and many were the conferences held as to what should be their course in the pending troubles. The

Government very unceremoniously relieved General Johnston, and soon after this event a farewell meeting was held in the house of Captain Hancock. What resulted is thus related by Mrs. Hancock, in the volume of interesting "Reminiscences" of her husband: "The most crushed of the party was Major Armistead, who, with tears, which were contagious, streaming down his face, and hands upon Mr. Hancock's shoulders, while looking him steadily in the eye, said: 'Hancock, good-by; you can never know what this has cost me, and I hope God will strike me dead if I am ever induced to leave my native soil, should worse come to worst.'" The dying words of Armistead, on Gettysburg battle-field: "Tell Hancock I have wronged him and have wronged my country," illustrate how great must have been the mental strain under which he labored during the continuance of the war, and what a sacrifice he made when he resigned his commission in the Regular Army, to take up arms in the defence of the dogma of State rights, which recognized allegiance to the National Government only as secondary to that of the State. Scores of other southern officers did the same, and that they acted from conscientious and honest motives cannot well be denied; but as in the case of Armistead, many of them felt that the South had adopted the wrong method for a redress of their supposed grievances, and that the war was forced upon them from other than patriotic motives. In the manner of his death Armistead's wish was gratified. How different was the last act of young Cushing, who commanded Battery "A" Fourth United States Artillery, whose life blood ebbed away at almost the same moment that Armistead received his death wound. Mortally wounded though he was, he summoned up all his strength and running his gun down into the very faces of the exultant foe, he turned to his commander and said: "Webb, I will give them one more shot," and when the last discharge was made, called out, "good-by" and fell dead by the side of his gun. With the spirit that pervaded these men, both armies fought at Gettysburg, and it is easily understood why the several encounters which took place on all parts of that field were so stubbornly and so vigorously contested.

The State of New Jersey has commemorated the services of her troops in enduring granite. To supplement this work by a faithful and accurate account of the exhaustive nature of these services has been the desire of the writer, who has received the cordial coöperation of many of the survivors, and is largely indebted also to Adjutant-General W. S. Stryker, his faithful assistant, Colonel James S. Kiger, Honorable William H. Corbin, Secretary of the New Jersey Battle-Field Commission, General Ezra A. Carman, General W. H. Penrose, Colonel William E. Potter, Major W. W. Morris, Captain William F. Hillyer, Thomas S. Marbaker, Historian Eleventh New Jersey Regiment, Captain H. F. Chew, George J. Hagar, Esq., and many others, members of the several regimental organizations, for valuable information and aid furnished. The government maps of Colonel J. B. Bachelder have also been consulted and to them the writer is largely indebted, as well as to Colonel Bachelder himself for very important information received. The maps on pages 155, 157 and 162 are from General Doubleday's book on "Chancellorsville and Gettysburg," Charles Scribner's Sons, publishers, who have kindly given permission for their use. Those on pages 250, 251 and 301 are inserted only for general reference and do not conform literally to the text. The portraits, monuments and small maps were all made especially for this book from original photographs and drawings. S. T.

ORANGE, N. J., July 1, 1888.

NOTE.—The wrong totals appear at foot of table on page 11. They should be: Officers, 512; men, 12,311; total, 12,823. These figures increase the percentage of waste as shown on page 12, line seven, from sixty to sixty-five per cent.

On page 64, first word, last line, should be *southwest*.

On page 139, eighth line, Harrisburg should be *Gettysburg*.

# CONTENTS.

CHAPTER I.—New Jersey Regiments in the Army of the Potomac from 1861 to June 30, 1863, their assignments to duty and the commands with which they served — Tables showing losses for two years............................................. 1

CHAPTER II.—Resume of historical facts—Public feeling in the South—Temper of the Rebel Army—Position of both armies in June, 1863—The fight at Franklin's Crossing on the Rappahannock—Gallant charge by the Twenty-sixth New Jersey 16

CHAPTER III.—Lee's plan of campaign—Disposition of his forces —General Hooker mystified but not deceived—The cavalry fight at Brandy Station—The First New Jersey Cavalry's brilliant charge............................................. 34

CHAPTER IV.—Ewell's dashing advance through the valley—Milroy surprised at Winchester—The Fourteenth New Jersey on Maryland Heights—History of the corps badge—The New Jersey troops and their commanders—An exhaustive march.............................................................. 64

CHAPTER V.—Ewell at Williamsport — Jenkins' raid in Pennsylvania — Consternation throughout the North—New Jersey Volunteers go to the defence of Harrisburg — Hooker advances to a new line of observation—Incidents of the march—Execution of deserters—An incident of President Lincoln's mercy and why it failed... ........................ 79

CHAPTER VI.—From the Rappahannock to Gum Springs—Experiences of the Seventh New Jersey Regiment and the Second Brigade—Useless night work—An all-night march.......... 99

CHAPTER VII.—Hooker's perplexities aggravated—A dashing cavalry exploit — Lee's army in Pennsylvania — The Union forces cross the Potomac—Stuart's raid—General Hooker resigns................................................................. 108

CHAPTER VIII.—The alarm in the North—New Jersey's Governor appeals to the President—The new Union commander—Movements of the armies—Reminiscenses of an officer of the Second New Jersey Brigade — The Thirteenth New Jersey at Littlestown—The night before the battle............ 122

CHAPTER IX.—The first day's fight at Gettysburg—Gallantry of Buford's troopers — Heroic resistance by the First Army Corps—Death of General Reynolds—Arrival of Howard and the retreat to Cemetery Ridge—Hancock's opportune arrival on the field.................................................................. 140

CHAPTER X.—The New Jersey troops coming on the field of battle —Rapid and exhaustive marching—The Eleventh Regiment undergo a fatiguing night march—The Second New Jersey Brigade march between the skirmish lines of both armies—The Twelfth Regiment in line of battle—The deployment of Sickles' line—The Thirteenth Regiment on Culp's Hill—Arrival of the First New Jersey Brigade at four o'clock—A forced march of thirty-five miles................................. 174

CHAPTER XI.—The second day's battle—Sickles' new line—Longstreet's attempt to turn the Federal left—The Second New Jersey Brigade, the Eleventh Regiment, and Battery "B," First New Jersey Artillery, in action—Hood repulsed at Little Round Top—A gallant and successful charge by the Twelfth New Jersey Regiment—Casualties among the New Jersey troops.................................................................. 193

CHAPTER XII.—The second day's battle concluded—The Twelfth Corps' position attacked by Ewell's troops—Green's heroic defence—The attack on Cemetery Hill—A fierce and deadly hand-to-hand struggle—Return of the Twelfth Corps to the right during the night.............................................. 259

## CONTENTS.

CHAPTER XIII.—The Third day's battle — The Twelfth Corps charge the enemy at Culp's Hill and regain their works—The Second Massachusetts and the Twenty-seventh Indiana Regiments charge the enemy supported by the Thirteenth New Jersey Regiment—Lee foiled in his attack on the Federal right............................................................ 268

CHAPTER XIV.—The third day's battle concluded—Longstreet's charge on Cemetery Ridge—Disastrous repulse of Pickett's and Heth's divisions—Dreadful execution with "buck and ball" by the Twelfth New Jersey—Hexamer's old battery ("A" First New Jersey) engaged—The First New Jersey Cavalry win new laurels.................................................. 277

CHAPTER XV.—After the battle—Scenes on the field—The care of the wounded—Effect of General Meade's order sending all wagons to the rear—Prompt and effective service at the Twelfth Corps Hospital—Retreat of Lee's army and the pursuit...................................................................... 317

CHAPTER XVI.—Organization of the Gettysburg Battle-Field Commission—A record of its work—Description of the monuments........................................................................ 333

BIOGRAPHICAL SKETCHES OF PORTRAITS............................. 359

# ILLUSTRATIONS.

AUTHOR...............................................*Frontispiece.*

|  | PAGE. |
|---|---|
| Map—Location of New Jersey Monuments...................... | xvii |
| Major-General Joseph Hooker...................................... | 13 |
| Advance of Twenty-sixth New Jersey Volunteers............... | 23 |
| Captain Samuel U. Dodd........................................... | 29 |
| Major William W. Morris........................................... | 35 |
| Colonel Percy Wyndham............................................ | 43 |
| Major-General H. Judson Kilpatrick............................. | 53 |
| Colonel Hugh H. Janeway.......................................... | 59 |
| Lieutenant Rochus Heinisch........................................ | 67 |
| Major-General George G. Meade................................. | 75 |
| Major-General A. T. A. Torbert.................................. | 83 |
| Colonel James N. Duffy............................................. | 89 |
| Lieutenant-Colonel William Henry, Jr........................... | 95 |
| Colonel Samuel L. Buck............................................. | 101 |
| Colonel Henry N. Brown............................................ | 109 |
| Lieutenant-Colonel Charles Ewing................................ | 115 |
| Brevet Major-General William J. Sewell........................ | 123 |
| Colonel George C. Burling.......................................... | 131 |
| Colonel Louis R. Francine.......................................... | 141 |
| Map—Position of Troops July 1................................... | 145 |
| Brevet Major-General John Ramsey.............................. | 147 |
| Map—Advance of Davis' and Archer's Brigades................ | 155 |
| Map—Defeat of Davis and Archer................................ | 157 |
| Brevet Major-General Robert McAllister....................... | 159 |
| Map—Advance of Heth's Division against Doubleday........ | 162 |
| Brevet Colonel John Schoonover................................. | 165 |
| Major John T. Hill.................................................... | 175 |
| Map—First Position Thirteenth Regiment New Jersey Volunteers | 182 |

|  | PAGE. |
|---|---|
| Brevet Brigadier-General Ezra A. Carman | 185 |
| Brevet Brigadier-General Frederick H. Harris | 191 |
| Brevet Major A. Judson Clark | 203 |
| Map—Position of Fifth, Sixth, Seventh, Eighth, Eleventh New Jersey Regiments—July 2 | 207 |
| Captain Ambrose M. Matthews | 211 |
| Brigadier-General William H. Penrose | 217 |
| Monument First New Jersey Brigade | 229 |
| Monument Fifth Regiment New Jersey Volunteers | 233 |
| Monument Sixth Regiment New Jersey Volunteers | 245 |
| Map—The Fight for Little Round Top | 246 |
| Map—Ruger's Division Twelfth Corps | 248 |
| Map—Longstreet in Position for Attack on Sickles | 250 |
| Map—Union Line after Sickles' Defeat | 251 |
| Monument Seventh Regiment New Jersey Volunteers | 255 |
| Map—Repulse of Louisiana Tigers | 265 |
| Map—Fourth Position of Thirteenth Regiment New Jersey Volunteers | 267 |
| Monument Eighth Regiment New Jersey Volunteers | 269 |
| Map—Twelfth Corps Charging on Culp's Hill | 272 |
| Map—Last Position Thirteenth Regiment New Jersey Volunteers | 273 |
| Monument Eleventh Regiment New Jersey Volunteers | 289 |
| Map—Repulse of Longstreet's Charge July 3—Position of Twelfth New Jersey Volunteers | 283 |
| Marker Twelfth Regiment New Jersey Volunteers at Bliss Barn | 291 |
| Brevet Lieutenant-Colonel William E. Potter | 295 |
| Map—The General Line of Battle at time of Pickett's Charge | 301 |
| Map—New Jersey Regiments—July 2 | 310 |
| Monument Twelfth Regiment New Jersey Volunteers | 311 |
| Monument Thirteenth Regiment New Jersey Volunteers | 319 |
| Surgeon J. J. H. Love | 323 |
| New Jersey Battle-Field Commission | 335 |
| Monument Battery "A" (Parsons') First New Jersey Artillery | 339 |
| Monument Battery "B" (Clark's) First New Jersey Artillery | 349 |
| Monument First New Jersey Cavalry | 357 |

## CHAPTER I.

NEW JERSEY REGIMENTS IN THE ARMY OF THE POTOMAC FROM 1861 TO JUNE 30, 1863, THEIR ASSIGNMENTS TO DUTY AND THE COMMANDS WITH WHICH THEY SERVED — TABLES SHOWING LOSSES FOR TWO YEARS.

THE patriotism of the citizens of New Jersey during the stormy period of 1861–65, was attested on many occasions, not alone by the valor of her soldiery on scores of battle-fields, but by the promptness with which the people responded to the call of the National Government for troops, and the thorough manner in which the several organizations were armed and equipped before leaving the State. No appeal by the general government was ever made to the State authorities for assistance in vain. Governor Olden coöperated heartily and cordially with the President and Secretary of War in all their efforts to suppress the rebellion in its infancy, and at the very outbreak of hostilities forwarded to Washington a brigade of four regiments, aggregating three thousand men, for three months' service under command of General Theodore Runyon. This brigade was fully armed and equipped at the expense of the State and was the first completely equipped body of troops to make its appearance at the National Capital, where it was greeted with the utmost gratification by the President. The Secretary of War feelingly appreciated the promptness of the State authorities in so generously and effectively aiding the National Government in its efforts to preserve its own integrity, and in a letter to Governor Olden cordially acknowledged the great service thus rendered, and in the name of the government tendered its sincere thanks to the people of the commonwealth.

The theory entertained by the National authorities that the rebellion would be crushed out in three months' time soon proved erroneous. The rebellious states waxed bolder and bolder in their defiance of the National Government and resisted every offer of peace so determinedly, that a call was issued for thirty-nine regiments of infantry and one of cavalry to serve for three years or during the war, the quota for New Jersey being three regiments of infantry. Before another month had expired a second demand was made upon the State, this time for five additional regiments, all to serve for the same period of time. Under these calls there were promptly raised two brigades of infantry and two batteries of artillery, as follows:

First Regiment—Colonel, William R. Montgomery.
Second Regiment—Colonel, George W. McLean.
Third Regiment—Colonel, George W. Taylor.

Fourth Regiment—Colonel, James H. Simpson.
Battery "A" First New Jersey Artillery—Captain William Hexamer, Commanding.

These regiments formed the First New Jersey Brigade, and were assigned to duty with Franklin's Division. General Philip Kearny was commissioned by Governor Olden and placed in command of the brigade. The Second Brigade was composed of the following:

Fifth Regiment—Colonel, Samuel H. Starr.
Sixth Regiment—Colonel, James T. Hatfield.
Seventh Regiment—Colonel, Joseph W. Revere.
Eighth Regiment—Colonel, Adolphus J. Johnson.
Battery "B" First New Jersey Artillery—Captain John E. Beam, Commanding.

This brigade was assigned to Hooker's Division where it became a great favorite and was eventually known as "Hooker's Old Guard." It formed the Third Brigade of the Second Division, Third Army Corps, and was commanded by Colonel Starr of the Fifth Regiment, the senior officer.

Rapidly as these organizations were formed the opportunities presented for enlistment were not sufficient to satisfy the desires of a great many who were anxious to go to the war. Thousands of Jerseymen enlisted in the regiments of other States, and whole companies left Newark, Elizabeth, Rahway, Orange and other places and were incorporated with

New York and Pennsylvania regiments and credited to those States.

The Ninth Regiment was specially authorized by the War Department as a rifle regiment, and in a short time its ranks were full. Under the command of Colonel Joseph W. Allen it proceeded to North Carolina, as part of the Burnside Expedition, gaining immediate renown at the Battle of Roanoke Island.

The War Department also gave direct authority for the raising of an infantry regiment in the State, to be known as the "Olden Legion." The Governor strenuously opposed this movement, and would have nothing whatever to do with it. Finally the State agreed to accept it and the Governor commissioned William R. Murphy its Colonel, and designated it as the Tenth Regiment.

In August 1861, a regiment of cavalry known as "Halstead's Horse" was ordered to be recruited in the State by the direct authority of President Lincoln, and the companies as soon as formed were forwarded to Washington. Like the Tenth Infantry, dissatisfaction, wrangling and vexation ensued, and finally the State authorities were prevailed upon to accept it, when it became the First New Jersey Cavalry with Sir Percy Wyndham as its Colonel.

On July 7th, 1862, a call was issued for three hundred thousand men to serve for three years or during the war, under which the following organizations were formed and sent to Washington:

Eleventh Regiment—Colonel, Robert McAllister.
Twelfth Regiment—Colonel, Robert C. Johnson.
Thirteenth Regiment—Colonel, Ezra A. Carman.
Fourteenth Regiment—Colonel, William S. Truex.
Fifteenth Regiment—Colonel, Samuel Fowler.

Instead of brigading these troops together, the exigencies of the service demanded their immediate presence in Washington as soon as possible after their muster-in. The Eleventh Regiment was assigned to Carr's Brigade, Sickles' Division, Third Army Corps; the Twelfth Regiment to the Second Brigade, Third Division, Second Army Corps; the Thirteenth Regiment to Gordon's Brigade, Williams' Division, Banks' Corps; the Fourteenth Regiment to a Provisional Brigade, Middle Division, Eighth Army Corps; and the Fifteenth to the First New Jersey Brigade, First Division, Sixth Army Corps.

The State had shown commendable promptness in forwarding its troops to the seat of war, and the repeated calls upon the people for volunteer soldiers were responded to with alacrity. The total number of three years troops furnished to the Government by New Jersey up to this period amounted to six hundred and twenty-eight officers and fifteen thousand two hundred and seventy-seven enlisted men; total fifteen thousand nine hundred and five. These figures are from the Adjutant General's report, the original muster of each regiment being as follows:

| ORGANIZATION. | OFFICERS. | MEN. | TOTAL. |
|---|---|---|---|
| First Regiment Cavalry | 44 | 998 | 1,042 |
| First Regiment Artillery Battery A | 5 | 151 | 156 |
| First Regiment Artillery Battery B | 5 | 159 | 164 |
| First Regiment Infantry | 38 | 996 | 1,034 |
| Second Regiment Infantry | 38 | 1,006 | 1,044 |
| Third Regiment Infantry | 38 | 1,013 | 1,051 |
| Fourth Regiment Infantry | 38 | 871 | 909 |
| Fifth Regiment Infantry | 38 | 823 | 861 |
| Sixth Regiment Infantry | 38 | 860 | 898 |
| Seventh Regiment Infantry | 38 | 882 | 920 |
| Eighth Regiment Infantry | 38 | 851 | 889 |
| Ninth Regiment Infantry | 42 | 1,115 | 1,157 |
| Tenth Regiment Infantry | 35 | 883 | 918 |
| Eleventh Regiment Infantry | 39 | 940 | 979 |
| Twelfth Regiment Infantry | 39 | 953 | 992 |
| Thirteenth Regiment Infantry | 38 | 899 | 937 |
| Fourteenth Regiment Infantry | 39 | 968 | 1,007 |
| Fifteenth Regiment Infantry | 38 | 909 | 947 |
| | 628 | 15,277 | 15,905 |

With the single exception of the Ninth Regiment these organizations all served, at one time or another, with the Army of the Potomac in the field, and deducting the number represented by the Ninth Regiment, the actual number of men furnished by New Jersey to that Army was five hundred and eighty-six officers and fourteen thousand one hundred and sixty-two enlisted men, a total of fourteen thousand seven hundred and forty-eight. The First and Second New Jersey Brigades followed the fortunes of the Army of the Potomac through all its checkered career from the Peninsula campaign under McClellan to the surrender of Lee at Appomattox, winning imperishable renown on scores of battle-fields for their bravery, endurance and fighting qualities.

The defeat of General Pope at the second battle of Bull Run filled the people of the North with dismay, and the authorities at Washington with fear for the safety of the Capital. On the 4th of August, 1862, the President issued a call for three hundred thousand men for nine months' service, a draft being ordered to take place on September 1st ensuing, if the number required were not sooner furnished by volunteers. The quota for New Jersey under this call was placed at ten thousand four hundred and seventy-eight, and orders were at once issued to proceed with the recruiting of this number. At the same time the State was engaged in filling its quota under the previous call of July 7th for three year troops, and in order to meet this extra emergency, city, township and county officials, offered liberal inducements for men to take service in these commands, and thus avoid the draft so imperatively ordered. On the third day of September the Adjutant-General announced the formation of eleven regiments for nine months' service, with an aggregate of ten thousand seven hundred and fourteen men, all volunteers, and being an excess of two hundred and thirty-six over the number called for. These regiments were numbered, officered and assigned to duty as follows:

Twenty-first Regiment—Colonel, Gillian Van Houten; assigned to Third Brigade, Second Division, Sixth Army Corps.

Twenty-second Regiment—Colonel, Cornelius Fornet; assigned to duty in the Defences of Washington, and afterward to the Third Brigade, First Division, First Army Corps.

Twenty-third Regiment—Colonel, John S. Cox; assigned to the First New Jersey Brigade, First Division, Sixth Army Corps.

Twenty-fourth Regiment—Colonel, William B. Robertson; assigned to duty first in the Defences of Washington, and afterward with Kimball's Brigade, French's Division, Couch's (Second) Corps.

Twenty-fifth Regiment—Colonel, Andrew Derrom; assigned to Second Brigade of Casey's Division, and afterward to First Brigade, Third Division, Ninth Army Corps.

Twenty-sixth Regiment—Colonel, A. J. Morrison; assigned first to Briggs' Brigade, Sumner's Corps, and next to the First Vermont Brigade (General Brooks), Second Division, Sixth Army Corps.

Twenty-seventh Regiment—Colonel, George W. Mindil; assigned to Casey's Division and next to Second Brigade, First Division, Ninth Army Corps.

Twenty-eighth Regiment—Colonel, Moses N. Wisewell; assigned to First Brigade, Third Division, Second Army Corps.

Twenty-ninth Regiment—Colonel, Edwin F. Applegate; assigned to various duties around Washington, and finally to Third Brigade, First Division, First Army Corps.

Thirtieth Regiment—Colonel, Alexander E. Donaldson, and Thirty-first Regiment, Colonel A. P. Berthoud, brigaded with the Twenty-second and Twenty-ninth Regiments, as part of the Third Brigade, First Division, First Army Corps.

With the addition of these troops the number of men contributed to the Government reached the very respectable figure of twenty-five thousand two hundred and fifty-seven, all volunteers, of whom twenty-three thousand one hundred and sixteen were accredited to the Army of the Potomac.

These new regiments, put right into the field with veterans who had served under McClellan on the Peninsula campaign and at Antietam, rendered valuable and efficient service under Burnside at the dreadful slaughter of Fredericksburg, with Hooker at the ill-fated battle of Chancellorsville, and with Sedgewick at Marye's Heights and Salem Church. They passed through all the rugged and trying experiences to be found in active campaigning in the immediate presence of the enemy, and had just become fully inured to the hardships and trials of a soldier's life when their term of service expired. At about the same time the terms of service of a large number of two years troops also expired, and with this large depletion, after the battle of Chancellorsville, the Army of the Potomac was weakened to a considerable extent. The casualties which the older three year regiments had sustained during their severe service, reduced some of them to mere skeletons, not a regiment of the original eight in both New Jersey brigades numbering more than four hundred men after the battle of Chancellorsville, while the average for all would not be greater than three hundred each. The official returns are not accessible for a verification of this statement, but the reports of the several New Jersey regiments made on the 30th day of June, 1863, just before the battle of Gettysburg opened, are sufficient for the purpose of comparison. The following data, taken from the original rolls at the War Department, Washington, and on file at the Adjutant-General's office, of this State, at Trenton, shows the strength of each New Jersey regiment and battery to have been on the date named:

NUMBER OF MEN OF EACH NEW JERSEY BATTERY AND REGIMENT, ARMY OF THE POTOMAC, PRESENT FOR DUTY JUNE 30, 1863.

| ORGANIZATIONS. | OFFIC'RS. | MEN. | TOTAL. |
|---|---|---|---|
| First Regiment Cavalry | 18 | 216 | 234 |
| First Regiment Artillery Battery A | 4 | 112 | 116 |
| First Regiment Artillery Battery B | 4 | 139 | 143 |
| First Regiment Infantry | 26 | 266 | 292 |
| Second Regiment Infantry | 28 | 377 | 405 |
| Third Regiment Infantry | 26 | 299 | 325 |
| Fourth Regiment Infantry (Train Guard) | 20 | 274 | 294 |
| Fourth Reg't Infantry (1st Div. 6th Corps) | 4 | 88 | 92 |
| Fifth Regiment Infantry | 15 | 206 | 221 |
| Sixth Regiment Infantry | 13 | 233 | 246 |
| Seventh Regiment Infantry | 22 | 309 | 331 |
| Eighth Regiment Infantry | 13 | 185 | 198 |
| Eleventh Regiment Infantry | | | 275 |
| Twelfth Regiment Infantry | 25 | 507 | 532 |
| Thirteenth Regiment Infantry | 28 | 332 | 360 |
| Fifteenth Regiment Infantry | 21 | 420 | 441 |
| Total | 267 | 3,963 | 4,505 |

The total strength of these commands as it appears by the preceding table, compared with the number of men furnished by the original muster of each regiment, will show the great depletion to which they had been subjected in their past service. The First and Second Brigades had suffered greatly from sickness brought on by exposure during the Peninsula campaign, and when to the casualties thus occasioned is added the losses by death, and those killed in action or dying from wounds received in battle, with the discharges made necessary by disability of various kinds, the percentage of waste during the previous two years' experience will be found very large.

To show the relative condition of the New Jersey troops at the beginning of the battle of Gettysburg with their entry into the service, the original figures of these fifteen commands are here reproduced:

ORIGINAL MUSTER.

| ORGANIZATIONS. | OFFICERS. | MEN. | TOTAL. |
|---|---|---|---|
| First Regiment Cavalry | 44 | 998 | 1,042 |
| First Regiment Artillery, Battery A. | 5 | 151 | 156 |
| First Regiment Artillery, Battery B. | 5 | 159 | 164 |
| First Regiment Infantry | 38 | 996 | 1,034 |
| Second Regiment Infantry | 38 | 1,006 | 1,044 |
| Third Regiment Infantry | 38 | 1,013 | 1,051 |
| Fourth Regiment Infantry | 38 | 871 | 909 |
| Fifth Regiment Infantry | 38 | 823 | 861 |
| Sixth Regiment Infantry | 38 | 860 | 898 |
| Seventh Regiment Infantry | 38 | 882 | 920 |
| Eighth Regiment Infantry | 38 | 851 | 889 |
| Eleventh Regiment Infantry | 39 | 940 | 979 |
| Twelfth Regiment Infantry | 39 | 953 | 992 |
| Thirteenth Regiment Infantry | 38 | 899 | 937 |
| Fifteenth Regiment Infantry | 38 | 909 | 947 |
|  | 436 | 10,503 | 10,939 |

Out of these ten thousand nine hundred and thirty-nine officers and men of New Jersey in the Army of the Potomac, mustered into the service at various times in 1861-62 to serve for three years or during the war, there were reported "Present for duty" on June 30th, 1863, but four thousand five hundred and five, a loss of about sixty per cent. The number of men on special service, and those "Absent without leave" during that period, would account for only a small fraction of this percentage, and the record of all these organizations will bear the closest scrutiny for trying and exhaustive service in campaigning and in actual conflict with the enemy. It had not been the policy of the State authorities to recruit men to fill up the losses in the old regiments, and they were continually being weakened by various causes.

The men who went to the war in 1861 and 1862, were governed by love of country and hatred of the heresy of Secession. They were the representatives of a principle, and embodied in their service the patriotic sentiment of the time. No danger was too great, no trial too severe, but found them ready and willing to undertake its performance, and in the case of hundreds of these patriotic men, when their term of service expired they reënlisted for the whole war. This was the class of men who confronted Lee's army on the heights of Gettysburg. They had become used to defeat, but they could not be dismayed. Their faith in the ultimate success of the cause they espoused never wavered, though the rebel army was devastating the

MAJOR-GENERAL JOSEPH HOOKER,
Commander Army of the Potomac.
Resigned, June 27, 1863.

loyal State of Pennsylvania. Each report that came to their ears of the destructive march of Lee's army through the North only nerved these men to a higher sense of the responsibilities which devolved upon them, and in spite of all the discouragements of the past the Army of the Potomac never felt itself better able to cope with its old antagonist than on those fateful days of July, 1863.

## CHAPTER II.

RESUME OF HISTORICAL FACTS—PUBLIC FEELING IN THE SOUTH—TEMPER OF THE REBEL ARMY—POSITION OF BOTH ARMIES IN JUNE, 1863—THE FIGHT AT FRANKLIN'S CROSSING ON THE RAPPAHANNOCK—GALLANT CHARGE BY THE TWENTY-SIXTH NEW JERSEY.

THE battle of Waterloo put an end to the ambitious career of Napoleon the First. Gettysburg destroyed the hopes of the South for the establishment of a Confederacy of States. And the South was full of hope in 1863. From the commencement of hostilities, two years before, the prestige of success—or rather that which amounted to the same thing, the failure of the National Government to crush out the rebellion in the East—was with General Lee and his army. The fortunate arrival of reinforcements at the first battle of Bull Run stemmed the tide of retreat in the southern army, and the advance of these fresh arrivals upon the demoralized Federals, turned their retreat into a rout and gave the victory to the Confederates. The Peninsula campaign resulted in fresh laurels for the southern troops, and General Lee's audacious advance through the valley, and the marshalling of his forces on the field of Manassas, a second time at Bull Run driving the Union army within the defences of Washington, gave added lustre to his growing fame. What feeling of opposition had existed in the South toward the schemes of the political leaders who had raised the standard of revolt against the National authority had been silenced by the victorious progress of the Army of Northern Virginia, and when the Maryland campaign was inaugurated it received the sanction of the Confederate authorities and the plaudits of the southern people. There was a general belief in the South that Lee's army once in the State of Maryland, thousands of sympathizers would flock to swell the ranks of the southern forces, and with this host of enthusiastic adherents an army of invasion could be formed which would compel the Government to recognize the Southern Confederacy and treat with it for a cessation of hostilities.

The sorest defeat for the South was not the loss of Antietam, it was the knowlege, dearly gained, that the people of Maryland were not so demonstratively sympathetic with the cause of the Confederacy as the leaders of public opinion in the South had supposed. The successful retreat of General Lee, with his whole army, into Virginia, was additional evidence of his military ability, and while "Maryland, my Maryland," was lost forever to the South, General Lee's army never admitted that Antietam was otherwise a sore defeat. It was practically a drawn battle, with the advantage, if any, on the side of the Army of the Potomac. Lee's defence of Fredericksburg Heights in the December which followed, and the defeat of the Union army with great loss—followed in May, 1863, with his remarkable victory at Chancellorsville—stimulated the war feeling of the South and awakened an enthusiasm such as had never before been witnessed there. So intense was the feeling, so confident the leaders, that the invasion of the North by the Confederate army was demanded by the press of the South and by public opinion. It was known that the term of service of many regiments in the Union army was about to expire, and the crushing defeats that had recently been sustained by the Army of the Potomac were not conducive to reënlistment. Besides this, a feeling of despondency had settled over the North, the faction that had been opposing the war were growing bolder in their utterances, and an invasion of the North, it was believed, would so excite the fears of these people that extraordinary efforts to arouse public opinion in favor of peace at any price would result. With a divided public opinion in the North, the southern army safely entrenched on northern territory, the actual transfer of the seat of war to northern soil must result, it was believed, in a settlement of the conflict, and on terms satisfactory to the South. The invasion of Pennsylvania was not for the purpose of receiving accessions to the southern army, but to conquer a peace. The movement had the sanction of military precedent, was cordially indorsed by the Confederate authorities, aroused the enthusiasm of the soldiery, and stimulated the overweening confidence of the southern people to a firm belief in its ultimate success. Armed reinforcements and recruits eagerly joined the forces of General Lee, and buoyant with hope, exultant and confident, the Confederate army left their camps on the Rappahannock, while the prayers and fervent hopes of a united South bid them God-speed in their mission.

The temper of the southern army at this time is thus tersely expressed by Alfriend: "The Army of Northern Virginia, a compact and puissant force, seventy thousand strong, which had never yet known defeat, instinctively expected the order for advance into the enemy's country. Never was the *morale* of the army so high, never had it such confidence in its own prowess, and in the resources of its great commander, and never was entrusted to its valor a mission so grateful to its desires as that tendered by President Davis 'to force the enemy to fight for their own Capital and homes.'"

The Union army on the first of June was posted on the north bank of the Rappahannock river, while the rebel army was on the south side, mainly concentrated about Fredericksburg. As preliminary to the general movement Lee, with strategic skill, began the massing of his forces at Culpepper, leaving A. P. Hill's division at Fredericksburg to mask the movement. General Hooker was wary and suspicious, and from the nature of the reports brought to him by his scouts, he was confident an important movement was contemplated by Lee. He ordered a reconnoissance in force by the Sixth Army Corps, Howe's division of which was to cross the Rappahannock June 5th, while Wright's and Newton's divisions were to take position on the north bank of the river, in support.

This was to be the initial movement of the Gettysburg campaign on the part of the Union forces, and by it the valor of New Jersey troops was once more to be tested. The Twenty-sixth Regiment, which formed part of Grant's brigade of Howe's division, had been mustered into the service on the 18th of September, 1862, and its term of service, nine months, was about expiring. It had taken part in the two previous engagements at Fredericksburg on December 13th and 14th, 1862, under Burnside, and May 3rd, 1863, under Hooker, and also in the engagement at Salem Church on May 4th, 1863, in which last battle the command sustained a loss of 124—killed, wounded and missing.

The point at which the crossing of the Rappahannock was to be made was known as "Franklin's Crossing," three miles below the town of Fredericksburg. General A. P. Hill, the Confederate commander, had constructed a line of earth-works along the south bank of the river which were occupied by a strong force, and when Howe's division reached the stream the engineer corps were preparing to lay the pontoons over which the command was to cross. It was five o'clock in the evening when the column reached the river bank, and artillery was at once posted in a commanding position to sweep the open plain between the enemy's works and the woods beyond. While these preparations were being made on the north side of the river, the enemy sent forth a strong reinforcement to the rifle-pits. As they deployed out of the woods and moved across the plain to the works near the river bank, the Union artillery opened fiercely upon them, but without repelling their advance. The fire from their works was fierce and accurate, and it soon became evident that nothing short of a direct assault could force them from their position. The efforts of the engineer corps to launch their boats were futile, and General Howe organized a storming column, consisting of the Fifth Vermont and Twenty-sixth New Jersey regiments, with instructions to cross the river in boats and drive the enemy from the rifle-pits. General Howe sent for Lieutenant-Colonel Martindale, then in command of the Twenty-sixth, and as he gave him the instructions he was to follow complimented him and his command very highly, saying, "In a few days your term of service will be over and you will return home to your friends with an untarnished reputation for gallantry and covered with glory." The column formed within seventy-five yards of the river bank, the Fifth Vermont on the right, the Twenty-sixth on the left, and under a severe fire from the enemy. The artillery ceased firing, the advance was begun, the Fifth Vermont moved rapidly down a narrow gulch to the river bank, while the Twenty-sixth went down a road cut parallel with the river and fully exposed to the enemy's fire. The Twenty-sixth rushed gallantly down, crossed the narrow margin of the flats that bordered the river, where they found that the engineers had launched but seven of the boats. The regiment was now in a perilous position. Crowded together in a small space at the river bank, they were exposed to a galling and murderous fire, and as the engineers boldly rushed to the river to aid in launching the rest of the boats several of their number were killed and wounded. To remain inactive now was suicide. Captain Samuel U. Dodd, of Company H, being on the right of the line, sprang into the first boat, followed by Lieutenant Dodd and as many of his men as could find room in it, and pushed out in the stream. Ordering his men to protect themselves below the gunwales of the boat, Captain Dodd directed its course to the opposite bank. He was a man of large stature, a conspicuous mark for the enemy's fire, and as the boat reached the middle of the river he received a mortal wound, dying the next day. Immediately following came a boat with the Major of the Fifth Vermont and a detachment from that regiment, next in order being Captain Stephen C. Fordham and Captain Peter F. Rogers with several men of the Twenty-sixth. Major William W. Morris, with men from several companies, filled another boat, and Captain Samuel H. Pemberton, in charge of the fourth boat, followed by three other

Advance of the 26th Regiment N. J. Vols. across the Rappahannock River, June 5, 1863.

boats filled with men of the Twenty-sixth, moved boldly to the opposite side. Lieutenant-Colonel Martindale superintended the launching of the other boats, and the men of Captains Hunkele, McIntee, Harrison, Sears and Pearson's companies did herculean work in dragging the immense frames to the river. It was nearly seven o'clock when the boats reached the opposite bank and, without waiting for the whole command to get over, a movement upon the works was at once begun. There was an eager rivalry between the Vermonters and Jerseymen as to which should gain the rifle-pits first. Major Morris, with a portion of the Twenty-sixth, charged rapidly up to the enemy's lines, as did the Fifth Vermont. The rebels saw that retreat across the plain was hopeless. The Sixth Corps artillery commanded the whole position between them and the woods beyond, and they surrendered. Major Morris, without waiting to note how many prisoners were captured, at once deployed his men as skirmishers along the Bowling Green road. Lieutenant-Colonel Martindale brought the rest of the regiment up as soon as they had crossed over and they were posted as pickets for the rest of the night. The action was spirited, brave and gallant, and to the Twenty-sixth is undoubtedly due the honor of being first in the enemy's works, though the report of Colonel Grant seeks to give that credit to the Fifth Vermont, who turned in to him all the prisoners taken. The casualties in the Twenty-sixth were 2 killed and 17 wounded, as follows:

*Killed.*

Company H—Captain, Samuel U. Dodd.
" I—Private, Joseph H. Ainsworth.

*Wounded.*

Company B—Corporal, William H. Brown; Privates, William Small, William Delaney, Martin V. B. Sandford, Dwight Stent, Henry L. Johnson.
" C—Robert Wallace.
" D—William Davis, David Mintonge.
" E—Henry Berner.
" F—Corporal, William Egbertson.
" G—Sergeant, George S. Force.
" H—David F. Horton.
" I—Joseph De Camp, George W. Griffin, Horace Goble.
" K—Aaron G. Mead.

The following is the official report of Lieutenant-Colonel Martindale, concerning the action of the regiment:

HEADQUARTERS 26TH NEW JERSEY VOLUNTEERS,
In the Field near Fredericksburg, Va.,
June 8th, 1863.

*Lieutenant C. H. Forbes, Assistant Adjutant-General:*

SIR—Of the part taken by this regiment in the recent operations across the Rappahannock, a report of which I am desired to forward, I have the honor to state as follows:

On the afternoon of the 5th instant the regiment was ordered to march from its camp near White Oak Church and move with the brigade toward Fredericksburg. Arriving near the old crossing point (Franklin's), next below the town, it was formed in line of battle under fire of the enemy's riflemen, who were posted in earth-works near the south bank. Here we suffered our first loss in killed and wounded. Immediately afterward the order was given to charge down the road to the river, under cover of a heavy fire from our artillery, push across the pontoons and carry the line of rifle-pits occupied by the enemy. This order was executed at once, in a spirited manner, under a galling fire from the enemy's earth-works. This regiment and the Fifth Vermont had been ordered to cross the river together, but the right of the Twenty-sixth New Jersey having reached the river bank a little in advance, its first two companies were the first to enter the boats, cross over and charge up the opposite bank. A portion of our right company (H) was the first of our regiment to enter the enemy's intrenchments, which they did at the same moment with the Fifth Vermont, capturing a considerable number of prisoners. A line of skirmishers was immediately pushed out to the front, and the whole regiment was deployed in and beyond the Bowling Green road until the morning of the 6th instant, when it was relieved, placed in line of battle, resting upon Deep Run, and so continued until the evening of the 7th, when the regiment was ordered back to the left bank of the Rappahannock. Our casualties were 2 killed and 17 wounded. Among the killed I am deeply grieved to be compelled to mention Captain Samuel U. Dodd, of Company H, who fell a sacrifice to his gallant and conscientious devotion to duty while bravely leading his company in the first boat across the river. The loss to his company and regiment is irreparable, but the good influence of his noble example and character will endure for all time.

It gives me particular pleasure to call your attention to the fidelity and good conduct of Major Morris, in every requirement of duty, both in crossing and forming upon the opposite bank, and particularly upon the trying and exhausting duty of the skirmish line.

Of the line officers, while many are justly entitled to great praise for meritorious conduct, I desire to call your particular attention to the conspicuous gallantry and spirited conduct of Captain Stephen C. Fordham, of Company A, who distinguished himself both in the attack upon the enemy's intrenchments and the advance to the extreme front of the line of skirmishers. Also to that of Lieutenant John Dodd, of Company H, who distinguished himself in like manner, and was the first man of either regiment to plant his foot upon shore in crossing the river.

I have the honor to be,
Respectfully your obedient servant,
E. MARTINDALE,
Lieutenant-Colonel Commanding Regiment.

The conspicuous gallantry of Captain Fordham is well illustrated by the following incident:

CAPT. SAMUEL UZAL DODD,
Co. H, 26th N. J. Vols., Inf.
(*From a War-time Photograph.*)

When the boat containing Major Morris and his men had reached within a few feet of the river bank Captain Fordham, who had accompanied a part of the regiment over in a previous boat, stepped from under the bank of the river and asked what the command should next do? The Major responded, "Wait, Captain, until I land." Just at that moment the Major of the Fifth Vermont, hearing Captain Fordham's call for orders, started up the road in the direction of the enemy's works. Captain Fordham saw the movement, and taking one man with him, started off to get in advance of the Vermonter, and as they came abreast of each other both moved rapidly for the enemy's position. This action nerved the rest to follow his example, and without waiting for the whole regiment to cross they started on a run and all together charged the position. Lieutenant Rochus Heinisch, of Company "A," Corporals William H. Brown and W. H. Whittemore, Company "B," were first into the enemy's works. Corporal Brown was wounded.

The charge of the Twenty-sixth was gallantly performed and has received the highest words of praise, but Colonel Grant, commanding the brigade, in his report of the affair, seeks to award the credit to the Fifth Vermont as being the first to enter the works. He says: "We left camp yesterday, soon after noon, and marched to the river, a distance of about five miles. The pontoons were on the ground ready to be taken down the bank and thrown across the river. The rebels had constructed rifle-pits in front of and commanding the point where the bridges were to be placed. These rifle-pits were occupied by rebel infantry. As soon as the artillery could be got into position it opened a terrific fire upon the rifle-pits. It had but little effect, however, except to keep back reinforcements that were coming to the assistance of those already in the works. But very few of those in the pits were injured by the artillery fire. They managed to keep up a galling fire upon the engineers that attempted to construct the bridges. It was determined to drive the rebels from the rifle-pits. The Fifth Vermont, Lieutenant-Colonel Lewis, and Twenty-sixth New Jersey, Lieutenant-Colonel Martindale, were ordered forward for that purpose. They rushed gallantly down the bank and, with the assistance of the engineers, and under a galling fire from the rifle-pits, they launched the pontoon boats into the stream, jumped into them and rowed across and landed upon the south bank. But a few companies of the Fifth had crossed when they sprang up the bank, and with shouts charged the rifle-pits, driving the enemy from them in great confusion, taking many of them prisoners. The Twenty-sixth New Jersey came gallantly to the support of the Fifth and did well, but it is believed the Fifth cleared the rifle-pits."

This is faint justice from a brigade commander for a gallant and most heroic service, and the evident intent to award the chief credit to the Fifth Vermont for a service performed by the Twenty-sixth New Jersey in conjunction with them, is not the work of a broad or generous disposition. An eye-witness of the fight, one of the Fiftieth Regiment, New York Volunteers, says of it:

"General Howe at once ordered the Twenty-sixth New Jersey to cross and storm the pits, and most gallantly and fearlessly did they go in. The rebels stuck to their position until those fearless Jerseymen set foot on the south side of the river, which was about half-past six o'clock, when, notwithstanding the shower of canister sent after them, they fled before the impetuous charge of those gallant Jersey Blues; indeed, they could not well leave before, for our cannon completely swept the plain and their pits was by far the safest place for them. Skirmishers were immediately deployed and soon brought in sixty or seventy prisoners, belonging principally to Florida regiments. My own position was such that I could see the whole affair. Our regiment suffered considerably—we lost 28 killed—many in our brigade who were killed or wounded are within a few days of the expiration of their terms of service; the same is true, as I am informed, of the Twenty-sixth New Jersey, but still neither the one or the other faltered in the least in going forward in the performance of their duties, and they deserve and should receive honor from all men."

## CHAPTER III.

LEE'S PLAN OF CAMPAIGN—DISPOSITION OF HIS FORCES—GENERAL HOOKER MYSTIFIED BUT NOT DECEIVED—THE CAVALRY FIGHT AT BRANDY STATION—THE FIRST NEW JERSEY CAVALRY'S BRILLIANT CHARGE.

WHETHER General Lee had forebodings of disaster when making his plans for an offensive campaign will, perhaps never be known, but certain it is that while everybody about him, and public feeling in the South, was full of confidence and hope, he was depressed in spirits. He evidently realized that the future of the Southern Confederacy depended upon the success of his operations. The situation elsewhere, from the southern point of view, was not the most encouraging. General Grant was hammering away at Vicksburg and the possibilities of its fall were alarming. General Longstreet thus summarizes the situation:

"While General Lee was reorganizing his army he was also arranging the new campaign. Grant had laid siege to Vicksburg, and Johnston was concentrating at Jackson to drive him away. Rosecrans was in Tennessee and Bragg was in front of him. The force Johnston was concentrating at Jackson gave us no hope that he

MAJOR WILLIAM W. MORRIS,
26th Regt. N. J. Vols., Inf.
(*From a War-time Photograph.*)

would have sufficient strength to make any impression upon Grant, and even if he could, Grant was in position to reinforce rapidly and could supply his army with greater facility. Vicksburg was doomed unless we could offer relief by a strategic move. I proposed to send a force through East Tennessee to join Bragg, and also to have Johnston sent to join him, thus concentrating a large force to move against Rosecrans, crush out his army and march against Cincinnati. That, I thought, was the only way we had to relieve Vicksburg. General Lee admitted the force of my proposition, but finally stated that he preferred to organize a campaign into Maryland and Pennsylvania, hoping thereby to draw the Federal troops from the southern points they occupied. After discussing the matter with him for several days I found his mind was made up not to allow any of his troops to go west. I then accepted his proposition to make a campaign into Pennsylvania, provided it should be offensive in strategy but defensive in tactics, forcing the Federal army to give us battle when we were in strong position and ready to receive them."

A successful invasion of Pennsylvania, and the defeat of the northern army, were the primary objects of the campaign. These would not alone counterbalance the effect that the fall of Vicksburg would have upon the southern mind, it would give the representatives of the South in foreign countries a vantage ground in securing the recognition of the Confederacy, which meant an open market in which to purchase supplies and munitions of war, and, perhaps, bring about the intervention of the great powers for a cessation of hostilities; peaceably if possible, by armed support if necessary. England and France were only awaiting an opportunity to extend a helping hand to the South. A victory for General Lee on northern soil would be all-sufficient. The plan of campaign was prepared, the preliminary movements had been made. General Lee had divided his army into three parts: Hill was left at Fredericksburg, Longstreet and Ewell moved toward Culpepper, from which point Ewell was to proceed to the Shenandoah Valley to clear the way for the balance of the army to follow. On the seventh of June General Lee's cavalry moved to the Rappahannock river, their artillery being posted so as to cover the crossing at Beverly Ford. On this same day General Wright's division, of the Sixth Corps, relieved the troops of Howe's division, at Franklin's Crossing, below Fredericksburg, Hooker thus keeping up a show of force sufficient to detain Hill, while Lee ordered Longstreet and Ewell to halt near the Rapidan river long enough to ascertain what the Union Commander's intentions were, and to be in supporting distance of Hill, if wanted. On the eighth of June Hooker directed Pleasonton—who had been placed in command of all the cavalry—to make a reconnoissance in the direction of Culpepper for the purpose of ascertaining the possible plans of the enemy. The resistance made by General Hill at Fredericksburg was obstinate enough to convince Hooker that the enemy were in strong force at that point, but his suspicions were not allayed. He believed that some movement of great importance was contemplated by Lee, and that movement, he rightly divined, was an invasion of the North.

The Cavalry Corps of the Army of the Potomac comprised three divisions, commanded as follows: First Division, General John Buford; Second Division, Colonel A. N. Duffie; Third Division, General D. McM. Gregg, and a Regular Cavalry Reserve with six batteries. For the purpose of this reconnoissance the corps was divided into two wings, the right comprising the First Cavalry Division and the Reserve Brigade, supported by a detachment of infantry under the command of General Ames, of the Eleventh Corps, the wing being commanded by General Buford. The left wing comprised the Second and Third Divisions of cavalry, with General D. A. Russell's detachment of infantry from the Sixth Corps, the whole commanded by General Gregg. General Pleasonton made his headquarters with Buford's wing. On the afternoon of the eighth of July the corps moved out on their mission, the right wing halting near Beverly Ford and the left wing at Kelly's Ford, on the Rappahannock. So far the advance toward Culpepper had progressed satisfactorily, but the next movement lead to a conflict where none was anticipated, the separated wings of Pleasonton having to encounter Stuart's whole force and engage him in separate conflict. General Buford crossed the river early on the ninth and met the enemy between the Ford and Brandy Station, but was compelled to retire by reason of the great superiority of numbers against which he was pitted. General Gregg crossed the river at Kelly's Ford between five and six o'clock in the morning and was moving toward Stevensburg, at which point he was directed to establish the left of his line, the infantry detachment under General Russell being ordered to move direct to Brandy Station. Gregg heard the firing of Buford's men, and after a march of five miles overtook Duffie's division, whose advance had reached Stevensburg without meeting the enemy, and he ordered them to move at once upon Brandy Station, taking the same road as the Third Division. When the head of Gregg's division reached the Station the enemy were there in great force, having only a short time before repulsed the First Division. In the charge of the Third Division upon Stuart's forces the First New Jersey Cavalry carried off the honors of the day for impetuous dash and consummate skill. Of the heroic part taken by this command in this, the first great cavalry fight of the war, no improvement can be made upon the realistic description given by Chaplain Pyne, in his "History of the First New Jersey Cavalry." He says:

"It was on the eighth of June that Gregg's division broke camp at Warrenton Junction, to march to Kelly's Ford. Arriving there after nightfall the men, formed in column of battalions, holding their horses during the night, bivouacked without fires or sound of bugles. In consequence of these and other precautions, Duffie's division was well on the road to Stevensburg, and Gregg moving toward Brandy Station, before the rebels had taken the alarm. Capturing or cutting off the videttes, Captain Yorke led the advance around the position of the rebel cavalry, and debouched through the woods beyond Brandy Station, while the enemy was still between that place and the Rappahannock river. As Jones' brigade hastily formed to receive us, the First New Jersey Cavalry dashed out of the woods, charging down among them. Without even an attempt to charge, the rebel line broke in confusion; and driving them back, pell-mell, the regiment pressed upon their rear. With a hundred and fifty prisoners, taken by a body of only two hundred and fifty-nine enlisted men, the regiment then rallied and re-formed for the greater work before them.

"Nearly half a mile apart, on two eminences of a continuous line of hill, stood a couple of country houses, surrounded by their customary farm buildings and enclosures, though both had been dilapidated by the frequent presence of the soldiery of both armies. At the one facing the right of the line General Stuart had established his headquarters, and each of them was protected by a battery of horse artillery. Leaving the First Pennsylvania Regiment to support his battery, Wyndham formed the First Jersey for a charge. Lieutenant-Colonel Broderick was at its

head, and in column of battalions it advanced, with
a steady trot, its line more accurate than ever on
parade. As it passed over the difficult ground in
the vicinity of the railroad, there was danger of its
front being compressed by the narrowness of the
defile. Without a pause, Hobensack led the left
squadron of the first line down the steep bank of
the cutting and up the other side—a steep descent
and rise of nine feet each way, taken by the whole
body without a waver or hesitation. While the
right squadrons of the other battalions followed
Broderick against Stuart's headquarters, the left
wings, under Lucas and Malsbury, accompanied
Hobensack and dashed at the hill on which stood
the other battery. So rapid was the advance of
both columns that the batteries of the enemy endeavored in vain to get range upon them; while our
own guns, admirably directed by Martin and his
officers, played with terrible effect upon the stationary rebel line. With a ringing cheer Broderick rode
up the gentle ascent that led to Stuart's headquarters, the men gripping hard their sabres, and the
horses taking ravines and ditches in their stride. As
the rebels poured in a random and ineffectual volley,
the troopers of the First Jersey were among them,
riding over one gun, breaking to pieces the brigade
in front of them and forcing the enemy in confusion
down the opposite slope of the hill. Stuart's headquarters were in our hands, and his favorite regiment in flight before us. At the same time, far

Colonel Percy Wyndham,
1st N. J. Cav.
(*From a War-time Photograph.*)

away at Beverly Ford, were heard the guns of Buford, as Pleasonton hurled his division, in column of regiments, against the shaken enemy. By the same orderly who carried off Stuart's official papers, Wyndham ordered up a section of his battery and the regiment of Pennsylvanians. Leaving the artillery to the support of the First Maryland, the noble Pennsylvanians came to the attack. It was time that they did so; for a fresh brigade of rebels was charging the hundred men of Broderick. Gallantly did the Lieutenant-Colonel meet the charge. As the enemy advanced, down against them rode our men: Broderick and his adjutant in front, Hart, Wynkoop, Cox, Jemison, Harper, Sawyer, Brooks and Hughes, all in their places, leading their respective men. With a crash, in went the little band of Jerseymen into the leading rebel regiment, the impetus of the attack scattering the faltering enemy in confusion right and left. Through the proud Twelfth Virginia they then rode, with no check to their headlong onset; and with dripping sabres and panting steeds emerged into the field beyond. No longer in line of battle, fighting hand to hand with small parties of the enemy, and with many a wounded horse sinking to the earth, they met a third regiment of the rebels, no longer faltering before an unbroken enemy, but rushing eagerly upon the scattered groups of combatants. Even in this emergency the confidence of the men was not shaken in their leaders. Against that swarm of opposers each individual officer opposed himself, with such men as collected around him; and slowly fighting, breaking the enemy with themselves into bands of independent combatants, the Jerseymen fell back up the bloody hillside. Not a man but had his own story of the fight to tell. Kitchen, left alone for a moment, was ridden at by two of the rebels. As one was disabled by his sabre, he spurred his horse against the other. As the animal bounded beneath the goad a bullet penetrated his brain, and, throwing his rider twenty feet beyond him, the steed, all four feet in the air, plunged headlong to the earth. As the adjutant, trembling from the fall, slowly recovered his senses, he saw another rebel riding at him. Creeping behind the body of his dead horse, he rested his revolver on the carcass to give steadiness to his aim, and frightening off his enemy, managed to escape to the neighborhood of the guns and catch a riderless horse to carry him from the field.

"In the middle of the fight Broderick's horse fell dead beneath him. Instantly his young orderly bugler, James Wood, sprang to the earth and remounted him. While the bugler himself sought for another horse, a rebel trooper rode at him with an order to surrender. As Wood was taken to the rear, he came upon a carbine lying upon the ground. Seizing it and leveling it at his captor, he forced the man to change places with him; and thus, with an empty weapon, repossessed himself of arms and horse, together with a prisoner. Jemison, on foot and alone, was chased around the house upon the hill, when he saw Broderick again unhorsed in the midst of a crowd of enemies, and Sawyer riding to the rescue. At the moment when Jemison was giving himself up for lost, he saw his pursuers stop, wheel and hurry away, and running himself around the corner, he beheld Taylor, sword in hand, leading the charge of the Pennsylvanians. Around the base of the hill the sturdy regiment swept along, driving the enemy before it, and making a complete circuit of the position, returned again toward Brandy Station.

" In the mean time, the left wing of the regiment had directed its efforts upon the other battery of the rebels. Keeping to the trot, their unbroken ranks moved steadily against the hill, on the top of which stood the cannoneers and a few horsemen observing their approach. As they came nearer, all these men disappeared except one, who maintained his position; and as they came within two hundred yards of the summit, this man lifted his hat, beckoning with it to those in the rear. In one moment the whole hillside was black with rebel cavalry, charging down as foragers, pistol and carbine in hand. Hobensack glanced along his squadron. Not a man was out of place, and every horse was taking the gallop without a blunder or overrush of speed. At the sight of this united band of enemies, the confused rebel crowd hesitated and shook. With an ill-directed, futile volley, they began to break away, and the next moment, a shrieking mass of fugitives, they were flying before the sabres of our men.

The rebel battery of four guns was left with but two men near it, and with their eyes fixed upon it our officers pressed upon the fugitives. When within a hundred yards of the guns, and when looking over the hill, Lucas could see yet another brigade coming in the distance to reinforce the broken enemy, an ejaculation from Hobensack caused him to turn his eyes to his own rear. There was the main body of the force that had broken the right wing coming into full line of battle upon their rear.

"'Fours, left-about, wheel!' was the instant order. 'Boys, there's a good many of them, but we must cut through. Charge!' and obliquely against their line rushed down the Jersey troopers.

"Enthusiasm and desperation supplied the place of numbers, and cutting their way out, the little band opened a path toward the section of our battery. Three times was the guidon of Company E taken by the enemy. Twice it was retaken by our men, and the third time, when all seemed desperate, a little troop of the First Pennsylvania cut through the enemy and brought off the flag in safety. Once the rebels who hung upon the rear attempted to charge our retiring men, but the wheel of the rear division sufficed to check their assault, and the left wing of the Jersey reached Clark's two guns, annoyed only by the revolvers of the rebels.

"Under cover of the fire of the artillery, and assisted by the charge of the First Pensylvania, Hart had succeeded in bringing off the remnant of the right wing.

He was the senior officer of that half of the regiment. Broderick was dying in the enemy's hands; Shelmire lay dead across the body of a rebel; Sawyer and Hyde Crocker were prisoners; Lieutenant Brooks was disabled by a sabre stroke on his right arm; Wyndham himself had just received a bullet in his leg. Men and horses had been fighting for over three hours, and were now utterly exhausted. Duffie was in line of battle two miles and a-half to the rear, but there was no support upon the field. Kilpatrick's brigade, which had charged on our right and rear, had beaten the rebels opposed to it, the First Maine bearing off a battle-flag, but it was now formed on our flank, some distance from the field, to cover us from being entirely cut off. The enemy were indeed terribly demoralized, and the charge of a dozen of our men again and again routed a hundred of the rebels; but now there were not a dozen horses that could charge—not a man who could shout above a whisper. The guns were across a ditch, which rendered their removal very difficult, and it was their fire which kept the rebels from crossing the hills to charge against us. So, with a desperate hope that Duffie might come up after all, our worn-out troopers stood by the gallant cannoneers of the Sixth New York (Martin's, formerly Bramhall's) Independent Battery—New Yorkers by commission, but Jerseymen of Rahway in their origin.

"Presently the apprehended moment came, and the last reserves of the rebels, fresh and strong, poured down on three sides upon the exhausted little knot of Jersey troopers. While cavalry fought hand to hand across the guns, the artillerymen continued steadily serving their pieces and delivering their fire at the enemy upon the hill. Time after time, as a rebel trooper would strike at a cannoneer, he would dodge beneath a horse or gun-carriage, and coming up on the other side, discharge his revolver at his assailant and spring once more to his work. At length, from mere exhaustion, Hart, Hobensack and Beekman, with their comrades, were forced back a little way from the guns, and while they were forming the men afresh the rebels rode again upon the cannoneers.

"As one of the gunners was ramming home a charge, a rebel officer cut him down with three successive sabre strokes. Then, springing from his horse, he wheeled the piece toward our troopers, not fifty yards away. Hobensack turned to Hart, stretched out his hand, and said: 'We must shut our eyes and take it. Good-bye!' and clasping each other's hands they awaited for their death. The roar of the piece thundered out, and the smoke wrapped them in its folds, but the charge flew harmlessly over their heads. The piece had been elevated against the hill, and the rebels had not thought of changing its angle. They were so savage at the harmlessness of the discharge that they actually advanced half-way toward our men, but beyond that they dared not come, and the Jersey regiment marched calmly off the field without an effort being made to pursue them.

"No other comment can be needed to tell the impression made by them upon the rebels. If there had been five hundred fresh men upon the field they might have swept the whole rebel cavalry force into the Rappahannock river.

"Of the three senior officers on the field, Wyndham received a ball in the leg, which unfitted him for months for active service, and Broderick and Shelmire never came off the field alive. As is frequently the case in cavalry combats, but little quarter was asked or given. Men fought as long as they could, and then fell beneath the sabre or pistol, the loss of the enemy almost trebling that of the National troopers.

"The name and character of Colonel Wyndham are known throughout the country; Broderick and Shelmire were known to few beyond their own immediate sphere of duty. Within that sphere they were valued, and their loss was severely felt."

General Gregg, in his report of the fight, says:

"Coming thus upon the enemy, and having at hand only the Third Division (total strength 2,400), I had either to decline the fight in the face of the enemy or throw upon him at once the entire division. Not doubting but that the Second Division was near, and delay not being admissible, I directed the commanders of my advance brigade to charge the enemy formed in columns about Brandy House. The whole brigade charged with drawn sabres, fell upon the masses of the enemy, and after a brief but severe contest, drove them back, killing and wounding many and taking a large number of prisoners. Other columns of the enemy coming up charged this brigade before it could reform and it was driven back. Seeing this, I ordered the First Brigade to charge the enemy upon the right. This brigade came forth gallantly through the open fields, dashed upon the enemy, drove him away and occupied the hill. Now that my entire division was engaged, the fight was everywhere most fierce. Fresh columns of the enemy arriving upon the ground received the vigorous charges of my regiments, and under the heavy blows of our sabres were in every instance driven back. Martin's battery of horse artillery, divided between the two brigades, poured load after load of canister upon the rebel regiments. Assailed on all sides, the men stood to the guns nobly. Thus, for an hour and a-half, was the contest continued, not in skirmishing but in determined charges. The contest was too unequal to be longer continued. The Second Division had not come up, there was no support at hand and the enemy's number were three times my own. I ordered the withdrawal of my brigades. In good order they left the field, the enemy not choosing to follow.

\* \* \* \* \* \* \*

" The Third Division behaved nobly, and where every officer and man did his duty it is difficult to particularize. I would, however, mention Colonel Percy Wyndham, First New Jersey Cavalry, commanding Second Brigade, and Colonel Judson Kilpatrick,

MAJOR-GENERAL H. JUDSON KILPATRICK,
Brigadier-General Commanding Cavalry Brigade.

Second New York, commanding First Brigade, who gallantly led their brigades to the charge, and throughout the entire engagement handled them with consummate skill. Colonel Wyndham, although wounded, remained on the field and covered with a portion of his command the withdrawal of the division. Captain J. W. Martin, commanding Sixth New York Battery of Horse Artillery, did most excellent service. His sections were charged by the enemy's regiments on all sides. Two of his pieces disabled and one serviceable fell into the hands of the enemy, but not until twenty-one of his men were cut down, fighting stubbornly, and nearly all of the horses killed. Although the loss of these pieces is to be regretted, still the magnificent defense of them establishes in the highest degree the soldierly character of the officers and men of the battery. The serviceable gun was spiked before the enemy got it."

It will be noticed that the men so honorably mentioned, Colonel Wyndhan, Colonel Kilpatrick, and the men of the Sixth New York Battery, were all Jerseymen. The latter command, while credited to New York, was raised almost wholly within the city of Rahway, this State. Of thirty-six men who went into the fight but six came out safely, and every one received some wound that he will carry through life. The charge by the First New Jersey was led by Colonel Wyndham in person, aided by Lieutenant-Colonel Broderick. At the first onset the enemy were driven from their guns, the support coming up were met and in a few minutes were driven back. Reinforced, it returned and was again repulsed.

The rebels were terribly punished. By their own confession they lost many more than their adversaries, and in the First New Jersey almost every soldier must have killed his man. Sergeant Craig, of Company K, is credited with three; Slate, of the same company, had several hand-to-hand combats with the enemy, and the instances of individual bravery and pluck were numerous. Every soldier had an exciting story to tell, and Adjutant Kitchen, who was in the thickest of the fray, thus describes what befell himself:

"The crowd with whom Broderick was engaged was a little distance from me, and I had just wheeled to ride up to his help when two fellows put at me. The first one fired at me and missed; before he could again cock his revolver I succeeded in closing with him. My sabre took him just in the neck, and must have cut the jugular. The blood gushed out in a black looking stream; he gave a horrible yell and fell over the side of his horse, which galloped away. Then I gathered up my reins, spurred my horse, and went at the other one. I was riding the old black horse that used to belong to the signal sergeant, and it was in fine condition. As I drove in the spurs it gave a leap high in the air. That plunge saved my life. The rebel had a steady aim at me; but the ball went through the black horse's brain. His feet never touched ground again. With a terrible convulsive contraction of all his muscles, the black turned over in the air, and fell on his head and side stone dead, pitching me twenty feet. I lighted on my pistol, the butt forcing itself far into my side. My sabre sprang out of my hand, and I lay, with arms and legs abroad, stretched out like a dead man. Everybody had something else to do than to attend to me, and there I lay where I had fallen.

"It seemed to me to have been an age before I began painfully to come to myself; but it could not have been many minutes. Every nerve was shaking; there was a terrible pain in my head, and a numbness through my side which was even worse. Fighting was still going on around me, and my first impulse was to get hold of my sword. I crawled to it, and sank down as I grasped it once more. That was only for a moment; for a rebel soldier, seeing me move, rode at me. The presence of danger roused me, and I managed to get to my horse, behind which I sank, resting my pistol on the saddle, and so contriving to get an aim. As soon as the man saw that, he turned off without attacking me. I was now able to stand and walk; and holding my pistol in one hand and my sabre in the other, I made my way across the fields to where our battery was posted, scaring some with my pistol and shooting others. Nobody managed to hit me through the whole fight. When I got up to the battery I found Wood there. He sang out to me to wait and he would get me a horse. One of the men, who had just taken one, was going past, so Wood stopped him and got it for me.

"Just at that moment White's battalion and some other troops came charging at the battery. The squadron of the First Maryland, who were supporting it, met the charge well as far as their numbers went; but were, of course, flanked on both sides by the heavy odds. All of our men who were free came swarming up the hill, and the cavalry were fighting over and around the guns. In spite of the confusion, and even while their comrades at the same place were being sabred, the men at that battery kept to their duty. They did not even look up or around, but kept up their fire with unwavering steadiness.

"There was one rebel, on a splendid horse, who sabred three gunners while I was chasing him. He wheeled in and out, would dart away, and then come sweeping back and cut down another man in a manner that seemed almost supernatural. We at last succeeded in driving him away, but we could not catch or shoot him, and he got off without a scratch."

Adjutant Kitchen was promoted Lieutenant-Colonel of the Second New Jersey Cavalry the following August, and served until June 30, 1864, when he resigned.

The First New Jersey Cavalry in this, as in every engagement in which it took part, was noted for the bravery of its men and the thoroughness with which they performed their duty. Its record is a noble and brilliant one, and no command shed greater honor upon its native State than this. The casualties in the

COLONEL HUGH H. JANEWAY,
Major Com'd'g 1st N. J. Cav.
(*From a War-time Photograph.*)

fight at Brandy Station were 52, of whom 6 were officers and 46 enlisted men as follows:

*Killed.*

Lieutenant-Colonel Virgil Broderick.
Major John H. Shelmire.
Company A—John Black.
" B—Joseph Howard.
" E—Sergeant James H. Palmatier; George T. Poulson.
" F—Sergeant Samuel Rainear.
" G—Augustus Ringleb.

*Wounded and Missing.*

Colonel Percy Wyndham, gunshot wound through fleshy part of leg.

Captain Henry W. Sawyer, wounded and prisoner.

Second Lieutenant Hyde Crocker, prisoner.

First Lieutenant Joseph Brooks, wounded, sabre cut of left arm.

Company A—Henry Cash, Ephraim Croasdale, Charles E. Wilson, missing.

Company B—First Sergeant Smighton P. Crossman, Private Aaron H. Rake, wounded; Jacob Casler, John Tynon, missing.

Company D—Octave Antonio, wounded and missing; Isaiah Buchanan, wounded in shoulder; Joseph Crane, missing.

Company E—First Sergeant Joseph Killey, slightly

wounded in head; Sergeant George W. Steward, gunshot wound in hip; Theodore L. Clement, Daniel McCormick, missing. (The last named deserted.)

Company F—Corporal Amos L. Poinsett, severely wounded in face and neck; Charles Cadott, wounded in leg; Daniel Cliver, wounded and missing; Sergeant Joseph F. Thibeaudeau, Corporal Ridgway S. Asy, Nathan Moore, John C. Dantz, missing.

Company G—First Sergeant Jeremiah P. Brower, Private James H. Stubbs, wounded and missing; Richard Darmstadt, wounded; Borden G. Joline, Marshall Summers, missing.

Company H—Timothy Mahoney, wounded in leg; Corporal John A. Schaffer, Privates William H. Jackson, Douglas E. Grey, missing.

Company I—Sergeant Frederick Schaal, gunshot wound left wrist; Sergeant Charles Earley, wounded and missing; Philip Hann, missing.

Company K—Sergeant Robert Tuthill, wounded in thigh; Sergeant Richard Decker, rib broken; John M. Hendershot, wounded in foot; *Henry Heater, severely wounded in the back, ball passing through and out at the abdomen; John Hanley, missing.

Company M—James Linley, Horace Van Order, missing.

---

*Heater recovered from his wound, was promoted Corporal July 1, 1863, Sergeant, January 1, 1864, and served his full term, being mustered out September 16, 1864.

RECAPITULATION.

|  | Killed. | Wounded. | Missing. | Total. |
|---|---|---|---|---|
| Officers | 2 | 4 | — | 6 |
| Enlisted Men | 6 | 19 | 21 | 46 |
| Total | 8 | 23 | 21 | 52 |

Among the Jerseymen of Martin's Independent Battery (Sixth New York) who did such heroic service the following casualties are reported :

*Wounded.*—Frank H. Bliss, William Bishop, Augustus B. Crane, Alfred T. Freeman, Robert H. Fowle, John Jordon.—6.

*Captured by the Enemy.*—Thomas Crane, Daniel C. Cripps, James Horton, Jonathan Hand, Daniel A. High, *Cornelius H. Miller, Rufus M. Miller, Thompson Thorn.—8. Total, 14.

---

*Recaptured at same fight.

## CHAPTER IV.

EWELL'S DASHING ADVANCE THROUGH THE VALLEY—MILROY SURPRISED AT WINCHESTER—THE FOURTEENTH NEW JERSEY ON MARYLAND HEIGHTS—HISTORY OF THE CORPS BADGE—THE NEW JERSEY TROOPS AND THEIR COMMANDERS—AN EXHAUSTIVE MARCH.

ON the tenth of June General Ewell advanced his troops through the Blue Ridge to Chester Gap, then pushed on to Front Royal, where he crossed the Shenandoah river, and by rapid marching through the Valley reached Winchester on the evening of June 13th, making seventy miles in three days. Lee's line of battle thus stretched over an interval of a hundred miles, from Fredericksburg to Winchester. This rapid marching had for its object the clearing of the Valley of whatever Union forces might have been established there, the most important point being Winchester, which was held by Milroy with about seven thousand men. Ewell had so skillfully performed his mission that Milroy was completely surprised.

Winchester is a railroad station about thirty miles southeast from Harper's Ferry. It was considered a good point for observation and not particularly valuable as a strategic position. General Milroy had constructed a stout line of intrenchments about the town, and he had a force of men sufficiently large for any ordinary defence of the place. In the neighborhood were many Union families who naturally relied upon the military forces for protection, and to whom they also were of great service. Berryville, southeast of Winchester, was occupied by Colonel McReynolds with a brigade, and Major Morris, with two hundred men, was stationed at another outpost, Bunker Hill.

While the movements of General Lee were in progress the authorities at Washington, on the 11th of June, ordered General Milroy to remove his armament and supplies to Harper's Ferry. Milroy at this time was ignorant of the advance of Lee's army to the north side of the Rappahannock river, though the fact was known to the government authorities. He was reluctant to obey the order, as he felt able to cope successfully with any force of the enemy likely, in his opinion, to attack his position, and he was permitted to remain, subject to conditions which would enable him to avoid an engagement with superior numbers.

General Hooker, ignorant of the designs of the enemy, had not yet made a general movement of his army. On the 10th of June, after the cavalry fight at Brandy Station, Generals Russell and Ames, with their detachments of infantry, had been ordered to join their commands, and the cavalry rendezvoused in the vicinity of Warrenton Junction. When Ewell's movement was observed, General Hooker, on the 11th, ordered the Third Corps to move from its camps in the vicinity of Falmouth to Hartwood Church, in close proximity to Kelly and Beverly Fords, which crossings they were to watch carefully, while the Fifth Corps, stationed in the neighborhood of Banks and United States Fords were to perform a like service there. On the 12th the lines were still further extended, the First Corps moving from the vicinity of White Oak Church to Deep Run, the Third Corps taking a new position at Bealton, Humphrey's division moving to the Rappahannock, while the Eleventh Corps moved from Brook's Station to the place vacated by the First Corps at Hartwood Church. The next day, June 13th, when Ewell was at Winchester, General Hooker had only begun to put his army earnestly in motion. Milroy was in exceeding great peril. Without any knowledge of the movements of either army he was undecided for a time what to do, but on the 12th he sent word to Colonel McReynolds, at Berryville, to keep a sharp lookout as a reconnoissance ordered by him had discovered that a large force of the enemy were moving on the Front Royal road, and to be prepared to fall back on Winchester should he be attacked by superior numbers. On the following day McReynolds fell back, his rear guard engaging the enemy, and succeeded in reaching Winchester before midnight, after a severe march of thirty miles. The detachment under command of Major Morris was also compelled, after a severe engagement, to rejoin the main body at Win-

LIEUT. ROCHUS HEINISCH,
Co. A, 26th Reg. N. J. Vols., Inf.
(*From Recent Photograph.*)

chester. Milroy's forces were being hemmed in on all sides by the superior numbers of Ewell, and these accessions to the troops at Winchester produced great embarrassment. Their presence augmented the difficulties which beset Milroy, and they were so exhausted after their arduous labors that Milroy was compelled to postpone action until they recovered sufficiently to endure further marching. Meanwhile Ewell was making the best use of his time and organized his forces for attack. The eastern side of the town was approached first, but the attack there was gallantly repulsed. The enemy, reinforced, made a more determined effort and succeeded in getting possession of part of the town, but they were driven out by artillery. Milroy then attempted to steal his way out, but every avenue of escape seemed to be cut off and as a last resort he determined to fight his way through the rebel lines. The enemy outnumbered him two to one, but a desperate charge upon their lines enabled the troops to break through. In the darkness the column became divided and Milroy succeeded in bringing safe to Harper's Ferry the greater part of his command. Colonel Ely's and Colonel McReynolds' brigades were, however, captured.* This cleared the Valley of all Union troops and made the further progress of Lee's army to Williamsport an easy matter.

---

*Milroy's losses were severe. General Lee reported that his troops captured "more than 4,000 prisoners, 29 guns, 277 wagons and 400 horses." These no doubt included seven hundred prisoners and five guns captured by General Rodes at Martinsburg.

The alarm that was felt in Washington by Ewell's presence in the Valley led to the receiving of marching orders by the Fourteenth New Jersey Regiment, Colonel William Truex, then stationed at the Monocacy river. Hurriedly, in light marching order, the regiment moved to the cars in waiting to carry them to Harper's Ferry, one company remaining behind to guard the bridge at the river. The regiment went into camp on Maryland Heights, with the troops of General Tyler, who had escaped from Martinsburg after a fierce encounter with Rodes' division of Ewell's corps. The Fourteenth encamped on the Heights for about two weeks. General Tyler was superseded by General French, who at once proceeded to fortify his position and make it impregnable from attack. At this arduous and fatiguing duty the Fourteenth were kept busily engaged and suffered great hardship and exposure.

On June 13th, General Hooker abandoned his position opposite Fredericksburg, the First Corps moving from Deep Run to Bealton, the Fifth from the fords on the Rappahannock toward Morrisville, Wright and Newton's divisions of the Sixth Corps from Franklin's Crossing to Potomac Creek, the Eleventh Corps to Catlett's Station, while the Twelfth Corps moved from Stafford Court House and Aquia Creek Landing to Dumfries, marching all night long. The storehouses and supply depots at Aquia Creek were burned. As soon as the Federal army disappeared from his front, General A. P. Hill broke camp at Fredericksburg and started to join Longstreet and Lee at Culpepper.

The New Jersey troops were distributed as follows in the several corps :*

---

*Each of the corps of the Army of the Potomac were designated by a badge, the First Division color being red, the Second Division white, and the Third Division blue. The flags of each division headquarters were designated as follows: First Division, a square flag, white, with red emblem in centre; Second Division, blue flag, white emblem in centre; Third Division, white flag, with blue emblem in centre. Brigade headquarter flags were triangular, the colors being arranged in the same manner. This method of distinguishing the various corps emanated from the simple device employed by General Kearny, while in command of a division on the Peninsula campaign, under General McClellan. Just before the battle of Williamsburg General Kearny caused the officers and men of his division to be supplied with a patch of flannel cut in the shape of a square (diamond) or lozenge, and in a general order directed that all the field and staff officers should wear a red diamond on the top of their caps, and the line officers the same in front, the enlisted men wearing it on the left sleeve of the coat. It was devised as a means of better distinguishing the officers and men, as the uniforms of both were so much alike at the time as to cause confusion. After the death of General Kearny, at Chantilly, General Birney, his successor, ordered that these patches should be worn in memory of their gallant old commander, but none were entitled to wear the badge but those who had been in action with the divsion. General Hooker, when he was placed in command of the Army of the Potomac, utilized the idea and caused each of his seven corps to be designated by a badge. The badges worn by the New Jersey troops were as follows :

2          3         6         12

SECOND CORPS—*Third Division, Second Brigade.*
Twelfth Regiment, Major John T. Hill.
THIRD CORPS—*Second Division, First Brigade.* Eleventh Regiment, Colonel Robert McAllister.
*Third Brigade.* Fifth Regiment, Colonel William J. Sewell.
Sixth Regiment, Colonel George C. Burling.
Seventh Regiment, Colonel L. R. Francine.
Eighth Regiment, Colonel John Ramsey.

*Second Army Corps Badge*—Trefoil. Twelfth New Jersey, Second Division: Blue.

*Third Army Corps Badge* — (Kearny's) Diamond, First Division: Red. Fifth, Sixth, Seventh, Eighth and Eleventh New Jersey Infantry. Artillery Brigade: Battery " B," First New Jersey Artillery.

*Sixth Army Corps Badge*—Greek Cross. First Division: Red. First, Second, Third, Fourth and Fifteenth New Jersey Regiments. Battery " A," First New Jersey Artillery.

*Twelfth Army Corps Badge*—Five Pointed Star. First Division: Red. Thirteenth New Jersey Regiment.

The designs for the other three corps were as follows:

1     5     11

*First Army Corps*—Disc, or lozenge. *Fifth Army Corps*—Maltese Cross. *Eleventh Army Corps*—Crescent.

In a short time the badge was universally adopted by the corps in all the armies of the Union, and became one of the most popular features of soldier life.

*Artillery Brigade.* Battery "B," First New Jersey Artillery, Captain A. Judson Clark.

SIXTH CORPS—*First Division, First Brigade.* General A. T. A. Torbert, commanding.
First Regiment, Lieutenant-Colonel Wm. Henry, Jr.
Second Regiment, Colonel Samuel L. Buck.
Third Regiment, Colonel Henry W. Brown.
*Fourth Regiment, Major Charles Ewing.
Fifteenth Regiment, Colonel William H. Penrose.
*Cavalry Detachment.* Company "L," First New Jersey.

TWELFTH CORPS—*First Division, Third Brigade.*
Thirteenth Regiment, Colonel Ezra A. Carman.

CAVALRY CORPS—*Second Division, First Brigade.*
First Regiment, Major M. H. Beaumont.
*Third Division.* Brigadier-General Judson Kilpatrick, commanding.

ARTILLERY RESERVE—*Fourth Volunteer Brigade.* Battery "A," First New Jersey, Lieutenant Augustin N. Parsons.

General Lee's plan of operations comprised, among other things, the drawing away of the Federal army from the Defences of Washington, thus to enable him to administer a severe blow to Hooker on Virginia territory. After Ewell had successfully driven Milroy from the Shenandoah Valley Hill moved to Culpepper,

---

*The Fourth Regiment on this campaign was detailed as guard to division trains, and at division headquarters.

and Longstreet, moving east of the Blue Ridge, occupied Ashby's and Snicker's Gaps, hoping by this manœuvre to entice Hooker to move against him at these points. General Hooker, however, did not bite at the bait thus temptingly held out, but skillfully covered the Capital from any likelihood of attack and moved his army to checkmate any possible designs Lee might have in that direction. On June 14th he had advanced his army in the following order: The First and Third Corps to Manassas Junction, the Fifth Corps to Catlett's Station, the First and Third Divisions of the Sixth Corps to Stafford Court House, the Eleventh Corps to Centreville, which place it reached next day. The Twelfth Corps arrived at Dumfries on the morning of the 14th, and remained there during the day. On the 15th, the day of Milroy's defeat, the Army of the Potomac moved rapidly to more advanced positions. The Second Corps, which had remained at Falmouth, moved to Aquia, the Fifth Corps joined the First and Third at Manassas Junction, the Sixth Corps moved to Dumfries, just as the Twelfth was moving out for Fairfax Court House. The Cavalry Corps, which had been rendezvousing at Warrenton Junction, moved to Union Mills and Bristoe Station.

The march of the Twelfth Corps, from Stafford Court House to Dumfries, on the 15th of June, was a memorable one to the Thirteenth New Jersey Regiment. Orders for a change of camp had been received on the morning of the 13th, and the Third Brigade broke camp at Stafford and moved to Brook's Station,

Major-General George Gordon Meade,
Commander Army of the Potomac.

where the rest of the day was spent in erecting new quarters. About seven o'clock in the evening orders. to move were again received, and in a short time the column was on the road, passing through Stafford about nine o'clock and continuing on all through the night until Dumfries was reached the next morning. The night was very dark, but for a good part of the way the road was illumined by the bright reflection which came from the burning buildings at Aquia Creek Station. The march to Fairfax on the 15th of June was also a severe one. The heat of the sun was intense, there was little water to be found anywhere on the route, and whenever the column halted for a brief rest, men would search in vain for a stream of water to quench their thirst. Occasionally a feeble stream would be found, but the sudden rush for water soon converted it into a mud-puddle, and thus the misery of thirst was only aggravated. The distance marched was about twenty-five miles, and so overpowering was the heat that three men of the Third Brigade—Charles E. Somerville, of the Thirteenth New Jersey, and two men of the One Hundred and Seventh New York—died from the exhaustion it caused.

General Hooker had designed to attack Hill at Fredericksburg and put his army in such position as to interpose between Lee's main army and Richmond, but he was overruled by General Halleck. Compelled therefore to fall back and await the development of Lee's plans, he moved his army with marked skillfulness and ability. All the authorities agree as to the general correctness of the views advanced by Hooker, but he was in almost every instance balked in his designs by the military authorities in Washington, and refused the coöperation which he deserved. He did not permit himself, however, to be influenced by the clamorous appeals sent to him; he was forced in a defensive position by Lee's movements, and as though aware of the intent of Lee to draw him into a battle, he steadfastly pursued the one course of covering the Capital against any possible designs the rebel chieftain might have in that direction, and putting himself in position to watch every movement his wily antagonist might make.

## CHAPTER V.

EWELL AT WILLIAMSPORT—JENKINS' RAID IN PENNSYLVANIA — CONSTERNATION THROUGHOUT THE NORTH—NEW JERSEY VOLUNTEERS GO TO THE DEFENCE OF HARRISBURG—HOOKER ADVANCES TO A NEW LINE OF OBSERVATION—INCIDENTS OF THE MARCH—EXECUTION OF DESERTERS—AN INSTANCE OF PRESIDENT LINCOLN'S MERCY AND WHY IT FAILED.

THE rebel leaders seemed to have everything their own way after the defeat of Milroy at Winchester. General Lee was the ruling spirit of his own army, and unlike the Union commander, was not hampered by those in power at the seat of government. He gave wide latitude also to his lieutenants, and thus practically there were four independent armies, acting with a common impulse. Ewell's brilliant exploit had won for him the admiration of his troops, and they hailed him as a worthy successor to the idolized "Stonewall" Jackson. The complete rout of Milroy's forces stimulated the advancing columns and emboldened them to a wonderful degree. The fleeing teamsters, contrabands and non-combatants generally who had escaped from Ewell's clutches, created consternation and dismay among the farmers of Western Maryland and the Cumberland Valley, by the wonderful stories their imaginations conjured up, and these in turn spread the alarm by gathering together their valuables, live stock, and portable property, and fleeing toward Harrisburg. The whole country was in a state of alarm, and Jenkins with two thousand of his impetuous cavalrymen, started on a tour of the Valley to prevent the loss of so much material and supplies, of which Lee's army stood in great need. He entered Greencastle on the 16th of June and at night of the same day halted at Chambersburg. He levied on everything of value he could find — horses, cattle, forage, medical stores, and went so far as to seize a number of free negroes whom he sent South to be sold as slaves. It is said in behalf of Jenkins' fairness toward the people whom he thus despoiled, that he paid for the goods in "honest" Confederate money. This is true only in part; he deliberately confiscated the greater part of the supplies seized, making no offer of compensation.

The alarm which prevailed throughout the North on the advent of Jenkins with his bold raiders in Pennsylvania, was increased by the apparent slowness with which the Army of the Potomac moved toward the enemy. This feeling found vent in hysteric appeals to the government and sharp criticism of the Union commander, as the defenceless condition of Pennsylvania made its territory a fine field for depredations of all kinds. On the 15th of June Governor Curtin addressed an appeal to the Governor of New Jersey for aid as follows:

HARRISBURG, June 15, 1863.
GOVERNOR JOEL PARKER:

This State is threatened with invasion by a large force, and we are raising troops as rapidly as possible to resist them. I understand there are three regiments of your troops at Beverly waiting to be mustered out. Could an arrangement be made with you and the authorities at Washington by which the service of those regiments could be had for the present emergency? Please advise immediately.

A. G. CURTIN,
Governor Pennsylvania.

On the same day a dispatch was received by Governor Parker from the Secretary of War, detailing the movements of the rebel forces in Virginia which had been sufficiently developed to show that General Lee with his whole army contemplated moving forward to invade the States of Maryland, Pennsylvania and other States. The President, to repel this invasion promptly, had called upon Ohio, Pennsylvania, Maryland and Western Virginia for one hundred thousand volunteers for six months, unless sooner discharged, and realizing the importance of having the largest possible force in the least time, desired immediate information as to what number, in answer to a special call of the President, the Governor could raise and forward, of militia or volunteers, without bounty, for the period named, and to be credited on the draft of the State.

These appeals were not as promptly responded to as the authorities hoped for. In Pennsylvania, where the greatest danger existed, the people seemed to feel their utter helplessness, and looked longingly, anxiously, for the advance of the Army of the Potomac. Philadelphia was lethargic to a wonderful degree, and General Couch, who had been sent to Harrisburg, for the purpose of organizing a defensive force for the safety of the Capital, found himself without troops, and with slight prospects for getting any. Governor Parker of New Jersey promptly replied to the appeal of Governor Curtin, promising all the assistance in his power, and on the 17th issued the following proclamation:

EXECUTIVE CHAMBER,<br>TRENTON, N. J., June 17, 1863.

Jerseymen! The State of Pennsylvania is invaded! A hostile army is now occupying and despoiling the towns of our sister State. She appeals to New Jersey, through her Governor, to aid in driving back the invading army.

Let us respond to this call upon our patriotic State with unprecedented zeal.

I therefore call upon the citizens of this State to meet and organize into companies, and to report to the Adjutant-General of the State as soon as possible, to be organized into regiments as the militia of New Jersey, and press forward to the assistance of Pennsylvania in this emergency.

MAJOR-GENERAL A. T. A. TORBERT,
Brigadier-General Commanding First N. J. Brigade.
(*From Photograph after the War.*)

The organization of these troops will be given in general orders as soon as practicable.

[L. S.] Given under my hand and privy seal this seventeenth day of June, eighteen hundred and sixty-three. JOEL PARKER.
        Attest:
S. M. DICKINSON, Private Secretary.

The presence in the State of a number of the nine months' regiments, whose terms of service had or were about expiring, caused the Governor to issue a special appeal to these troops as follows:

STATE OF NEW JERSEY,
EXECUTIVE CHAMBER, TRENTON,
June 17, 1863.

Soldiers! The Governor of Pennsylvania has requested your services to assist in repelling an invasion of that State. Your term of service has expired. You have performed your duty, and your gallant conduct has reflected honor on yourselves and the State that sent you forth.

It will take time to organize and send other troops to the aid of Pennsylvania. You are already organized and drilled. The hard service you have seen in Virginia has made you veterans—far more efficient than new troops can possibly be.

I regret any necessity that may detain you from your homes, but can this appeal from a sister State, in her hour of danger, be disregarded?

Your State and United States pay will be continued.

You will not be required to go out of the State of Pennsylvania, and will return as soon as the emergency will admit. Your response to this appeal will add to the fame you have already achieved.

JOEL PARKER.

On the very day the proclamation was issued, the Twenty-third Regiment, then in camp at Beverly undergoing the necessary preliminaries for being mustered out, were called together, and its Colonel, E. Burd Grubb, made a straightforward, practical and patriotic appeal to his men, who responded at once. Numbers of men who were not in camp at the time hastened to join their comrades, and that same evening the regiment, three hundred strong, marched through Philadelphia to the Harrisburg depot, receiving a grand ovation on the way. The next day they reached the threatened city, being the first armed force to arrive, but to the surprise of the men of the Twenty-third they were received with exceeding coolness. From the "Notes of an officer" in Foster's "New Jersey and the Rebellion," the following extract is taken: "Our men were refused canteens of water by the citizens, and one person who did not conceal his secession proclivities came very near being 'torn out,' so exasperated were our troops at his undisguised sympathy with the rebels. It required all Colonel Grubb's influence to prevent violence. The fellow at last procured a flag, hung it out, promised to behave in future, and was finally let off, a pretty badly scared man, who took good care not to ventilate any more disunion sentiments during the occupancy of the city by the Jersey Blues." A very different reception was experienced by Captain William R. Murphy, of Company A, First New Jersey Militia, whose command also volunteered for the emergency. In a dispatch to Governor Parker he says:

"At Philadelphia and here (Harrisburg) we have received every attention because we are Jerseymen. 'A citizen of New Jersey' is a prouder title than that of a 'Roman citizen.'"

The Twenty-seventh Regiment, Colonel Geo. W. Mindil, on arriving at Cincinnati, learned of the threatened invasion of Pennsylvania, and the command was immediately tendered to the President who accepted it, and it remained in the vicinity of Pittsburg and Harrisburg until the danger had passed. Ten companies of New Jersey Militia and one battery of light artillery also volunteered for the emergency. These companies came from all parts of the State, three from Trenton, commanded by Captains William R. Murphy, Company A; George F. Marshall, Company B; James C. Manning, Company C; Company D of Lambertville, Captain Hiram Hughes; Company E of Morristown, Captain George Gage; Company F of Newark, Captain William J. Roberts; Company G of Mount Holly, Captain J. Fred. Laumaster; Company H of Newark, Captain Timothy Colvin; Company I of Trenton, Captain Joseph A. Yard; Independent Company of Camden, Captain James M. Scovel; Light

Battery of Rahway, Captain John R. Chapin. These commands all reported to General Couch at Harrisburg, and the militia companies were organized into two battalions, commanded respectively by Captains Murphy and Laumaster.

These commands remained in the State until all danger was over, and received the thanks of Governor Curtin for their valuable and patriotic services.

While Jenkins' raid was in progress Ewell remained at Williamsport to rest his men, amuse himself by a feint upon Harper's Ferry, but principally to await the arrival of Longstreet's corps, which had been making a rather bold attempt to draw on a battle with the Army of the Potomac.

This apparant inaction on the part of the enemy was a source of mystery to the Union commander. He was flooded with dispatches from Washington, which reflected the excited views of the people North, together with orders for the movement of his army which, in turn, were countermanded soon after. The North was alarmed, reasonably so. The Government at Washington appeared to be panic-stricken. Hooker alone seemed to have his head firmly set upon his shoulders. It was not yet clear to his mind that an invasion of Pennsylvania, further than a cavalry raid on a large scale, was intended, and he therefore determined to halt his army, then approaching Centreville and Manassas, and await developments. The information he sought came to him most unexpectedly.

The Union cavalry had given little attention to the

COLONEL JAMES N. DUFFY,
Lieutenant-Colonel 3d New Jersey Volunteers,
Assistant Inspector-General on Division Staff.
(*From a recent Photograph*)

rebel horsemen since the fight at Brandy Station, quietly following the movements of the army in its march toward Washington. Longstreet, unobserved, had taken position along the easterly slope of the mountains, and to Stuart's cavalry had been detailed the duty of guarding his flanks and defending the gaps. General Pleasonton had been scouting along the Blue Ridge with Gregg's division of cavalry, when, on the 17th of June, he decided to go through Aldie Gap. The rebel cavalry had no suspicion that Pleasonton was in that vicinity, and had made a long march of forty miles for the purpose of occupying it themselves. Kilpatrick's brigade was in the advance, and the opposing forces soon met in deadly conflict.

Kilpatrick's force was a small one comprising the Second New York, First Maine and Harris Light—in the latter command were two companies from northern New Jersey, recruited by Kilpatrick himself. The First Rhode Island had been detached that morning with orders to join him at Middleburg. Forming the Second New York Kilpatrick boldly charged the enemy. This small force could not long withstand the shock, and as they galloped back to find a rallying point, the First Maine, supported by the Harris Light, rode upon the enemy with such tremendous force as to drive them from their defensive position, capturing a battalion of dismounted men before they could reach their horses, while the mounted rebels were sent reeling down the hill. They made no stop until they reached Middleburg, where Stuart had encountered

Duffie's division. The next day, the 19th, Pleasonton occupied Middleburg and Philemont, and after a series of brilliant encounters with the enemy succeeded in holding the positions he had gained. Stuart was forced to fall back behind Longstreet's infantry column, and the latter was compelled to take a more westerly route for his line of march.

Hooker promptly availed himself of the advantages thus gained by Pleasonton. On the 18th he occupied the gaps, the Twelfth Corps being ordered to Leesburg, the Fifth to Aldie and the Second to Thoroughfare Gap. The other corps of the army were formed in a second line in reserve.

An amusing, if ghastly, incident is related by a former Sergeant of Company K, Twelfth New Jersey, which occurred on the march to Thoroughfare Gap, with the Second Army Corps. The heat was oppressive. Men became utterly exhausted not alone from the severe marching, but their inability to get water. The streams were all dried up, and the little water the men had in their canteens had been churned to a disagreeable and nauseating degree of temperature. While the column was crossing Bull Run battle-field, murmurings of discontent arose from the ranks, the men being exceedingly fatigued and in a complaining mood. As the column moved on the body of a dead soldier was discovered, one of the arms protruding from the mound of earth which covered the remains and pointing upward. A soldier with a penchant for absurd remarks — and there were many such in the army — caught a glimpse of the uplifted arm and shouted out: "Say, boys, see the soldier putting out his hand for back pay!" The remark was infectious. Men forgot all about their sufferings, and the ghastly joke broke up all the disaffection which had previously existed.

The Union army halted on the line just established for several days. The position was an admirable one, fully protecting the Capital and giving the army a good base for future operations. In the event of Lee moving still further from Richmond Hooker possessed splendid opportunities for attacking him in the rear and threatening his line of communications. This Hooker was desirous of doing, but all his requests for coöperative movements were refused, and his suggestions treated with contempt. His relations with the government were of the most unpleasant nature, and he was continually thwarted in his designs.

The halt of the army at this juncture was not unwelcome to the troops. Ignorant of the intense excitement throughout the country, accustomed to place little reliance in the "grapevine" stories which reached them, they surrendered themselves to the comforts of camp life, utterly unmindful of the desperate activity which at that time was making of Harrisburg a fortified city, and even awakening Philadelphia to a sense of insecurity. The customary duties of camp life were at once instituted, and for the first time in its history an execution for desertion took place in the Army of the Potomac. Three men of the Twelfth Corps, two belonging to the Forty-sixth Pennsylvania and one to the Thirteenth New Jersey, were shot in the presence of the whole of the First Division on the 19th of June, at Leesburg. The reasons which impelled this action were given by General Slocum in an address at Gettysburg, on July 1, 1887, at the unveiling of the monument of the Thirteenth Regiment. As the incident related furnishes additional evidence of the kind heart of President Lincoln, it is worthy of reproduction. Desertions had been alarmingly frequent, particularly under General Burnside, and heroic measures were necessary in order to put a stop to them. General Slocum said :

" Mr. Lincoln, in the kindness of his heart, was constantly pardoning these men. He could not sign a man's death warrant.

" The corps commanders of the Army of the Potomac had a little conference, and they agreed that they would take the thing into their own hands and put a stop to it. They agreed that they would shoot somebody as speedily as they could. We all pledged ourselves to that. It so happened that I had at the time three of these men in my corps. They were tried; they were convicted upon incontestable evidence, and when we got up here to Leesburg, before the battle of Gettysburg, as all of you remember who were there, their graves were dug and the men were placed at the head of the graves and they were shot. They were sentenced to be shot between the hours of nine and

LIEUTENANT-COLONEL WILLIAM HENRY, JR.,
Commanding First Regiment N. J. Volunteer Infantry.
*(From a War-time Photograph).*

one. I gave the order that the troops should be brought out, and the moment the hands of the clock pointed to nine those men should be executed. I did so because I anticipated that a telegram would come from Mr. Lincoln, if he could possibly reach me. The wire had been built well up: they were within a few rods of me; I knew what was coming. Before ten o'clock I received a message from Mr. Lincoln saying if such a man, giving his name, has not been shot, ' you will suspend his sentence.' I sat down and telegraphed back to Mr. Lincoln, 'The man has been executed, pursuant to his sentence.' Then we came up here and fought the battle of Gettysburg. Great battles were fought out west; the whole country was in a state of intense excitement; and when we were ordered west after the battle of Gettysburg we went up to Washington to take the cars. I went to bid Mr. Lincoln good-bye; it was the last time I ever saw him. As I entered his room he said to me, without hardly waiting for me to greet him, ' General Slocum, the last message that I received from you gave me more pain than anything that has occurred since I took my seat as President.' I was astonished at his words and I said with surprise, ' Mr. Lincoln, I don't remember; what was it?' Said he, ' You were up there at Leesburg and I telegraphed you to suspend the sentence of a man who was condemned to death, and,' said he, ' the wife and the sister of that man sat here at this table opposite me and I had to open your telegraphic answer and read it to them.' Said he, ' it caused me more pain than almost anything that has occurred since I became President of the United States.'

"Now, think of it, gentlemen; think of what had intervened—three or four months, all crowded with great events, and yet the first thing that came into the mind of that great man when he saw me was this incident, this failure of his to save the life of one man."

During the time which intervened between the beginning of the campaign and the halt of the army on the line extending from Leesburg to Thoroughfare Gap, most of the nine months regiments returned to New Jersey. They were mustered out of the service at the following places:

Twenty-first Regiment, on June 19, 1863, at Trenton.
Twenty-second, on June 25, at Trenton.
Twenty-third, on June 27, at Beverly.
Twenty-fourth, on June 29, at Beverly.
Twenty-sixth, on June 27, at Newark.
Twenty-seventh, on July 2, at Newark.
Twenty-eighth, on July 6, at Freehold.
Twenty-ninth, on June 30, at Freehold.
Thirtieth, on June 27, at Flemington.
Thirty-first, on June 24, at Flemington.

The Twenty-fifth Regiment, which had served with the Ninth Corps, at Newport News and Suffolk, was mustered out on June 20, at Beverly.

# CHAPTER VI.

FROM THE RAPPAHANNOCK TO GUM SPRINGS—EXPERIENCES OF THE SEVENTH NEW JERSEY REGIMENT AND THE SECOND BRIGADE—USELESS NIGHT WORK—AN ALL-NIGHT MARCH.

IN THE foregoing pages the larger events of the campaign have been detailed with considerable minuteness and the army, as a whole, treated as a great machine, subject to the direction and control of its commander-in-chief; but this machine is composed of a large number of individual parts, and the manner in which they performed the severe tasks given them is a matter of great interest. At this first break in the progress of the army a favorable opportunity presents itself to introduce the recollections of some of those who participated in the march, enduring its fatigues, deprivations and hardships.

The Second New Jersey Brigade, Colonel George W. Burling, commander—comprising the Fifth, Sixth, Seventh and Eighth New Jersey Regiments, the One Hundred and Fifteenth Pennsylvania, and the Second New Hampshire—formed the Third Brigade of the Second Division, Third Corps. An officer of this gallant brigade who was wounded at Gettysburg details in the following interesting manner the experiences of that command:

"On the eleventh day of June, 1863, the Second Brigade broke camp near Falmouth, Va., and with the rest of the Third Corps, under command of General Sickles, marched up the Rappahannock river toward McLean's Ford, and Rappahannock Station on the Orange and Alexandria Railroad, arriving at the latter place at sunset the next day, and bivouacking on the north bank of the river. The only incidents of the march of these two days were the oppressive heat and the intolerable choking dust of the latter part of the march, especially when the column turned off upon a by-road, which led through a dense young growth of trees, to go to McLean's Ford. The close proximity of the river to our halting place, gave the men an opportunity to indulge in the luxury of a bath, and to relieve the choking, parched sensation with good drafts of coffee, before sinking down by their stacks of muskets for the long, good, undisturbed night's sleep. It was refreshing to the tired foot soldier to be allowed to sleep until he had enough, without being rudely awakened in the early morning by the sound of the "assembly." That was one of the few times in our experience in the Army of the Potomac that we were not aroused from our slumbers by some command, before we had fully rested from the fatigue of a long march.

"A slight stir was occasioned soon after sunrise by the galloping of horses about the field. The neighing

Colonel Samuel L. Buck,
Com'd'g 2d Regt. N. J. Vols., Inf.
(*From a War-time Photograph.*)

of the animals, and the shouts of the awakening soldiers as the horses jumped over the long lines of sleeping men in their wild career, caused no little excitement and apprehension; but no one was touched by the terrible hoofs of the mad beasts, which seemed almost as miraculous as that so many should escape injury in battle with a shower of deadly missiles flying all around.

"The regiments of the brigade were moved out of the open field during the day to the shelter of the surrounding woods, from the increasing heat of the Summer's sun. It was sultry and hot.

"At sundown a detail from the Seventh was made, of which Captain William R. Hillyer, of Company K, had charge, to construct a line of rifle-pits to command the approaches to the river. Having been supplied with picks and shovels the detail accompanied by the engineer proceeded to the river, on the bluffs overlooking which the pits had been marked for excavation. It was very slow work. The stiff, unyielding red clay seemed to resist all efforts to make an indentation into it with the picks, wielded by the nerveless arms of tired soldiers. The urging and stimulating commands of Captain Hillyer, with the constant shaking of the drowsy workers, scarcely sufficed to produce more than a beginning of the ditch laid out. The night's work was useless, and the men all felt that the task was an unnecessary one. Another element conducive to drowsiness was the inky blackness of the night, made more complete by the glimmering of myriads of fireflies, whose brilliant scintillations only rendered the shallowness of their illuminating power more conspicuous by the failure to penetrate the intense blackness in which they sparkled so continuously.

"Just here it is in place to remark that at that period of the war the veterans in the ranks had learned to scent danger far more keenly than those high in authority. They seemed to know intuitively when danger lurked about them and were better able to discriminate between useless and necessary toil and hardship. Their keen intelligence and sharpened instincts plainly satisfied these tired and worn-out soldiers that the task given them to do was utterly useless, and therefore no amount of threats or suggestive warnings had any stimulating effect upon them. Nothing could move them to tax their exhausted energies. We all knew before we began our labors that Lee's army was not contemplating any movement against Rappahannock Station, and it was no surprise that work on the pits ceased at daylight, when we were called into camp. We already knew that Lee was in the Valley.

"The entire day of the 14th was spent in camp and at 9 o'clock at night marching orders were received. To the squad of men who had spent the whole of the previous night on fatigue duty, the prospect of an all-night march was not pleasant to contemplate. However we joined the columns and with the rest of the corps moved up the railroad in the direction of

Manassas Junction. The aggravating halts to cross sloughs and brooks in single file, the hurrying to close the gaps thus made in the line, the roughness of the road, cut in many places through the thick scrub growth, beside the railroad bed, caused the weary hours of the night to slip rapidly by, and the early morning sun caught the column but ten or twelve miles on the road and more thoroughly worn out, than a twenty-mile march by daylight would have caused. We were at least eight hours in making this distance. Halting, stumbling over stumps and into ruts and mudholes, dozing as we walked in the ranks, and awakening by bumping against the knapsack of the man ahead.

"As daylight appeared and the sun rose, and the column still trudged on with no apparent intention of halting, the dusty, exhausted ranks sent up the shout of 'Coffee! coffee!' which passed along the column until it finally convinced the leader thereof that the earnest demand for refreshment should be heeded. About 7 o'clock, when the heat had already become unbearable, we turned into a field by the side of a clear stream near Warrenton Junction or Catlett's Station, stacked arms, refreshed ourselves with a good wash, cooked coffee, and stretching shelter tents to protect us from the broiling rays of the June sun, we were all soon asleep.

"At noon the march was resumed and taking the railroad track moved toward Bristoe Station and Manassas Junction. But oh! the sultriness of that long afternoon! The parched lips that gasped for water! The dozens of men overcome by the heat who dropped down by the wayside, especially in the long stretches of treeless and breezeless plantations that the column was compelled to cross! Of the Seventh Regiment, comprising about two hundred and fifty officers and men, there certainly were not twenty-five who followed the Colonel's horse into bivouac at Manassas Junction, when the command halted there at nine o'clock on the night of the fifteenth of June. But the stragglers came in as fast as their strength could carry them, and by morning all were ready for another start except the dozen or so made sick by the heat and march of the day before.

" This exhaustive ordeal was followed by two nights of good rest, and on the seventeenth, refreshed and buoyant, a change in the temperature also favoring us, we went along at a swinging gait across Bull Run, over the battle ground of '61, up the heights of Centreville, where we halted and rested another day. On the nineteenth we marched across Fairfax County toward the mountains in the distance. That day the column kept well together. There was no straggling and no annoyances from dust or heat.

" Hooker's manœuvering of his army was occasioned by his lack of knowledge of Lee's intentions, based upon the supposition that Washington was Lee's objective point, and to keep his army between Lee and Washington ready to be interposed upon any route of approach to that city which the enemy might select.

Thus it was that we first covered the fords of the upper Rappahannock, and now at Gum Spring, where we went into camp on the evening of the nineteenth, the passes to the Valley were fully masked, while Hooker in his headquarters at Fairfax Court House, received hourly intelligence from the cavalry outposts in the gaps of the movements of the Confederate army through the Valley.

"The signal stations at Aldie, Goose Creek and Fairfax Court House formed an unbroken chain. The Seventh New Jersey was detached from the brigade to guard the signal station from bushwackers, or Moseby's guerillas, who, we were all well aware, were all around us in their peaceful homes in the garb of honest farmers, and innocent of all hostile intent, as long as we were in force among them and on the alert. From the rocky promontory at Goose] Creek, on which the signal station was placed, there was spread out below us the Valley of the Potomac, Leesburg, Edward's Ferry and the mountains in the distance. It was a beautiful prospect and thoroughly appreciated by the men of the Seventh who had been for two years shut up in the pine woods and lowlands of Virginia."

## CHAPTER VII.

HOOKER'S PERPLEXITIES AGGRAVATED—A DASHING CAVALRY EXPLOIT—LEE'S ARMY IN PENNSYLVANIA—THE UNION FORCES CROSS THE POTOMAC—STUART'S RAID—GENERAL HOOKER RESIGNS.

THE Army of the Potomac was daily undergoing serious depletion by the withdrawal of large numbers of the nine months' regiments owing to the expiration of their terms of service. To supply their places General Hooker made urgent appeals to the government for reinforcements, but he was only partially successful. Stannard's Vermont Brigade, a nine months' command, was ordered to him and assigned to Doubleday's division of the First Corps, Lockwood's Maryland Brigade was ordered to the Twelfth Corps, and Crawford's Pennsylvania Reserves at Alexandria were also directed to be sent to him. Stahl's division of cavalry, six thousand strong, were added to the Cavalry Corps. The hysterical cries of inaction which poured down upon Hooker, while he did not permit them to influence his actions, did produce a marked effect upon the government, and the administration without giving him credit for any sagacity whatever found much fault with him, and at the same time would

COLONEL HENRY W. BROWN,
Colonel Com'd'g 3d Regt. N. J. Vols., Inf.
(*From a War-time Photograph.*)

not give him the help he needed.  His suggestions were treated as of little account.  In the very beginning of the campaign when he had proposed to attack Hill at Fredericksburg and get between Lee and Richmond, the President wrote to him :

"If you find Lee coming to the north of the Rappahannock, I would by no means cross to the south of it. In one word, I would not take any risk of being entangled upon the *river like an ox jumped half over a fence, liable to be torn by dogs front and rear, without a fair chance to gore one way or kick the other.*"

Later, on June 10, the President wrote:

"Lee's army and not Richmond is your true objective point.  If he comes toward the upper Potomac, follow on his flank on the inside track, shortening your lines while he lengthens his.  Fight him when opportunity offers.  If he stays where he is *fret him and fret him*."

Yet, when General Hooker sent for Crawford's Pennsylvania Reserves to join his army, which had been ordered to him, the Military Governor of Alexandria, where the brigade was stationed, detained them there in defiance of Hooker's order, and was sustained by General Halleck in this act of insubordination.*  There were in the immediate defences of Washington a large body of troops under Generals Heintzelman and Schenck, and General Hooker's suggestion that they be sent to the front where they could be of direct service against the enemy, was refused.  A request

---

*Comte de Paris.

by General Hooker to General Heintzelman that the latter send a force of two thousand men from Poolesville, Md., to the passes of South Mountain, and thus aid in keeping Lee's column still further to the west, was likewise refused on the ground that the passes were not part of the Defences of Washington. Hooker was certainly in an unenviable position.

Pleasonton's cavalry performed the serviceable task of "fretting" Stuart—forcing him to combat wherever he could find him. A brilliant passage at arms between the troopers of these rival chieftains took place at Upperville on June 21st. Gregg's division engaged the enemy in front, while Buford swept entirely around their flank and threw his whole line of battle upon their weakest point. Chaplain Pyne thus describes the scene:

"Every field was the scene of a sanguinary contest, and every stone wall was made a fresh line of defence. On one occasion a regiment of rebels pouring into a field commenced forming line behind a wall, as the Eighth Illinois were forming on the other side of it. The race for first formation was one for life and death; and the eager horses came bounding into their places with a speed that partook of desperation. At length the Illinois regiment opened a deadly fire from their carbines. The rebels gallantly attempted a reply but the effort was too much for their failing endurance. Breaking in disorder, they were chased by Buford's exulting men, leaving twenty men stone dead in that short minute of fire. From that moment there was no longer a pretence at resistance. At full gallop the enemy hurried into and through Ashby's Gap, leaving nearly all their wounded, a crowd of prisoners, two guns, and several colors in our hands as trophies of the victory. The Confederate cavalry had lost its prestige forever."

Pleasonton at once started to rejoin the army, and this movement was interpreted as a retreat by the enemy. The First New Jersey Cavalry covered the rear, and though followed by the rebels in a spiritless manner no encounters of any moment took place. On one occasion when the cavalry had almost reached the limit of their day's march, the enemy opened upon them with artillery, a piece of shell striking Louis Vandegrift, of Company D, First New Jersey, fatally wounding him. Orders had been received to fall back when Vandegrift was hit, but before vacating the ground his comrades concealed his body in a corner of the fence. After the line halted for the night five volunteers rode back to the spot, and while four of them faced the enemy, the other one dismounted and placed the body on his horse. Thus guarded the five gallant fellows rejoined their commands and Vandegrift was given a soldier's burial. This was the only casualty in the course of the movement.

The retrograde movement of Pleasonton convinced Lee that Hooker would not engage him in battle south of the Potomac, and he accordingly gave the order for the long contemplated invasion. On the 22d of June, Ewell crossed the Potomac river and

Jenkins with his cavalry brigade was ordered forward to Chambersburg, which place Rodes and Johnson's divisions reached the next day, Early's division taking the road to York by way of Gettysburg. Jenkins left Chambersburg on the arrival of these troops and proceeded toward Harrisburg, which place Ewell had been directed to take possession of if possible. On the 23d, Lee having been apprised of Pleasonton's retreat ordered the corps of Longstreet and Hill to cross the Potomac, the former at Williamsport, the latter at Shepherdstown, which was consummated on the 24th and 25th, both forces uniting at Hagerstown, in support of Ewell's advance. On the 27th, two-thirds of Lee's army was massed near Chambersburg, with Ewell proceeding on his northern mission.

General Hooker was apprised of Ewell's advance on the 23d and on the 25th had knowledge of the proposed movement of the two remaining corps, and being now fully satisfied that Washington was safe from a surprise movement by Lee gave orders for the advance of his army on a line parallel to that of the enemy, taking the east side of the South Mountain. On the 26th the Twelfth Corps crossed the Potomac at Edwards' Ferry, with orders to proceed to Harper's Ferry, and act in conjunction with the forces there against Lee's communications with Richmond, and follow up his rear through the Cumberland Valley. The rest of the army proceeded on the line as marked out, the First Corps halting at Middletown on the 27th, the Second at Barnesville, the Third at Middle-

LIEUT.-COL. CHARLES EWING,
Major Com'd'g 4th Regt. N. J. Vols., Inf.
(*From a War-time Photograph.*)

town, the Fifth at Ballinger's Creek, the Sixth bringing up the rear at Poolesville. The Twelfth Corps reached Knoxville, three miles from Harper's Ferry on its special errand. The First New Jersey Cavalry, which covered the rear of the army, was the last body of troops to cross the river.

Lee was kept in entire ignorance of Hooker's prompt action, by the absence of Stuart with his cavalry, who, with the permission of his chief, had started to make a circuit of the Union army. Stuart's intention was to turn the left flank of Hooker, and delay, if not prevent his crossing of the Potomac river. This raid, so full of discomfiture, disappointment and vexation, absolutely barren of any important result, was of great value to the Union cause. Leaving behind him the brigades of Jones and Robertson, who were to keep close watch of the Union army and follow its movements, Stuart on the night of June 24th set off on his famous raid. Moving in a southerly direction he encountered the Second Corps at Haymarket, which compelled him to make a wide detour to conceal his movement, and on the 27th, when Lee's troops were near Chambersburg and Hooker's army had all crossed the Potomac and were far away in Maryland, his two columns were at Burke's and Fairfax Stations. Following in the rear of the Union army he reached Drainesville on the day the Sixth Corps left it, and discovered the important fact that Hooker instead of waiting to have his flank turned had moved off, Stuart did not know where. Under the impression however that the Union troops were marching in force toward Leesburg, he, with great difficulty, crossed the Potomac near Drainesville, intending to rejoin Lee by marching through Maryland. He was simply following in the rear of Hooker's army, who had two days the start of him.

Ignorant of the ridiculous position he was in, his troopers began to pick up small detachments of Union soldiers, capturing wagon trains, creating a panic among teamsters, and committing depredations almost within sight of the Capital. On his northward march he did considerable damage to railroad tracks and bridges, and burdened himself with a long train of captured wagons, filled with supplies of all kinds, and with which he was anxious to get to Lee's lines. But he was ignorant of its whereabouts, and on the 29th moved toward Westminster, where he was confronted by a squadron of Union cavalry, who stoutly contested his advance, and inflicted considerable loss upon him before they gave way. On the 30th Stuart started for Hanover, hoping to find Early there or to get some information as to his whereabouts, but as he ascended the small hills overlooking the town, to his dismay he saw a column of Union cavalry marching through the place, going north. Here was a dilemma. Retreat was out of the question, and as he seemed to be surrounded by enemies in whatever direction he moved, he determined, with becoming audacity, to attack Kilpatrick's column, and gain possession of the Gettysburg Road. His encounter with Kilpatrick, at first successful, was turned into defeat by the timely arrival of reinforcements, and taking a more easterly route he marched his men all night long, arriving in Dover on the morning of the first, only to learn that Early had occupied all that territory but had departed suddenly. Moving on the afternoon of the 1st of July to Carlisle he encountered General W. F. Smith's troops from Harrisburg, who had taken possession of the town, and remaining only long enough to demand its surrender under threat of bombardment he started for Gettysburg where he arrived on the afternoon of the 2d of July, and greeted his chief for the first time in seven days. His men were worn out and exhausted after their long, arduous and fatiguing journey.

In thus digressing to follow Stuart in his erratic movement and bewildering surprises, the regular course of events with the main bodies of troops have been interrupted. The orders for the Union army for June 28th directed the First Corps to Frederick City, the Second to Monocacy Junction, the Third to Woodsboro, the Sixth to Hyattstown, the Eleventh to Middletown, and the Twelfth to Frederick City. The contemplated movement on the rear of Lee's army was thus abandoned, by the refusal of General Halleck to permit the troops at Harper's Ferry to be placed under Hooker's control and that officer resigned his command, which was promptly accepted.

It is very evident that the removal of General Hooker was a subject that had for some time been in contemplation by the government. He was deliberately refused every important thing he asked for, and realizing that without the active support and coöperation of the government, the army would be crippled in an encounter with the enemy, he promptly resigned. The feeling of the government as it existed toward Hooker is fully explained in the following extract from Mr. Blaine's "Twenty Years in Congress":

"The indispensable requisite to Union success was a commander for the Army of the Potomac in whose competency the administration, the people, and most of all the soldiers, would have confidence. In the judgment of military men it was idle to entrust another battle to the generalship of Hooker, and as the army moved across Maryland, General Hooker was relieved and the command of the army assigned to General George G. Meade."

General Hooker would evidently have been relieved had he not resigned, but it was clearly a mistake to have retained him so long in command without giving him the support and coöperation he deserved. His request for the utilization of the forces at Harper's Ferry was refused. General Meade was permitted to use them without a murmur. The Pennsylvania Reserves, refused to Hooker, joined Meade on the march. In fact Meade, whose competency to command had yet to be proved, who had yet to win the confidence of the soldiers as a leader, was to be as strenuously upheld in all his acts as Hooker had been repressed. The difficulty of choosing a successor to Hooker had for some time been a source of trouble to the Secretary of War, and it is related that when the messenger whom Secretary Stanton had sent with the order putting Meade in command of the army, returned, the Secretary was impressed with the great fact that General Meade, while he had no desire to succeed to the command of the army, made no comment on the removal of Hooker. This may or may not be true, but General Meade very wisely made no change in the personal staff, retaining that of General Hooker's as his own.

## CHAPTER VIII.

THE ALARM IN THE NORTH—NEW JERSEY'S GOVERNOR APPEALS TO THE PRESIDENT—THE NEW UNION COMMANDER—MOVEMENTS OF THE ARMIES—REMINISCENSES OF AN OFFICER OF THE SECOND NEW JERSEY BRIGADE—THE THIRTEENTH NEW JERSEY AT LITTLESTOWN—THE NIGHT BEFORE THE BATTLE.

THE alarm which prevailed in Pennsylvania when Jenkins made his raid of the 17th subsided on his return to Williamsport, only to break out afresh and with increased anxiety when the forward movement of Lee's army began in earnest. The Twenty-third New Jersey Regiment had returned home and on the 27th of June was mustered out; the Twenty-Seventh Regiment remained until the 26th of June when it left Harrisburg for Newark, where it was mustered out on July 2d; the militia under Captain Murphy had received orders from Governor Parker to return, but the changed situation caused him to remain until all danger was over. With Longstreet and Hill at Chambersburg, Ewell with two divisions at Carlisle while Early was moving toward York, destroying the

BVT. MAJOR-GEN. WILLIAM J. SEWELL,
Colonel Com'd'g 5th Regt. N. J. Vols., Inf.
*(From Photograph Since the War.)*

Northern Central railroad, and levying contributions on the people, and Jenkins with a large cavalry force moving directly on Harrisburg, the invasion assumed immense proportions.

The finest agricultural region of the North lay at the mercy of the rebel army. If Lee's horses laughed and his men became merry at the bounteous plenty which surrounded them they met their Bartholomew a few days later. The tendency to pillage and destroy was great, and many unnecessary burdens were placed upon these peaceful people; but war is a terrible, earnest thing, and General Lee endeavored to mitigate its severities by issuing strict orders as to the manner in which supplies should be taken. If the revengeful spirits of his men overcame their respect for their commander's instructions, that was a matter beyond his immediate control.

Governor Curtin called anew for troops and issued a proclamation for the raising of sixty thousand men. Vain call. There were no arms with which to supply so large an army except old flint locks and shot-guns, and the time was short for the proper organizing of such a host. But some came. New York, West Virginia and Philadelphia responded, and additional appeals were made to New Jersey for aid. The attempt to muster into the United States service all the troops which had volunteered for the emergency, seemed to Governor Parker a serious thing, as it would take from his control the militia of the State then serving in Pennsylvania, and his own fears that New

Jersey was imperilled led him to telegraph to President Lincoln direct as follows:

EXECUTIVE CHAMBER,
TRENTON, June 29, 1863.
*To the President of the United States:*
The people of New Jersey are apprehensive that the invasion of the enemy may extend to her soil. We think that the enemy should be driven from Pennsylvania. There is now certainly a great apathy under such fearful circumstances. That apathy should be removed. The people of New Jersey want McClellan at the head of the Army of the Potomac. If that cannot be done, then we ask that he may be put at the head of the New Jersey, New York and Pennsylvania troops now in Pennsylvania defending these middle States from invasion. If either appointment be made the people will rise *en masse*.

I feel it my duty, respectfully, to communicate this state of feeling to you.

JOEL PARKER.

The President replied as follows:

WASHINGTON, June 30, 1863.
*To Governor Parker:*
Your dispatch of yesterday received. I really think the attitude of the enemy's army in Pennsylvania presents us the best opportunity we have had since the war begun.

I think you will not see the foe in New Jersey.

I beg you to be assured that no one out of my

position can know so well, as if he were in it, the difficulties and involvements of replacing General McClellan in command, and this aside from any imputations upon him.

Please accept my sincere thanks for what you have done and are doing to get troops forward.

A. LINCOLN.

The invasion, however, came to an abrupt and sudden termination. On the 28th of June General Lee had been reliably informed of the presence of the Army of the Potomac at Frederick. This was startling news, as he had supposed that that army was still south of the Potomac, held in check by the ambitious and daring Stuart. He saw at once that his communications were endangered, and, as Hooker had predicted, an attack in Lee's rear would compel him to turn back and give battle, or at least bring the invasion to an end. Realizing the great peril of his position he determined upon the no less bold and audacious plan of threatening Baltimore, and thus he simply did what General Meade was preparing to meet, though not exactly in the manner in which he was compelled to. Lee at once sent couriers to all his corps commanders to concentrate their troops at Gettysburg, and on the 29th the rebel columns headed southward.

The change of commanders in the Army of the Potomac from General Hooker to General Meade was effected quietly and with no intermission in its work. The march was continued as though nothing unusual had happened, but there was a deep feeling of regret at the resignation of General Hooker. The frequent changes that had taken place in the head of the Army of the Potomac, from the time McClellan had been relieved by order of the President, had almost destroyed the feeling of hero worship which existed in its early history. The army had developed into a self-reliant body of men, bent upon a certain mission the success of which outweighed all personal considerations, and its emotional nature though not wholly destroyed, had been disciplined into wholesome restraint. McClellan, who organized the army, had won the affections of the men. They followed him with enthusiasm through all the vicissitudes of the Peninsula campaign; they hailed his return to command, after the defeat of Pope, with joy and gladness, and their final parting with him was like the separation of life-long friends. Under any other form of government, a change of this nature, in the very midst of an active campaign and on the eve of an important military movement, might have led to serious consequences; but McClellan's ready acquiescence in the orders of his government had much to do with allaying personal feeling in so important a matter. General Burnside, who succeeded him, was known to the men of the Army of the Potomac as a patriotic and loyal man of great personal bravery, and of commanding presence. His modesty of demeanor, coupled with his gallantry and bravery, caused him to be received with great cordiality, and with the same fidelity it had shown toward McClellan, the Army of the Potomac moved with Burnside and fought the disastrous battle of Fredericksburg, where on Marye's Heights it vainly expended its force in a succession of assaults which stand unrivalled evidences of soldierly performance of duty and personal valor. The supersedure of Burnside by Hooker, who had won the significant cognomen of "Fighting Joe," by many deeds of daring in the Peninsula, restored the confidence of the army which had been seriously impaired by the Fredericksburg disaster. The unfortunate result of the Chancellorsville campaign did not destroy the confidence of the army in Hooker's ability, and it entered upon the Gettysburg march with all its old-time ardor and spirit. The change, sudden as it was, whereby General Meade succeeded to the command of the army, caused only a momentary feeling of regret to pass through the ranks. Hooker was beloved, Meade was little known, except as the commander of one of the best corps in the army. This fact reconciled the troops at once to his appointment. He had never won distinction, or made himself conspicuous, as had Hooker or Kearny or Hancock; but his qualifications, so greatly the reverse of those which made them thus prominent, stamped him as a man of sterling worth; his personal bravery was undisputed, and his heart was in full sympathy with the government. The characteristics of the several corps commanders were discussed frequently on a march, and they were generally "sized up" with great accuracy. It was the prevalent belief that Meade was a "safe" man, but not a brilliant or inspiring commander. The army was willing to take him on trial.

General Meade's first action on assuming command was to recall General Slocum and the Twelfth Corps, from its special mission in coöperation with the forces of General French at Harper's Ferry, and to order the latter to occupy Frederick when the army advanced. As strong evidence that General Hooker's removal had been contemplated for some time past, the action of General Halleck is significant. His first dispatch to the new commander of the army, placed under his control, with unlimited power, not only the troops of General French, which were refused to Hooker, but also the forces of Generals Schenck and Couch. For the first time in its history the commander of the Army of the Potomac was such in fact as well as in name.

The responsibilities of General Meade were great and he realized it. Retaining the personal staff of General Hooker as his own, he thus came into the possession of information which was of great assistance to him, but he was still ignorant of the intentions of Lee. Having abandoned Hooker's idea of attacking Lee on the line of his communications with Richmond, he so disposed his forces as to interpose them between the rebel army and the cities of Philadelphia, Baltimore and Washington, should Lee attempt an advance on either place. His orders to the several corps commanders for the 29th of June were for the First and Eleventh Corps to move to Emmetsburg; the Third

COLONEL GEORGE C. BURLING,
6th Regt. N. J. Vols., Inf., Commanding 2d N. J. Brig. (3d Brig., 2d Div., 3d Corps.
(*From a Photograph after the War.*)

and Twelfth to Taneytown; the Second to Uniontown; the Fifth to Liberty, and the Sixth to New Windsor. The orders to the cavalry were for Buford to guard the left flank of the army by moving toward Fairfield, Gregg's division to protect the right flank at New Windsor, while Kilpatrick was to cover the centre by an advance to Littlestown. The army moved in three columns, the First and Eleventh Corps forming the left, the Third and Twelfth Corps the centre, and the Second, Fifth and Sixth Corps the right columns.

The country through which the army was now passing teemed with a loyal and patriotic people. The presence of the Army of the Potomac was greeted with every manifestation of delight. To men who had spent the greater part of their soldier life in the pine forests of Virginia, where population was sparse, and what there was of it hostile to the cause they represented, and whose professed loyalty to the government was in most cases a subterfuge to secure protection for their property, the change to the open country of Western Maryland, and among a people who showed by their demeanor that they were friends to the Union cause, was exceedingly gratifying. An officer of the Second New Jersey Brigade in a letter to the author thus details his recollections of events on this march, the correctness of which every soldier in the Army of the Potomac, at that time, will verify:

"On the 25th of June the Second Brigade crossed the Potomac river at Edward's Ferry, marched rapidly up the tow-path of the Ohio and Chesapeake canal, which here followed the course of the river, and bivouacked where night overtook us—on the bank of the stream. The marching was rapid, no rests were taken, and every man seemed to be left to himself to plod along as well as possible. When night came on every man halted where he was, picked out a good spot for his night's rest and without any formality spread his blankets and soon fell into a deep and refreshing sleep. The bank of the river, for ten or fifteen miles, was lined with straggling regiments. No details for picket or guard were made, the canal on one side and the bank of the river on the other precluding the necessity for sentries, and abandoning themselves wholly to the novelty of the situation, all were soon wrapped in deep slumber. The next morning witnessed a grand scurrying along of ten thousand lost warriors, eager to join their colors lest 'absence without leave' might be scored against them. Officers and enlisted men were all in the same list, and it was impossible to say whether colonels and brigadier-generals had lost their commands, or regiments and brigades had lost their commanders. It was an open question and has never been settled. Nevertheless, as the sun mounted up into the sky there was a mysterious gravitating of the units of military commands into their proper bodies, and a gradual augmenting of companies, regiments and brigades as the minutes and hours flew by, so that by the middle of the forenoon we were once more pushing along in solid columns and with no straggling. We crossed the

Monocacy river on the canal aqueduct, took the road for Point of Rocks, climbed up the hills, in a sheltered depression on the north side of which we bivouacked for the night.

"The next day we marched northward through the beautiful valley to Middletown, then turned eastward over the mountains by the pike to Frederick City, stripping the cherry trees on every hand and enjoying a royal feast of that delicious fruit which abounded in profusion and perfection just at that time. Here it was that the Army of the Potomac first realized what it was to march through a country inhabited by a loyal and patriotic people. Our progress was an ovation of cheering, sympathetic, grateful greetings from a happy, peaceful populace, unscathed by the devastation of war. The cherry trees were the only property of the farmers of Maryland that the toil-worn, hungry veterans were permitted to depredate upon, and they were stripped clean by the fortunate divisions of the army that chanced to be in the van.

"The welcoming demonstrations of the people of Maryland aroused great enthusiasm in the Army of the Potomac. The profuse display of the Stars and Stripes from almost every house, the waving of handkerchiefs, and the smiles of fair ladies, the hearty hospitality as exhibited by the generous distribution of biscuits, milk, pies, cakes, and chickens, hastily cooked, to the appreciative soldiers was a revelation to the Army of the Potomac all the more astounding because of its contrast with the reception of the Massachusetts troops two years before in the city of Baltimore, and the well-tested disloyalty of that city and southern Maryland in the intervening years. The rivers of fresh milk that poured down the throats of the fifty thousand veterans of the army in those two or three days cannot be computed in gallons or in value, and it was all the more refreshing and grateful because it was a generous gift from the farmers to their defenders. That night we encamped on the north side of Frederick, after passing through that city amid the waving of innumerable flags and the cheering of the delighted populace. The next morning came the thunderbolt into camp which announced the resignation of the gallant fighter and beloved commander of our old division, Joe Hooker, and the appointment of General Meade as his successor.

"On June 29th we marched north toward Taneytown, the residence of the late Chief Justice of the United States, who rendered the famous Dred Scott decision, one of the fire-brands that helped to kindle the flames of rebellion. We also passed the home of Philip Barton Key, who was killed by our corps commander General Daniel E. Sickles, in Washington several years before the war, both being members of Congress at the time."

The demonstrations of welcome which greeted every corps of the army acted as an inspiration upon the men. Fatigue was forgotten, and the one all-pervading desire was to meet the rebel army while it was on northern soil. As the column of Meade's army reached northward, all unconscious of the direct approach of Lee southward, the rebel chieftain was likewise moving without any knowledge of the whereabouts of Meade, whom he still supposed to be forty miles or more away, at Frederick and vicinity. The orders General Meade gave for his army brought them in the following position on the 30th of June: The First Corps at Marsh Run, the Third at Bridgeport, the Fifth at Union Mills, the Sixth at Manchester, the Twelfth at Littlestown. The Second Corps remained at Uniontown and the Eleventh at Emmetsburg, while the cavalry was operating on the flanks of the army, Kilpatrick encountering Stuart at Hanover, while Buford was scouting about the mountains near Fairfield, Gregg covering the extreme right by moving on Manchester. In accordance with General Meade's instructions, a portion of General French's command took position at Frederick City.

The advance of the Twelfth Corps from Taneytown to Littlestown on the 30th of June brought the Thirteenth New Jersey Regiment to the front, their position for the day being the extreme right of the line. The march was void of incident until within about a mile of Littlestown when the column halted, owing to a report from Kilpatrick's cavalry that a large cavalry force of the enemy was near the town. The presence along the road of a large number of ablebodied citizens, who had left Littlestown, was a source of much comment and no little amusement to the veterans, and as they loaded muskets preparatory to a possible encounter with the enemy, the non-combatants expressed doubt of the ability of the Army of the Potomac to cope with the rebel forces. Moving forward at a rapid gait the Third Brigade of the Twelfth Corps reached the outskirts of Littlestown, and three regiments of the brigade with Winegar's battery went on a double quick through the town and to the fields beyond.

The approach of the Union army was hailed with joy by the people of Littlestown who heartily welcomed them by furnishing the soldiers with abundant supplies of food. To the tired army this generous hospitality was appreciated, and when at night the Thirteenth Regiment with the First Division of the Twelfth Corps went into camp on the farms of Spangler and Le Fevre on the McSherrystown road, they felt it no hardship to obey the strange and before unheard-of order: "No rail fences are to be disturbed and no rails burned for any purpose whatever." This order was religiously obeyed, and the people of Littlestown to this day bear testimony to that fact. These incidents gave strong indication of near approach to the enemy, and the Army of the Potomac was on the alert and ready.

At Harrisburg General Couch had succeeded in getting a few thousand militia organized and with General W. F. Smith kept close watch of the enemy's movements, reporting to Washington the information thus obtained. By this means General Meade was kept informed as to the progress Lee was making, and on the 30th had received notification of the withdrawal of Ewell's forces. When Ewell received orders from Lee to return at once to Carlisle, he had disposed his forces for the purpose of advancing upon and capturing Harrisburg, and as he moved backward General Smith, with such cavalry as he could muster, closely followed him. Ewell had no sooner left Carlisle for Harrisburg than General Smith occupied the place, and when Stuart a short time after came to the town in search of Ewell, after his long and exhaustive ride, he found the Union forces in possession.

General Lee's orders to his army were for Heth's division with eight batteries of artillery, followed by Pender's division, with Hood and McLaws *en echelon* behind him to march to Gettysburg. Ewell's division was scattered, Johnson's division was sent to Greenwood, and he was greatly delayed in rejoining his command. This was the situation on the night of the 30th of June.

## CHAPTER IX.

THE FIRST DAY'S FIGHT AT GETTYSBURG—GALLANTRY OF BUFORD'S TROOPERS—HEROIC RESISTANCE BY THE FIRST ARMY CORPS — DEATH OF GENERAL REYNOLDS — ARRIVAL OF HOWARD AND THE RETREAT TO CEMETERY RIDGE -- HANCOCK'S OPPORTUNE ARRIVAL ON THE FIELD.

GETTYSBURG! The terrible three days' conflict on the heights surrounding this little town, from the masterly and heroic achievements of Buford's cavalry and the First Army Corps at Willoughby Run, to the spectacular and brilliant charge by Pickett's Virginians of Longstreet's corps on the third day of July, has been a theme of controversy among the chief participants and inspired the pens of the most gifted writers to a description in detail of all the momentous events which there happened. Swinton, in his admirable "History of the Army of the Potomac," gives a critical review of the battle; Doubleday, who commanded the First Corps, after the lamentable death of Reynolds, in its desperate struggle with superior numbers of the enemy, has written a graphic and unvarnished account of that magnificent engagement; Walker in his "History of the Second Army

COLONEL LOUIS R. FRANCINE,
7th Regt. N. J. Vols., Inf.
(*From a War-time Photograph*—1863.)

Corps" pays a glowing tribute to the men who composed that gallant body of soldiers, and Longstreet has given his version of the battle from his knowledge of Lee's plans, and in vindication of his own course, which has opened a controversy along the southern line of the argument that seems to grow more aggressive with time. The Comte de Paris, from the standpoint of an impartial and disinterested observer, has furnished the most complete and thorough record of the battle, and his unbiassed views on all the disputed questions which have arisen will be accepted as being nearer correct and just than those of interested controversialists. To the mind of the layman, these points of dispute are of little account. The advent of the rebel army to the close proximity of Harrisburg; the great destruction it did do and was capable of doing; the doubt and uncertainty which prevailed as to the ability of the Army of the Potomac to repel the invasion and drive the southern army back to its own soil, these were the questions of great concern then. The fact that the invasion was stayed and the Union arms victorious over an exulting foe, is sufficient cause for satisfaction now, and the army which accomplished it is deserving the admiration of mankind.

If there be such a thing as chance in the affairs of nations, good fortune had certainly smiled upon the preliminary movements of the Army of the Potomac. The Quixotic raid of Stuart, whose long absence lured the rebel commander into a belief that his principal antagonist was unable or unwilling to follow him, was the first of a series of fortunate blunders which contributed to the success of the Union army.

As has been already noticed General Lee had ordered the concentration of his army at Gettysburg, for the double purpose of protecting his own line of communications, and being in position to threaten the cities of Baltimore and Washington. He was thus contemplating just such a move as General Meade had been preparing for, and both Generals were desirous of fighting on a defensive line. Lee hoped by manœuvering to compel Meade to attack him, and under the impression that the Union army was in the neighborhood of Frederick, the movement of his army toward Gettysburg was conducted in a leisurely and confident manner. When General Meade gave orders for Reynolds with the left wing of the army to occupy Gettysburg on the first of July, he was also in ignorance as to the whereabouts of Lee, or what his intentions were, and when, later in the day, on the 30th, he received information from General Halleck that the rebels were moving southward, he resolved to take up a defensive position on the line of Pipe Creek, toward which the army was to fall back should they encounter the enemy in great numbers. He was still unaware of the close proximity of the rebel army and did not change his orders for the day. Thus both armies were moving simultaneously toward a common centre neither of them dreaming that the bloodiest drama of the war was about to be enacted at the very place each desired to occupy.

Gettysburg is the county seat of Adams County, and from it many roads radiate in all directions like spokes from a hub. At the north of the town the three roads, known as the Harrisburg, Carlisle and Mummasburg roads, all concentrate, while the York and Bonaughtown roads join at the east. On the western border the Chambersburg and Fairfield roads unite, while on the south the Emmetsburg, Taneytown

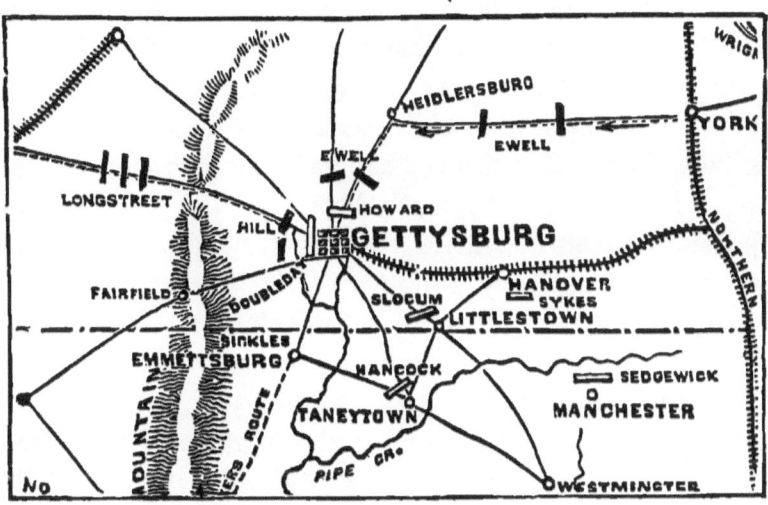

POSITION OF BOTH ARMIES ON THE MORNING OF JULY I.
UNION, WHITE; REBELS, BLACK.

and Baltimore roads, on all of which the Union army was marching, converge. Both armies were surely but gradually coming together, and the well-matured plans of the Union commander were to be overruled. The topography of the country about Gettysburg was admirably adapted for a battle-field and the many eminences afforded splendid opportunities for effective artillery display. It is very evident General Meade, though a Pennsylvanian, did not have any personal knowledge of the natural advantages the country about Gettysburg afforded for military operations.

General Meade was fortunate in having able and experienced corps commanders to assist him in this trying emergency. The cavalry arm of the service was well officered and ably commanded, by men who had all been tried in desperate encounters with the enemy, and they were nerved to any ordeal that might present itself, while, as for the troopers themselves, they had measured sabres with their opponents and did not fear them, and as will be seen in the pursuit of this narrative, they boldly and spiritedly resisted the infantry columns of the enemy, and with marked effect. Watchful, sleepless, Pleasonton's cavalry seemed to be everywhere and always just where it was most needed. On the 28th of June, the day that Meade took command, Gregg's division was on the right of the army, Buford guarding the left flank, while Kilpatrick covered the centre. Buford had sent Merritt's brigade of Regulars to Mechanicstown, southeast of Emmetsburg, while he accompanied the brigades of Gamble and Devens, on a spirited reconnoissance down the west slope of South Mountain. On the following day he moved up the valley northward to Waynesboro, recrossed the mountain range, and at night halted on the Fairfield road along which, in the distance, he saw the fires of Davis' brigade of

BVT. MAJOR-GEN. JOHN RAMSEY,
Colonel Com'd'g 8th Regt. N. J. Vols.
(*From a War-time Photograph.*)

Heth's rebel division of Hill's corps. At break of day on the 30th he dashed into the presence of the enemy, who retreated northward after exchanging a few shots, and satisfied of his inability to successfully cope with them, returned to Emmetsburg where he reported to Reynolds the events which had transpired. That officer having received orders for the left wing of the army to proceed to Gettysburg the next day, ordered Buford to take immediate possession of the town, and hold it until the arrival of the First Corps.

This important duty could not have been entrusted to a better or more capable man. Buford had distinguished himself in many previous engagements with the rebel cavalry, but his stubborn resistance to the infantry columns of Lee's veterans on the first day of July, was an exhibition of daring and skillful generalship which entitles him to rank with the bravest and best of those who fought so desperately and well on that memorable field.

The encounter with Buford's cavalry on the Fairfield road did not seem to produce any special excitement in the rebel lines, as on the 30th of June when Heth's division reached Cashtown, he dispatched Pettigrew's brigade, with a large wagon train, to Gettysburg for the purpose of making a requisition on the town for shoes and clothing. Pettigrew was about entering the town, when Buford came thundering along with his four thousand troopers, and the rebel scouts had barely time to notify Pettigrew of his approach, and thus enable that officer to fall back to a safe position on Marsh Creek. Halting his column there, Pettigrew notified Heth of the occupancy of the town by the Union cavalry. General Buford did not attempt to follow up Pettigrew, but took position on the west and north of the town, posting videttes far ahead on all the roads that were intersected by his line. Buford knew that the rebel army was close by and he anticipated a desperate and a serious struggle. He at once notified Meade and Reynolds of the disposition he had made of his forces, and calmly awaited the advance of the enemy's infantry.

At an early hour on the morning of July 1st Heth's division moved from Cashtown toward Gettysburg, and gathering up Pettigrew's division marched forward rapidly, anticipating nothing more serious than a brush with militia. But their first encounter with Buford's brave cavalrymen who had been posted in the most advantageous manner along Willoughby Run, amazed them. Buford stoutly contested every inch of ground, and held the advancing columns in check. Indeed, the numerical strength of the enemy was so great that by a persistent advance they could have swept Buford's forces away, but the ignorance which prevailed throughout the whole rebel army as to the whereabouts of the Army of the Potomac, caused them to move with caution. The Union cavalry made so determined and stubborn a resistance, however, that Heth supposed he had encountered a strong body of infantry. Reinforcing his line he again advanced, and Buford putting in his last reserve, and personally directing the fire of his artillery, prolonged the struggle until the troops of Reynolds came in sight.

When Buford saw the desperate conflict his men were waging against superior numbers he doubted his ability to hold the position a great while longer, and started for the seminary building to get a view, if possible, of the First Corps. He was quickly apprised of its approach by the appearance of General Reynolds himself, who had galloped forward in advance of his troops as soon as he heard the booming of Buford's guns. The cavalry had made a gallant and glorious fight, and the check the rebel advance had received saved to the Union army the line of hills south of the town on which the decisive battle was finally fought.

When the sound of conflict reached the ears of General Reynolds, he lost no time in hurrying forward his men. Giving orders to prepare for immediate action he started off on a gallop to find Buford, on a ride that would have been immortalized in verse had the drama, in which he was so prominent a figure, not assumed proportions of such great magnitude. The regiment in the advance of the First Corps that day, was the Ninety-fifth New York, Colonel George H. Biddle. In its ranks were a goodly number of New Jersey boys, mostly from the city of Newark, whose patriotism had exercised so controlling an influence over their emotions that they went into New York city and enrolled themselves in the first regiment which took their fancy. While, therefore, no distinctively New Jersey regiment was engaged in the first day's battle at Gettysburg, the State was most nobly represented by more than a score of brave fellows, "natives all and to the manner born."

The march to the scene of action was an inspiriting sight. General Reynolds was one of the ablest and best known of all the corps commanders. Possessing rare personal courage, coupled with military ability and skill of a high order, he was well adapted to initiate the great battle about to take place. A native of Pennsylvania, he was incensed at the presence of the rebel army there, and was anxious to engage them in battle at the very earliest opportunity. His men were all infected with the same spirit, and they moved to the sound of Buford's artillery with that steady, quickened motion which betokened confidence and gave evidence of the desperate earnestness which so distinguished them a few hours later. The Comte de Paris in describing the spirit which animated the Army of the Potomac says:

"The Federal soldiers and their leaders are fired by extraordinary zeal; like Antæus, who gathered new strength whenever he touched the earth, it seems that the idea of fighting on the soil of the free States, in the midst of a friendly population threatened with a terrible invasion, doubles their energy and their activity. The hesitations, the delays, and the frequent discouragements which seemed to paralyze the best conceived plans in Virginia, have given place to a noble emulation which urges them to dispute with each other the honor of dealing the swiftest and heaviest blows to the enemy. Without taking any account of their numbers, Reynolds himself notwithstanding the immense responsibility weighing upon him, gives them an example of this zeal by contributing more than any one else to inspire them with it. Sad and dejected, it is said, before the meeting of the two armies, he has become invigorated as soon as he felt his proximity to the adversaries with whom he desired to come to blows since the opening of the campaign."

Buford and Reynolds ascended to the cupola of the Lutheran Seminary from which an extended view of the country for miles around was obtained. Wadsworth's division of the First Corps was observed moving with rapid strides toward the sound of battle and it was seen to move to the left without entering the town, and advance up the easterly slope of Seminary Hill. Wadsworth's command consisted of two brigades under Generals Cutler and Meredith and as they moved to position an aide of General Howard made his appearance and asked for instructions for the Eleventh Corps. General Reynolds directed that General Howard bring his corps forward at once and "form them on Cemetery Hill as a reserve," * and

---

* General Howard has no recollection of having received any such orders, but as he did get orders to come forward, and as his corps was to occupy *some place* in rear, as a support to the First Corps, nothing is more probable than that General Reynolds directed him to go there; for its military advantages were obvious enough to any experienced commander. Lieutenant Rosengarten, of General Reynolds' staff,

then accompanied Wadsworth to place his men in position.

The place chosen for the battle-ground was on the west side of the town along the course of the stream known as Willoughby Run, its course at this point being almost due north and south. The Chambersburg and Fairfield roads both cross the stream, and uniting near the town form an angle of considerable extent. These roads also cross two elevations of ground, or ridges, running parallel with the stream, the one further west from the town being the scene of the first day's fighting. On the heights nearest the town is situated the Theological Seminary, from which the ridge derives its name. The steeple of this building was used by the commanders of both armies as an observatory. The rebels were advancing on the Chambersburg road in strong numbers when Wadsworth arrived, and Reynolds in person posted the Second Maine Battery in the road, and threw forward the Fourteenth Brooklyn, Colonel Fowler, and the Ninety-fifth New York, Colonel Biddle, (both under

---

states positively that he was present and heard the order given for Howard to post his troops on Cemetery Ridge. The matter is of some moment, as the position in question ultimately gave us the victory, and Howard received the thanks of Congress for selecting it. It is not to be supposed that either Howard or Rosengarten would misstate the matter. It is quite possible that Reynolds chose the hill simply as a position upon which his force could rally if driven back, and Howard selected it as a suitable battle-field for the army. It has since been universally conceded that it was admirably adapted for that purpose.—*Doubleday.*

Fowler's command,) in advance on the left, the other three regiments of the brigade—One Hundred and Forty-seventh New York, Seventy-sixth New York, and Fifty-sixth Pennsylvania—being placed in line on the right of the road. Gamble's brigade of cavalry were withdrawn and formed in column on the left of the infantry, Deven's brigade, further to the right

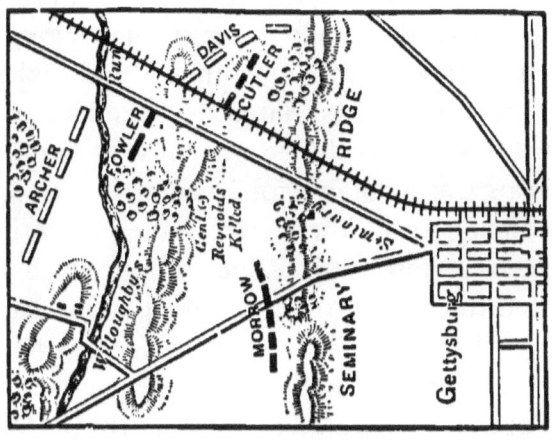

ADVANCE OF DAVIS' AND ARCHER'S REBEL BRIGADES.
UNION, BLACK ; REBELS, WHITE.

facing north, still awaiting the approach of the enemy from that direction.

The battle which was here waged with persistent fury, was a fitting prelude to the desperate conflict which succeeded it, and but for the gallant resistance made by the veterans of the First Corps in this initiatory contest, the admirable position on the hills south of Gettysburg would undoubtedly have been lost to the Army of the Potomac. Both armies thus confronted each other, and were coming closer together in such manner that a conflict was inevitable. To hold the enemy in check until the rest of the army could arrive and take position on the ridge in rear of the town, the admirable advantages of which had presented themselves to both Buford and Reynolds, was the imperative duty of the First Army Corps. How well they succeeded, how desperately they fought, how tenaciously they held their ground against overwhelming numbers, relinquishing it only when overpowered, is graphically related by Doubleday.

The army of General Lee was close at hand. Hill's whole corps was available for immediate action. Ewell was advancing from the north, with his entire command except Johnson's division, and the small body of men posted to contest their advance could have been swept away like leaves before the wind; but the rebel leaders were not anticipating a meeting with the Army of the Potomac. Ewell had passed through Gettysburg two days before, at which time no one knew anything about Meade's army, and General Lee consequently felt no particular anxiety concerning it. The obstructions so far encountered were to his mind "some gentlemen militia," who would be ready to depart as soon as it became a little warm for them.

Davis' rebel brigade, which had been thrown forward, to clear the road, formed behind a ridge, and was unperceived by Cutler's men. When they advanced into view the left of their line came square upon the right flank of Cutler's small force, which was compelled to fall back, and was ordered to re-form on Seminary Ridge. The Fifty-sixth Pennsylvania first perceived the enemy and opened fire, but they were soon overpowered and with the Seventy-sixth New York Regiment succeeded in getting away, continuing their retreat to the outskirts of the town ; but the One Hundred and Forty-seventh New York Regiment, not receiving the order to fall back—its Colonel having

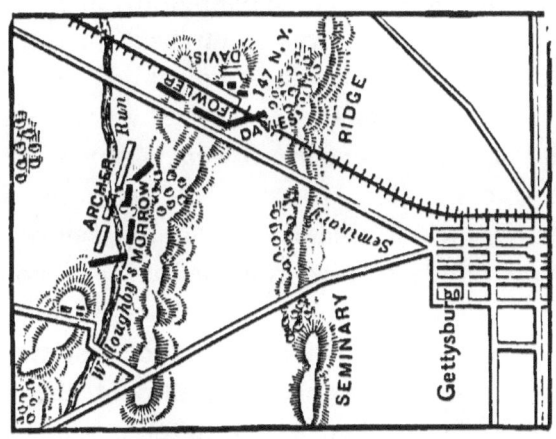

DEFEAT OF ARCHER'S AND DAVIS' BRIGADES.

been killed before the order could be given — was being hemmed in on all sides and made a desperate fight. As this movement of Davis' brigade also uncovered the right flank of Colonel Fowler's two regiments, while Archer's rebel brigade was advancing to envelop their left, they fell back in good order. Meredith's "Iron Brigade," commanded by Colonel Morrow—its permanent commander having been wounded by a shell—had been formed in line on the west slope of Seminary Ridge, and as Archer's brigade, preceded by skirmishers, was advancing to get possession of a small wood between the two roads, Colonel Morrow was ordered by General Doubleday to secure the position and hold it at all hazards. Enthusiastically they moved to the task, the Sixth Missouri Regiment being detached and with the headquarter guard composed of the One Hundred and Fifty-ninth Pennsylvania, forming a reserve. The "Iron Brigade" was composed of the Second Wisconsin, Colonel Lucius Fairchild; Sixth Wisconsin, Lieutenant R. R. Dawes; Seventh Wisconsin, Colonel W. W. Robinson; Twenty-fourth Michigan, Colonel Henry A. Morrow; Nineteenth Indiana, Colonel Samuel Williams — five regiments in all. Advancing boldly toward the enemy the Second Wisconsin enveloped their right flank, capturing Archer himself and more than a thousand of his men. Surprised at this extraordinary movement the remnant of Archer's troops fled precipitately, being pursued to the opposite side of Willoughby's Run by the victorious Unionists.

There was now time to pay some attention to the attack on Cutler, as Davis' men were exultant over their success, and were pursuing the flying regiments to Gettysburg. Lieutenant-Colonel Dawes with the Sixth Wisconsin, advanced against the exposed flank of Davis, and Colonel Fowler with the Fourteenth Brooklyn and Ninety-fifth New York, joined forces with him. Noticing this movement Davis stopped

BVT. MAJOR-GEN. ROBERT MCALLISTER,
Colonel Com'd'g 11th N. J. Vols., Inf.
(*From a Steel Engraving.*)

his pursuit of Cutler's men, and rushing into the railroad cut, where the grading afforded them shelter, they made a desperate resistance, but they had entered a trap. Fowler confronted them above, and Dawes opened a murderous fire upon them with a section of artillery which enfiladed their position, and he also formed his men across the cut, by Colonel Fowler's order to fire through it, thus having them completely at bay. The One Hundred and Forty-seventh New York was released from its perilous position, and two-thirds of the enemy surrendered, the rest escaping by scattering over the country.

These brilliant exploits were saddened by the death of General Reynolds, who was instantly killed by a musket ball immediately after deploying the men of Cutler's brigade. General Doubleday at once took command of the corps, and during the respite occasioned by the inaction of the enemy re-formed and strengthened his lines.

General Heth had halted his column to await the result of the action of his two brigades, and the news he received was far from encouraging. Replacing his defeated and dispirited troops with the fresh men of Pettigrew and Brockenborough supported by Pender's division, he advanced to a renewal of the fight.

Doubleday anxiously awaited the arrival of his other two divisions, Robinson's and his own commanded temporarily by General Rowley. At this time General Howard had arrived upon the scene, having preceded his corps, and noting the precipitate retreat of the two regiments of Cutler's brigade, magnified their disorderly haste into a rout of the First Corps, and so notified General Meade. At eleven o'clock to the great relief of General Doubleday the remainder of the First Corps came up. The enemy had established their line in a commanding position, and their artillery was advantageously posted, so as to sweep the Chambers-

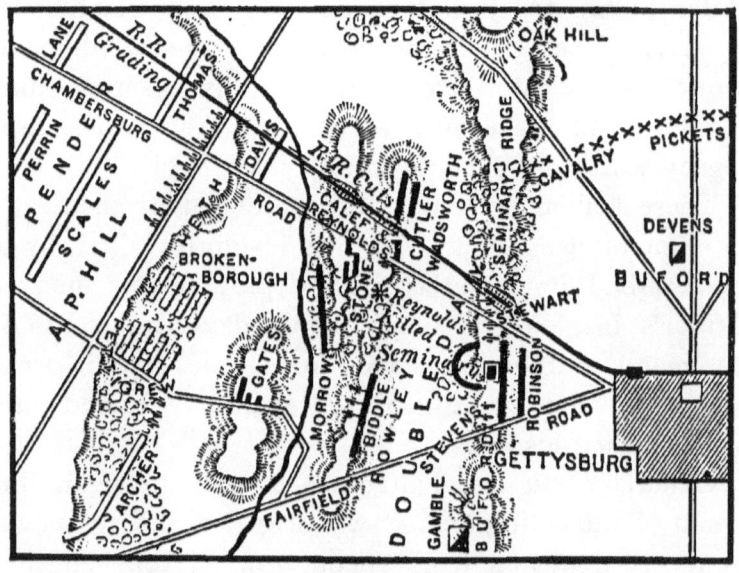

SECOND ADVANCE OF HETH'S TROOPS AGAINST THE FIRST CORPS.
DOUBLEDAY'S MAP.

burg road. A severe artillery duel took place at this point, the batteries of Calef and Reynolds doing splendid execution. Doubleday posted his troops in the following order to meet this new attack: Stone's brigade, of Rowley's division, being placed to the right of the woods occupied by Morrow, and Colonel

Biddle's brigade on the left, with Robinson's division in reserve at the seminary, on the west of which Robinson's men threw up a semicircular line of breast works, which served an admirable purpose later on.

The battle which ensued was one of the most desperate of the three days' contest. Howard upon receiving the news of the death of General Reynolds, assumed command of the left wing, turning over the command of the Eleventh Corps to General Schurz, General Barlow taking command of the division. He also notified General Meade of the sad event and sent orders to Sickles at Emmetsburg and Slocum at Two Taverns to hasten to the field. Between twelve and one o'clock the Eleventh Corps made its appearance on the scene of action and the divisions of Schimmelpfennig and Barlow were orderd to the support of Doubleday, and were directed to extend his line to the right, Steinwehr's division, with the reserve artillery being ordered to Cemetery Hill, as a reserve.

A new danger however threatened the Union line before these dispositions could be made. Buford, who had been anxiously watching the road from the north, where Deven's cavalry brigade had been posted, informed Doubleday of the approach of Ewell's troops from that direction, and Howard ordered the Eleventh Corps to change front and keep Ewell from assailing the First Corps in flank. This relieved the cavalry, who withdrew and formed still farther to the right.

The movements of Ewell's two divisions had been

well timed and both Rodes and Early came in sight of Gettysburg at almost the same moment. Before their exact whereabouts were known to the Union troops Rodes had posted a battery on Oak Hill, an eminence to the right of and almost on a line with that occupied by the troops of Doubleday. When the Eleventh Corps line had been established to meet Ewell, it left a wide interval between the left of Barlow and the right of Cutler's brigade of the First Corps, which necessitated the use of all of Doubleday's reserves, besides attenuating his general line of battle.

Noting with satisfaction the arrival of Ewell on the right flank of the Union line, Hill moved promptly to attack Doubleday with his whole force. Under cover of the dense woods Rodes succeeded in joining his line to that of Hill, while his artillery played effectively upon Doubleday's guns on the Chambersburg road. Rodes attacked Cutler's right flank vigorously. Doubleday proved equal to this emergency however. He ordered Baxter's brigade to fill the gap between Cutler and the Eleventh Corps, and as Baxter advanced boldly up the Mummasburg road, Rodes sent O'Neal's brigade in upon his flank. O'Neal was repulsed with heavy loss, and Iverson's rebel brigade was ordered to assail both Cutler and Baxter. Doubleday ordered in another brigade, and Robinson sent forward Paul's brigade, which took up position with Baxter. Doubleday had so far held his own against superior numbers. All the positions south of the Chambersburg road

BVT. COL. JOHN SCHOONOVER,
Adjt. 11th Regt. N. J. Vols., Inf.
(*From a War-time Photograph.*)

had been retained, but the enemy was pressing him hard on the right. Iverson's attack upon Robinson's two brigades failed and his force was almost annihilated, his loss being heavy in killed and wounded and over a thousand men were taken prisoners. Daniel came to Iverson's rescue, but arrived too late, and his advance was checked. O'Neal, Iverson and Daniel were each in turn defeated, and Heth, who made a vigorous demonstration against Meredith was also repulsed. Growing desperate the rebels determined to assault in force, and Ramseur, who had come up to assist Daniel, was aided by the advance of the three brigades of Pender's division, thus throwing upon the weakened, but obstinate Union line, a numerical force that by pressure alone must carry the position. Assistance was also coming to the enemy in another shape. Early's entire division was advancing to the front, and they poured down upon Barlow's division in great numbers, who resisted stoutly, but were obliged to fall back, leaving their wounded in the hands of the enemy, the heroic Barlow being among them. Schimmelpfennig was attacked by Doles' brigade, and retreated in hot haste, and as this division broke a general retreat was ordered by Howard. Schimmelpfennig's flight compelled Robinson to abandon his position, and Doubleday having used up all his reserves was at last compelled to fall back. Halting and re-forming his line in the semi-circular entrenchment thrown up by Robinson's division Doubleday, aided by Buford, who formed his cavalry in line of *battalion in mass to keep open the line of retreat, held the enemy in check for a short time.

The position of the First Corps was exceedingly critical, and its escape from annihilation is due to the great presence of mind and the skillful generalship of General Doubleday. As the columns of retreating Unionists mixed together in the town, men became separated from their commands, thousands were picked up by the enemy on the streets, and the roads leading to the rear were thronged with a motley crew of frightened and demoralized soldiers, whom no power seemed able to hold in check.†

A new actor now appeared upon the scene. When General Meade, at his headquarters in Taneytown, received the message from Howard that the First Corps were flying from the field, there was forced upon him the necessity of immediately deciding whether to

---

*General Francis A. Walker in his "History of the Second Army Corps" relates this incident: "When last it was my privilege to see General Hancock, in November, 1885, he pointed out to me from Cemetery Hill the position occupied by Buford at this critical juncture, and assured me that, among the most inspiring sights of his military career was the splendid spectacle of that gallant cavalry, as it stood there unshaken and undaunted, in the face of the advancing Confederate infantry."

†The Comte de Paris estimates that of the 16,000 men who went into action on the Union side no more than 5,000 were left in fighting condition. The First Corps was reduced to 2,450 men. Out of the 11,000 missing nearly 4,000 had been left on the field of battle, and about 5,000 were taken prisoners; the rest had scattered.

fight the battle where the conflict had begun or adhere to his original plan of forming a line on Pipe Creek. Instead of going to Gettysburg himself he sent for General Hancock, who had just arrived in Taneytown with the Second Corps, and appointed him to the command of the left wing, thus superseding both Howard and Sickles, who ranked him by seniority, and delegated to him the practical selection of the battle-field, whether to order up the whole army to Gettysburg and there join issue with the enemy, or to fall back to the position originally determined upon. When Hancock arrived upon the scene the confusion of retreat had not subsided. Streams of frightened men were passing down the Taneytown and Baltimore roads to the rear, and the powerlessness of Howard to restore confidence to the men was apparent. Hancock addressed himself at once to the task, and his presence was immediately felt by the troops. Brave, even to rashness, his manner and bearing made their impress felt. Men, who first thought only of flight, halted, cheered for Hancock, and sought their colors. His presence was worth a corps of men at that moment, and, though Seminary Ridge was lined with rebel infantry, and Ewell's troops were advancing through the town toward Cemetery Hill, Hancock re-formed the line with the Eleventh Corps on the right of Steinwehr's fortified position, the First Corps on the left and all the artillery at command posted in advantageous positions, thus presenting a bold front to the victorious foe. Noting the rising ground on the right

—Culp's Hill—toward which Ewell was moving, he posted Wadsworth's division there, and formed the cavalry on the left of Doubleday. The transformation was complete. Order had been restored out of chaos, and as Lee and his officers gazed upon this new line of battle, which had formed under the very muzzles of their guns, they mistook the deployment of this small force in a thin line to the right and left for the arrival of reinforcements, and hesitated to attack. Ewell was desirous of doing so, but Lee would not imperatively order it, and after a short contest with Wadsworth's men, the enemy halted. This was another of the blunders which aided the Union cause on this campaign. Had Ewell advanced at once, Culp's Hill would have fallen into his possession and he would thus have commanded the roads on which Meade's army was then moving.

The enemy however had had more fighting than they expected to experience. Their losses had been severe, and though they had met and defeated but two army corps, the fact—of which they had at last become cognizant—that the Army of the Potomac was in front of them, led to a magnifying of the importance of their victory. From prisoners they had no doubt learned that Meade's army was well on its way to Gettysburg, and as Lee had been deceived by the show of force on Cemetery Hill, he preferred to await the arrival of all his army before attacking.

On the morning of July 1st Sickles had received orders from General Meade to fall back to a position on the Pipe Creek line of battle, but learning subsequently that the First and Eleventh Corps, which with his own comprised the left wing of the army, were engaged with the enemy, he promptly moved toward the sound of action. He had resumed command of the Third Corps only a few days previous, and was naturally anxious to meet the enemy. Detaching De Trobriand's brigade from Birney's division, and Burling's brigade—composed of the Fifth, Sixth, Seventh and Eighth New Jersey Regiments, the One Hundred and Fifteenth Pennsylvania and the Second New Hampshire—from Humphreys' division with orders to remain at Emmetsburg, he moved promptly forward with Birney's division, and arriving on the field was assigned to position on the left of the First Corps.

The Twelfth Corps advanced from Littlestown on the morning of July 1st and at noon halted at Two Taverns, about five miles southeast from Gettysburg. While here word was received from Howard as to the engagement then in progress, and the order to march was soon given. Geary's division moved directly for Gettysburg by the Baltimore pike, and Williams' division, taking a road leading to the right advanced rapidly toward the sound of artillery. Proceeding some distance, skirmishers were sent forward, and as Benner's Hill loomed up in their front a body of horsemen were seen on its summit closely scanning the country around. Ewell's scouts were soon encountered and a few shots were exchanged when orders were received to bring on no engagement at that place. It had been the intention of General Williams to take possession of the hill, but as it had become known that Gettysburg was in the hands of the enemy, the line was withdrawn and position for the night taken on the east side of Rock Creek. The Thirteenth New Jersey Regiment supported Winegan's Battery ("M" First New York) during the night. Geary's division was posted on the left of the army, his line extending from the left of Sickles' line to the summit of Little Round Top, the Twelfth Corps thus holding both the right and left flanks of the Army of the Potomac on the night of July 1st. General Slocum arrived upon the scene about half-past five, and General Hancock, in accordance with instructions received, turned over the command to him, and started for Taneytown to report to General Meade.

Hancock had performed labors almost herculean. The very magnetism of his presence among the defeated and retreating troops gave them renewed confidence and courage, and when he had assigned the last body of troops to their position for the night, and saw that the force was strong enough to resist any attack that might be made until the rest of the army could be brought up, he started on his ride to Taneytown. During the afternoon he sent two dispatches to General Meade in which he favored the position secured as the best on which the battle should be fought, though the left was liable to be turned. On his way to headquarters he halted the

Second Corps, commanded by General Gibbons, which he met about three miles from the battle-field, as a protection to the left of the line.

The line of battle for the night extended from the rising ground east of Rock Creek, to Culp's Hill, to Cemetery Hill and along the ridge west of the Taneytown road to the summit of Little Round Top. The Fifth Army Corps was on its way from Bonaughtown, and the Sixth Corps just entering Manchester, thirty-four miles distant, had started on its long march for the battle-field.

Among the interesting incidents of the first day's battle is the record of John Burns, a resident of Gettysburg. General Doubleday in his official report of the battle says: " My thanks are specially due to a citizen of Gettysburg, named. John Burns, who, although over seventy years of age, shouldered his musket and offered his services to Colonel Wister, One Hundred and Fiftieth Pennsylvania Volunteers. Colonel Wister advised him to fight in the woods as there was more shelter there, but he preferred to join our line of skirmishers in the open fields. When the troops retired he fought with the 'Iron Brigade.' He was wounded in three places."

## CHAPTER X.

THE NEW JERSEY TROOPS COMING ON THE FIELD OF BATTLE — RAPID AND EXHAUSTIVE MARCHING — THE ELEVENTH REGIMENT UNDERGO A FATIGUING NIGHT MARCH — THE SECOND NEW JERSEY BRIGADE MARCH BETWEEN THE SKIRMISH LINES OF BOTH ARMIES — THE TWELFTH REGIMENT IN LINE OF BATTLE — THE DEPLOYMENT OF SICKLES' LINE — THE THIRTEENTH REGIMENT ON CULP'S HILL — ARRIVAL OF THE FIRST NEW JERSEY BRIGADE AT FOUR O'CLOCK — A FORCED MARCH OF THIRTY-FIVE MILES.

IT was nearly dark when General Hancock started for the headquarters of the army at Taneytown and reported to General Meade, whom he found about ready to proceed to Gettysburg, where he arrived about one o'clock a. m., on July 2d. Humphreys' division of the Third Corps left Emmetsburg for the battle-field at three o'clock a. m., Burling's brigade with De Trobriand's brigade of Birney's division remaining behind to guard the outlet of the mountain and watch the Hagerstown road for any movements of the enemy in that direction. After a long and exciting march the division arrived on the field

MAJOR JOHN T. HILL,
Com'd'g 12th Regt. N. J. Vols., Inf.
(*From a War-time Photograph*--1863.)

at midnight and owing to the darkness could not be given a place in line and was massed in rear of Birney's division.

The Eleventh New Jersey Regiment, belonging to Carr's brigade of Humphrey's division, experienced all the inconveniences of this march. They had bivouacked in a wheat-field near Emmetsburg when the news reached them that the First and Eleventh Corps had met the enemy near Gettysburg and were being driven back. Orders to press forward rapidly were received, and soon the column was in motion. On crossing Marsh Run, the troops took a road to the left, and were marching toward Black Horse Tavern, on the Fairfield road, which was occupied by the enemy; but General Humphrey discovered, in time to conceal his presence from them, that he was on the wrong road, and accordingly caused the column to "about face" and retrace their steps. This long detour was a severe strain upon the men, but without further mishap they bivouacked east of the Emmetsburg road about one a. m., and was subsequently massed in rear of Birney and facing west, the Eleventh New Jersey being next to the last regiment in the line.

The next New Jersey regiment to arrive was the Twelfth, which with the Second Corps had halted for the night about three miles south of the battle-field. The column moved at daylight, and was rejoined by General Hancock before it reached the field, which took place about 7 a. m., and was placed in position on the left of Doubleday's division of the First Corps.

(General Newton was now in command of the First Corps, General Meade having assigned him there on learning of the death of General Reynolds.) In the order of alignment Hay's division—to Smith's brigade of which the Twelfth New Jersey belonged—was on the right, Gibbons, the centre, and Caldwell's division, the left. This displaced the Third Corps, which formed into column and moved still further to the left.

This movement so full of momentous and important results then unforeseen, has led to a controversy that will cease only when all the actors have passed off this world's stage. General Geary, who had occupied Little Round Top on the night of the first, had been ordered to the right of the line, and soon after daybreak (5 a. m.) vacated the position, which was the vital point of the whole line, and to regain and keep possession of which, brought on one of the most desperate struggles of the whole war. Sickles' orders were to prolong the line of the Second Corps, his left to rest upon Little Round Top.* This is the great bone of

---

* General Meade, in his official report says: "The Second and Third Corps were directed to occupy the continuation of the Cemetery ridge on the left of the Eleventh Corps."

The Comte De Paris, in his work on Gettysburg, says:

"Between six and seven o'clock in the morning Meade sent his son to Sickles with orders to take the position which Geary had just left. The order was most positive, and Meade has been blamed for not having attended to the execution of said order in person. * * * When Colonel Meade arrived between eight and nine o'clock, to ascertain if the order which he had brought from his father had been executed, Sickles answered him that he could not distinguish the posi-

contention: What were Meade's orders to Sickles? Without entering into the discussion, which has developed a wonderful amount of misunderstanding, it is clear that General Sickles did not deem his orders so explicit as to prevent the exercise of his own judgment in the matter.

The ridge on which Sickles was directed to form

tion in which he was to replace Geary. Nevertheless, like an obedient lieutenant, he had not waited for fresh orders, to extend his line to the left, and before nine o'clock Birney was deploying Graham's and Ward's brigades in the direction of Little Round Top."

Doubleday gives this version: "Sickles, however, denies that any position was ever marked out for him. He was expected to prolong Hancock's line to the left but did not do so for the following reasons: First, because the ground was low, and second on account of the commanding position of the Emmetsburg road, which ran along a cross ridge oblique to the front of the line assigned him, and which afforded the enemy an excellent position for their artillery; third because the ground between the valley he was expected to occupy, and the Emmetsburg road constituted a minor ridge, very much broken and full of rocks and trees which afforded excellent cover for an enemy operating in his immediate front."

Swinton in his History of the Army of the Potomac, says: "Sickles had been instructed to take position on the left of Hancock, on the same general line, which would draw it along the prolongation of Cemetery Ridge toward the Round Top. Now the ridge is, at this point, not very well defined; for the ground in front falls off into a considerable hollow. But at the distance of some four or five hundred yards in advance it rises into that intermediate crest along which runs the Emmetsburg road. General Sickles, thinking it desirable to occupy this advanced position — which he conceived would, if held by the enemy, make his own ground untenable—assumed the responsibility of pushing his front forward to that point."

descended into low ground which extended for four or five hundred yards to Little Round Top. In his front the ground ascended gradually, and on the crest of this rising ground ran the Emmetsburg road. Sickles first formed his line as directed, Birney's left resting at the base of Little Round Top and connecting with Humphrey's division on the right.

The Second New Jersey Brigade (Burling's) of Humphrey's division and De Trobriand's brigade of Birney's division, which had been left at Emmetsburg to guard the mountain passes, received orders at two o'clock a. m. to rejoin the Third Corps, and began their hurried march. To them also had come the startling intelligence of a battle at Gettysburg, the death of General Reynolds, and that the First and Eleventh Corps had been driven back. At three o'clock, the column was marching quietly and swiftly through the streets of Emmetsburg. A short halt was ordered after a brisk march to enable the men to make coffee. The heat of the day before, and the sultriness of the morning, together with the long fast and the rapid marching had well-nigh exhausted the men, and the prospect of a "rest" was joyously welcomed. The little fires were soon blazing cheerily, but before the first cup of water had reached boiling point, an aide came galloping down the road with peremptory orders to push forward as rapidly as possible. Not a moment was to be lost. "Fall in!" "Take arms!" "Right, face!" "Forward, march!" rang out over the field from the throats of regiment and company commanders.  There was a speedy mounting of horses, the rumbling of artillery was heard on the pike, and once more the column of Jerseymen pushed rapidly on. Crossing Marsh Run, Berdan's sharpshooters, who had been ordered to reconnoitre the rebel position, were seen lying along the fence in the road and firing occasionally at the enemy's skirmishers, in the edge of the strip of woods at the west.  The column had reached the Union line just in time.  Soon after the brigade had passed this point Longstreet had extended his lines across the road preparatory to his fierce charge upon Sickles' position.  It was a narrow escape from isolation, if not capture, as the small brigade would have been overwhelmed had they come in contact with the rebel column, which would have been the inevitable result had they remained long enough at "rest" to have cooked and drank their coffee.  Moving leisurely up the pike to about the point where Pickett's division crossed it the next day in making his famous charge, the rail fence was thrown down, and marching across the fields to the slope of Cemetery Ridge, Burling's brigade halted, and at nine o'clock ate their breakfast without interference.  In the mean time men were sent forward to throw down the rail fences that stood between the ridge and the pike.  The brigade was once more at home with its old command.

When General Meade had completed his reconnoissance and given his orders to the several corps, Geary was ordered to take position on the right of the line, where Williams' division was to join him.  By this move the Twelfth Corps was to be again united. Promptly on receipt of his orders Geary moved out and took position on Culp's Hill, joining Wadsworth's division of the First Corps. At eight o'clock, Williams' division (commanded by General Ruger) crossed Rock Creek and moved up the west bank of that stream forming on the westerly side of Culp's Hill, and then moving by the right flank took position as follows: McDougall's brigade (the First) joining Geary, the One Hundred and Seventh New York of Colgrove's brigade extending the line to the edge of the woods, while the Thirteenth New Jersey Regiment was formed in rear in close column by division. On the right of the Thirteenth New Jersey was an open space of about one hundred yards, through which coursed a small stream having its rise at Spangler's spring west of the Thirteenth Regiment's position. This open ground was marshy, and the rest of Colgrove's brigade was formed in the edge of McAllister's wood, on the south. As soon as the line was established the men began constructing lines of breastworks out of the fence rails, old stumps, dead limbs of trees, stones and whatever

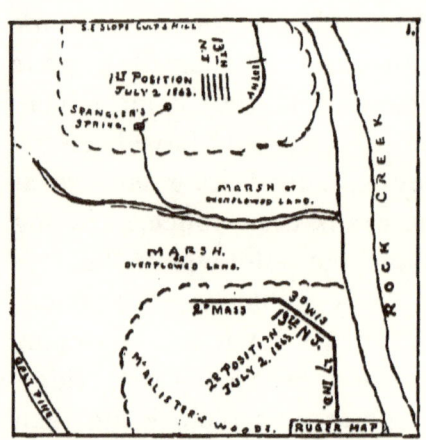

could be found that would impede the progress of a bullet. Lockwood's brigade, which had joined the Twelfth Corps on the morning of the second, was posted to the right of Colgrove, its right resting near the junction of the Baltimore pike with Rock Creek. The Fifth Corps was massed near the bridge over Rock Creek, on the Baltimore pike, in supporting distance of the Twelfth Corps. By twelve o'clock the Union line of battle was intact, extending from Culp's Hill on the right to the base of Little Round Top on the left, the summit of which was used as a signal station. The Sixth Corps was still on its long march from Manchester.

The line of battle as formed resembled more closely than anything else, an immense hook, Cemetery Ridge forming the shank, Cemetery Hill the heel, and Culp's Hill the end of the hook. It was an admirable defensive position, as it could be easily reinforced at any point by short marches, and its vulnerability was not to remain long untested.

The course of Lee in so long remaining silent was a source of mystery to the Union commander, and he determined to assault the enemy on the right with the Twelfth and Fifth Corps, supported by the Sixth Corps on its arrival, and the order for the movement was given. General Slocum and General Warren made a reconnoissance of the position and reported against it, and it was abandoned.

General Lee, though quiet, was not inactive. He had visited Ewell during the night and ordered him to attack the Union right, but that officer objected on the ground that the Federals were massed in his front, and said that he should intrench his position. The rebel army kept coming into line as the night advanced, and they were exultant over the victory of the day before, and confident of a more glorious result on the morrow. General Lee himself was infected with the same spirit, and awaited the approach of daylight with every expectation of success. Knowing of the great alarm the presence of his army in Pennsylvania had occasioned throughout the North, it only needed a victory over the Army of the Potomac on northern soil to bring about the full realization of his hopes. He saw peace won at last, the Southern Confederacy an established fact, his army victorious and marching triumphantly to their homes. Infused with such a spirit, army and commander felt themselves invincible. At daylight the rebel line extended from Benner's Hill, where Johnson's division was posted, Early joining him and fronting the ridge between Culp's and East Cemetery Hill, while Rodes' division occupied the town, and connected with Hill's corps on Seminary Ridge, which was disposed as follows: Pender's division on the left, Heth on the right, Anderson in rear between Marsh Creek and Willoughby Run. Longstreet with two divisions of his army were close by and moving forward, and by nine o'clock the rebel forces were all at hand and ready for action, except the division of Pickett, which was on its way from Chambersburg, and Stuart's cavalry who were moving to take position on the left.

BVT. BRIG.-GEN. EZRA A. CARMAN,
Colonel Com'd'g 13th Regt. N. J. Vols., Inf.
(*From a War-time Photograph.*)

On the Union side the same confidence was manifested by the troops, and as each corps came upon the field they reëchoed the words of Doubleday's heroes of the day before, *"We've come to stay!"* Thus both sides were nerved to the most desperate resolve, and how well they maintained it the record of the next two days gives abundant testimony.

Small things produce remarkable results at times. As the Thirteenth New Jersey Regiment with the First Division of the Twelfth Corps was making their exhaustive march on July first under a broiling sun from Two Taverns, men fell out of the ranks in squads by the roadside for a brief rest. Four or five women from Gettysburg, who had fled on the approach of the rebel army stood by the side of the road, and involuntarily began waving their bonnets and aprons. The men at first waved their hands in token of recognition, next they took off their caps to them, and finally the column broke into a hearty cheer. Tired and exhausted men rallied under the inspiring huzzas, rejoined the column and moved briskly toward the enemy.

At two o'clock in the afternoon the advance brigade of the Sixth Army Corps, came upon the field, and at 6 p. m. the entire corps had reported after a forced march variously estimated at from thirty to thirty-five miles. This corps had done some remarkable marching during the past three days, and with their presence on the field, the whole Army of the Potomac was now at hand. The First New Jersey Brigade, General A. T. A. Torbert, commander, comprising the First,

Second, Third and Fifteenth Regiments (The Fourth Regiment was on duty at division headquarters, three companies serving as Provost Guard and seven companies guarding the ammunition trains) composed the First Brigade, of the First Division, and reached the battlefield at 4 p. m. The brigade with its corps had marched fifty-five miles in three days, bivouacking on the night of June 30th at Manchester after a march of twenty-three miles on that day. The brigade was encamped in a meadow near the town, and the tired, weary men sought their soft and rich beds at an early hour expecting to have a good night's rest, but it was not to be. About 10 p. m. the camp was suddenly aroused by the shrill, clear notes of the "Assembly." Every man jumped to his feet and seized his arms. Soon the order came to march, and the " Forward " sounded. " Where ? " " What is all this for ? " were the questions asked but no one could answer. The orders had been to march to Taneytown, and the observant men in line noticed that the column was countermarching on the same road they had gone over. Ere long the column turned into the broad Baltimore pike and headed westward. All night long the steady tramp, tramp, was kept up, and when daylight broke, the march was still continued. There was no halt for breakfast, or coffee, but no one murmured or complained, and on they went, until about one o'clock, when to the joy of every one the head of the column was seen to be filing into an open field. A shout went up! This meant coffee and a little rest. Long lines stretched across the field, and the smoke of small fires soon showed what was being done, but hardly had the rear of the column gained its place before a horseman was seen coming at full speed down the pike; his horse white with foam told all; his mission was one of urgent importance. Riding up to where General Sedgwick was standing he delivered his dispatch—the Adjutant-General promulgated it orally: "The Corps is wanted at Gettysburg in the shortest possible space of time." A thrill went through every man's heart. Coffee in various stages of brewing was emptied on the ground, and stacks were broken ere the message was finished. From mouth to mouth went the summons: "Our comrades at the front want us," and but one thought animated all. Away the column went, and on gaining the pike, the stride of the men in their eagerness to get forward kept the officers' horses on a dog-trot. No more glorious sight ever met the eye of a soldier than this one as he looked back over that magnificent body of men as they marched up that pike on the afternoon of July the second. Ten miles were passed over and Rock Creek was reached, but one mile from the line of battle. A short halt to fill canteens with water was made. The great journey was over. The most wonderful march ever made by so large a body of troops had been accomplished—thirty-five miles in eighteen hours! The New Jersey Brigade rested near the centre of the line of battle for nearly two hours, when they were ordered to the left of the line where they arrived at dark. General Torbert reports that there were but twenty-five men absent when the march was ended and these reported to their commands during the night.

A strong picket line was sent out from the brigade, under command of Lieutenant-Colonel Wiebecke of the Second Regiment, composed of Company D, Captain Lipfert, and Company E, Lieutenant Gustavus Peine, of the Second Regiment, and details from the First, Third and Fifteenth Regiments. They became warmly engaged with the enemy during the third and sustained a loss of eleven men. Colonel Wiebecke with the gallantry and heroism that always characterized him in action won high encomiums from his superior officers for the gallant services rendered on this occasion.

BVT. BRIG.-GEN. FRED. H. HARRIS,
Captain Co. F, 13th Regt. N. J. Vols., Inf.
(*From a Recent Photograph.*)

## CHAPTER XI.

THE SECOND DAY'S BATTLE — SICKLES' NEW LINE — LONGSTREET'S ATTEMPT TO TURN THE FEDERAL LEFT — THE SECOND NEW JERSEY BRIGADE, THE ELEVENTH REGIMENT, AND BATTERY "B," FIRST NEW JERSEY ARTILLERY IN ACTION — HOOD REPULSED AT LITTLE ROUND TOP — A GALLANT AND SUCCESSFUL CHARGE BY THE TWELFTH NEW JERSEY REGIMENT—CASUALTIES AMONG THE NEW JERSEY TROOPS.

WHEN the line of the Third Corps had been established by the deployment of Birney's division in the position vacated by Geary, its right rested on the left of the Second Corps and its left at the base of Little Round Top. This rocky eminence, owing to the indefinite instructions given to General Sickles remained unoccupied, and its importance was apparently not then appreciated by him, or he may have thought other troops would form on his left to cover it. But, whatever the cause, · it was unoccupied except by the Signal Corps. Randolph's, and Clark's (" B," First New Jersey) batteries were placed in position in Birney's front, and were commanded by the ridge along which ran the Emmetsburg road. Seeley's, Smith's and Winslow's batteries of the Third Corps were parked within convenient distance. The skirmishers placed along the Emmetsburg road and to the front of it had been engaged in a desultory firing during the entire morning, and the army was momentarily expecting an attack from the enemy. The firing kept increasing in volume along Birney's front, and at noon he sent forward one hundred of Berdan's sharpshooters, supported by the Third Maine Regiment, with instructions to push as far forward as possible and feel the enemy's right. They advanced promptly to their work and soon became heavily engaged. The rebel skirmish line was driven back and a large body of men were found moving in column toward the Federal left. The reconnoitering force were in turn driven back with great loss, and General Birney informed General Sickles of his discovery, who ordered him to change front to meet the expected attack.

This movement, which led to such important results, has now become the subject of an excited controversy among military critics. The simple facts in the case seem to be these: Between Cemetery Ridge, on the prolongation of which the Union line of battle was formed, and Seminary Ridge, occupied by Lee's army, was a subordinate ridge of ground, along the crest of which ran the Emmetsburg road. The low ground, between Cemetery Ridge and Little Round Top which Sickles occupied, was commanded by this inferior elevation. The trend of this rising ground is southwesterly, and the most commanding position along its course is the Peach Orchard at the junction of a cross road with the Emmetsburg road. From the Peach Orchard running easterly, the high ground continues for a short distance and then ends abruptly at a rocky depression known as the Devil's Den, between which and the Round Top, there is a defile or gorge through which runs a small stream known as Plum Run. General Sickles had previously informed Meade of the nature of the ground in his front and solicited permission to make the change, requesting that a staff officer be sent with him to examine the position. General Hunt, Chief of Artillery, made a reconnoissance of the entire line, extending his tour to the summit of Little Round Top, and returned to General Meade, whom he requested to personally examine the left of the line before approving of Sickles' proposed advance. General Meade had in the mean time called a council of corps commanders at his headquarters near Zeigler's Grove, and was awaiting the presence of Sickles in obedience to the call. Sickles, not hearing anything from General Hunt, gave the order to Birney to advance to the new ground, and ordered Humphreys to take position on the Emmetsburg road connecting with Birney at the Peach Orchard. He then started for Meade's headquarters, but before he had time to dismount the sound of Clark's guns announced to the assembled corps commanders that the "ball had opened." Meade then accompanied Sickles to the threatened point of attack, and while he did not approve of the movement, saw there was no time to make a change, as Sickles expressed himself willing to do.

The change of front General Birney was directed to make brought his division along the left arm of the angle extending from the high ground above the Devil's Den to the Peach Orchard, at the intersection of a cross-road with the Emmetsburg road, General Ward's brigade being on the left of the line, De Trobriand in the centre, and Graham on the right. Ward's left regiment, the One Hundred and Twenty-fourth New York, was the extreme left of the line and was placed on the high ground west and north of the Devil's Den. This exposed flank was protected only by Smith's (Fourth New York) battery of rifled guns, which commanded the gorge, with the Fourth Maine Regiment still farther to the left at the base of Little Round Top, supporting it. On the right of Smith's battery was a thin belt of woods, and into the open ground (a wheat-field) beyond it Winslow's battery of light twelve-pounders was placed. Graham's line was formed along the Emmetsburg road, its left being at the Peach Orchard and refused so as to form an angle at this point. De Trobriand formed across the extreme point of the wheat-field to make connection with Ward and Graham, and in position to reinforce either, as circumstances might require. Humphreys advanced his division to the Emmetsburg road, leaving only Burling's brigade in support, which was soon after sent to reinforce Birney's weak line. By this movement a wide gap was made between the left of the Second Corps and Humphreys' right, which Gibbons filled by sending forward two regiments of his division.

The position of the Third Corps was now complete, and it was strengthened by the batteries of Bigelow, Phillips, Hart and Clark (" B " First New Jersey), in the open ground north of the cross-road and in rear of the Peach Orchard, and protected by a slight intrenchment dug along the road which gave to it the name of the "sunken road." Ames' battery occupied the Peach orchard, supported by the Third Maine and Third Michigan Regiments, which formed in front of the Orchard facing south, while Randolph's, Seeley's and Turnbull's batteries were placed along the Emmetsburg road fronting west. Sickles had been directed to call upon Sykes for a division of the Fifth Corps, and Hancock also ordered a division of the Second Corps to respond to any call for aid.

Meade and his corps commanders expected an attack by Lee at some point in the line at an early hour, and his desire to anticipate such a move was his reason for his order directing the Twelfth and Fifth Corps to charge the enemy's left on the arrival of the Sixth Corps. That movement appears to have been abandoned by the adverse reports of Generals Slocum and Warren, and Meade therefore changed his plans to an offensive movement by his left, which he was not, however, permitted to make. Lee's delay in attacking the Federal position was a source of astonishment to the Union army and incomprehensible to Meade, who had been expecting an advance against the Union right as more likely than at any other point, and the continued silence of the Confederate leader gave rise to a number of conjectures as to his possible intentions.

General Lee was not idle, however, but time, which was of so much value to him, was being ruthlessly wasted. After the abandonment of the plan whereby Ewell was to attack the Federal right, he had formed a plan of attack on the left of Meade's army, Ewell to assault the right at the sound of Longstreet's guns while Hill was to make a vigorous demonstration on the centre. Ewell had expressed the belief that he could successfully assault the right as soon as Longstreet should break through the Union left. No time seems to have been fixed upon for the beginning of this movement, and every hour's delay only strengthened the Union line. General Lee informed Longstreet of his proposed attack, but that officer attempted to dissuade him from it. A long time seems to have been spent in controversy, and finally Longstreet plead for more time until McLaws' division, which had been on picket should arrive.

Lee had abandoned the "offensive-defensive" plan of operations, and to the objections of both Longstreet and Hood to the proposed movement said: "The enemy is here, and if we do not whip him he will whip us." * Lee was sanguine of success. His troops had been victorious the day before, and they, as well as himself were filled with a belief in their invincibility.

---

* Hood in his letter to Longstreet.

Three-quarters of an hour were lost waiting for the arrival of McLaws, and when at last he reported, a further delay of several hours occurred in the march of the troops. This was occasioned by the instructions of General Lee which called for the masking of the movement from the Federals, the design being to fall suddenly and impetuously on the left flank of the Union army, which Lee supposed rested on the Emmetsburg road.

One incident was in Lee's favor. The Union cavalry which should have been placed on Sickles' left, had by a misunderstanding been ordered elsewhere, and there was nothing apparently to prevent a surprise movement but the skirmish line of the Third Corps. The situation seemed favorable for a repetition of "Stonewall" Jackson's flank movement by which the Eleventh Corps was put to flight at Chancellorsville ; but there was an important obstacle to its success, which Longstreet made a wide detour to overcome. This obstacle was the Signal Station on Little Round Top. The officer in charge discerned the marching column of the enemy, and at once notified General Sickles and General Meade of the fact. General Meade sent General Warren, of his staff, to the Signal Station, and Sickles ordered Birney to develop the enemy's right with the result as previously described. There was no chance now for a surprise.

Longstreet observed the signal station on Round Top, and knowing that the movement could no longer be concealed, formed his troops for the assault.

Hood's division was placed on the right in the following order:

Laws' brigade, supported by Benning, on the right; Robertson, with Anderson's brigade in his rear, on the left.

McLaws' division formed on the left of Hood, Kershaw's brigade in front and Semmes' brigade in rear of Kershaw, constituting his right; Barksdale, supported by Wofford, the left.

Hood's division was to attack first, by crossing the Emmetsburg road and advancing along the line, taking the left of the Union line in flank and rear. As soon as that was accomplished, McLaws was to deploy across the road in two lines of battle and drive the Federals from the Peach Orchard. These instructions were not carried out in the manner designed, and the battle was fought on a plan which developed itself.

General Hood, on whom devolved the opening of the fight, had received word from his scouts who had ascended Round Top, of the defenceless condition of Little Round Top, and the apparent ease with which the Federal army could be attacked in rear by passing completely around the larger mountain, and he vainly sought to secure a modification of the order, and to be permitted to move to the south of Round Top for that purpose. Three separate requests were sent to Lee, and finally Longstreet went to Hood and repeated the order of General Lee, which was to be strictly obeyed.

Birney's infantry line was a weak one, but his front

at the angle was well covered with artillery while Smith's battery to the extreme left had a commanding position. Birney having discovered the position of the rebel column, at two o'clock ordered Clark's battery ("B" First New Jersey) to open upon them, and after the firing of a few rounds they disappeared. About three o'clock a rebel battery opened fire on Clark's position, from the Emmetsburg road, about one thousand four hundred yards to the front, and the fire was effectively replied to, the battery soon ceasing to annoy them. The enemy, however, were massing their artillery under cover of which the infantry attack was to be made. The batteries of Reilley and Latham covered the front of Laws' and Robertson's brigades, and further to the left thirteen batteries were placed along the front of Seminary Ridge, their fire converging at the Peach Orchard and enfilading Sickles' line in both directions. At half-past three the columns of Hood were seen passing along Birney's front to the left. The whole artillery line on Seminary Ridge opened upon Birney's position, their fire taking Graham's brigade and Humphreys' division — then advancing to their new line on the Emmetsburg road—in flank. The Confederate infantry preceded by a strong line of skirmishers, advanced to the Federal position. The artillery which accompanied the rebel line opened fire vigorously upon Smith's battery near the Devil's Den which replied effectively.

Ward's line was a very thin one and the left

extremely weak. There was but one regiment to resist the whole of Laws' rebel brigade—the Fourth Maine—and Hood having disregarded Lee's orders—either because he was surprised at finding a line of battle extending from the Peach Orchard to the base of Little Round Top to oppose him, or believing the latter to be the key to the whole battle-field and easily taken, as his scouts had reported it defenceless—directed Laws to bear to the right, and Robertson noting the movement also bore in the same direction, and fell with crushing force upon Ward's line at its weakest point. Sickles at once called upon Sykes for the division which had been ordered to his support.

When Humphreys moved forward to the Emmetsburg road, as directed by General Sickles, Carr's brigade was in the advance, followed by Brewster, Burling's brigade being in the rear. The severe artillery fire upon the fated Peach Orchard was then in progress. Seeley's battery which had been ordered to take position on the right of a log house on the Emmetsburg road, was transferred to the left of the building and its fire soon silenced the guns in its front. Turnbull's battery from the artillery reserve took the place vacated by Seeley. In the alignment of Carr's brigade, the Eleventh New Jersey Regiment was brought to the Emmetsburg road, its right resting on the Smith, or Essex house, and extending nearly parallel with the road and about twenty paces to the east of it. In the rear of the Smith house was

BREV. MAJOR A. JUDSON CLARK,
Captain Com'd'g Battery B, 1st N. J. Artillery.
(*From a War-time Photograph – 1862.*)

an apple orchard, and to the left or south of it, a small peach orchard.* The Eleventh Regiment was the extreme left of the brigade and joined the troops of the First Division.

Soon after Humphreys had disposed his line to meet the expected attack of the enemy, he sent Burling's brigade to the support of Birney, as already stated. This brigade moved down to the rear of the right of Birney's division, where it was massed in a piece of woods south of the Trostle house, and on the margin of the road leading to the Peach Orchard. General Birney ordered Burling out of the woods into an open field and immediately on unmasking, the enemy opened a terrific cannonade on his left flank. For half an hour the brigade was exposed to a severe storm of shot and shell, when, at the solicitation of his regimental commanders, he moved the brigade back about one hundred yards where they could have the protection of a slight rise in the ground. This movement, under the heavy fire of the enemy, was made in perfect order, but it attracted the attention of Captain Poland of General Sickles' staff, who not understanding it rode furiously up to Burling and demanded to know by whose orders he had moved his brigade. " By my own," replied Bur-

---

*This fact has given rise to the belief that the position of the Regiment was in Sherfey's Peach Orchard which was some distance further to the left, and at the junction of a cross-road which runs from the Taneytown to the Emmetsburg road.—*Marbaker, Historian Eleventh Regiment.*

ling. " Take your command back to the position you left, sir," was Poland's excited reply, and Burling at once started to obey, but just at that moment an order was received from General Birney to detach two regiments to go to the support of General Graham. The Second New Hampshire and the Seventh New Jersey, Colonel Louis R. Francine, were detailed for that purpose. The Second New Hampshire was ordered to the support of Ames' battery in the Peach Orchard, and in taking position its right wing fronted the Emmetsburg road, and its left the cross-road in rear of the orchard, thus forming an acute angle. The Seventh New Jersey was ordered to the support of the remaining batteries, and took position to the rear of Clark's battery ("B" First New Jersey). It had been at this place only a short time when the terrific and deafening cannonade, which preceded the advance of the enemy, began. The fire from the rebel batteries was sharp and effective. Many of the shells burst directly over the regiment and several men were killed and wounded as they lay in the ranks. Trying as the ordeal was the men of the Seventh bore it bravely. Unable to engage the enemy they courageously submitted to the dreadful down-pour of missiles which broke upon them and from which their position permitted of no escape.

The Fifth New Jersey Regiment, Colonel William J. Sewell, was next detailed. Reporting to General Humphreys the Fifth was ordered to relieve the Sixty-third Pennsylvania, on picket duty on the Emmetsburg

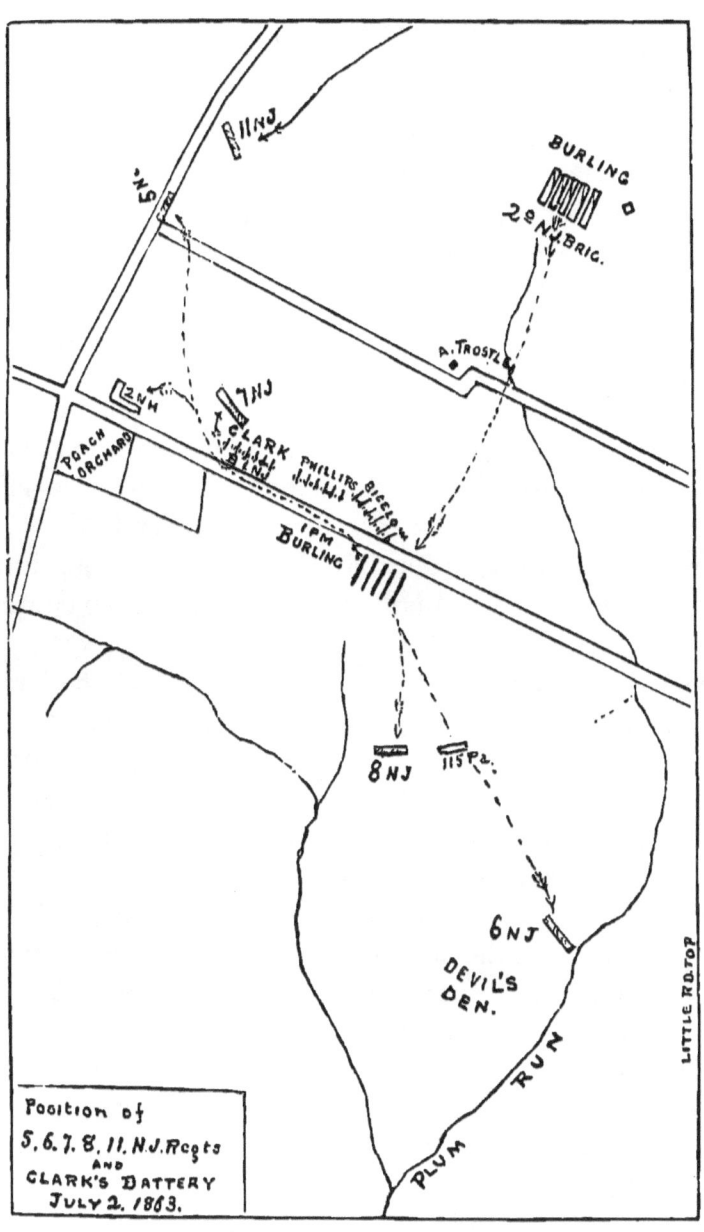

road. Colonel Burling was now left with but three regiments of his brigade.

The fighting on Ward's front to the left had been furiously kept up. The men of Robertson's brigade threw themselves upon the Federal line, and sought to envelop it by turning the left, the batteries of Smith and Winslow opened upon them, at first with case-shot, as they came nearer with shell, and when within three hundred yards with grape and canister. The infantry reserved their fire until the enemy were but two hundred yards away, when they poured a terrific volley into them checking their advance and throwing them into great disorder. Between the opposing lines was a stone fence and both sides waged a sharp contest for its possession. The battle was a frightful one. It seemed as though both Confederates and Federals were determined to fight until death before giving way. For more than an hour the lines alternately advanced and retreated, but Robertson, in his eagerness to interpose between Ward's left and the gorge, so extended his lines as to expose his flank to the fire of De Trobriand's brigade who was on the right of Ward. So deadly was the fire from this unexpected quarter that the left of Robertson's line was thrown back, and in order to avert disaster Robertson summoned up the rest of his brigade to meet De Trobriand's fire, which relieved Ward from the enormous pressure upon him and he promptly advanced and recovered the ground which he had lost.

Anderson's brigade at this juncture of affairs moved

down to the attack on De Trobriand, but he was also repulsed with heavy loss. Benning's brigade came in to Anderson's assistance and the fighting was renewed with great desperation on both sides.

Laws' brigade, General Hood accompanying it, with two regiments of Robertson's brigade moved directly across the gorge and attempted to scale the rocky sides of Little Round Top. Ward had no troops to prevent the movement, and there was nothing apparently to prevent the capture of this important position.

General Warren had not been long on Little Round Top before he saw the great importance of this summit to the Union army. As he saw the movement of Hood toward it he directed the signal officers to keep on waving their flags while he went for troops to defend it, and galloping out to the road he saw Barnes' division of the Fifth Corps moving to Sickles' assistance. These reinforcements should have been at Sickles' line an hour before, but they were in time to save Round Top. At the urgent request of Warren, General Sykes detached Vincent's brigade, and detailed Hazlett's battery to accompany them. Warren returned to his post and looked upon the frightful scene below. The incessant roar of artillery and musketry; the rapid movement of troops—now blue, now gray—as they emerge from the shelter of woods and rocks, or plunge recklessly into each other's ranks; the yells, the shouts, the cheers which arise above the sound of musketry—all these are seen and heard, but to Warren, who sees the enemy moving up the steep sides of the hill he occupies, the terrible conflict below becomes painful, as he anxiously awaits the arrival of Vincent. Noticing a body of troops on the road he once more starts for help, and at his urgent solicitation Colonel O'Rorke, of the One Hundred and Fortieth New York Regiment, follows him on a double-quick. During Warren's absence Vincent emerges on the spur of Little Round Top, and before him is spread a panorama of exceeding beauty and, just at that moment, of terrible grandeur, but he has no time to devote to its contemplation. As he posts his regiments along the rocky summit, Laws' enthusiastic Alabamians and Texans are pushing their way up the slope. Vincent's men are soon in position, the Sixteenth Michigan on the right, Forty-fourth New York and Eighty-third Pennsylvania in the centre, and the Twentieth Maine, Colonel Chamberlain, on the left. The enemy advance inspired by the sanguine words of their impulsive leader, and attack Vincent's centre. The rebels stumble and fall over the rocks and stones which impede their advance, but they push on, sheltering themselves as best they can from the close fire of Vincent's men. Unable to scale the obstructions in front, Hood extends his left to outflank the Sixteenth Michigan, which makes a gallant resistance but is being overpowered. Just at this moment, O'Rorke, with his brave New Yorkers, arrives on a run, and without any attempt at formation, they rush madly, bravely, desperately upon the enemy, and check their movement, capturing many prisoners as

CAPT. AMBROSE M. MATTHEWS,
Co. I, 13th Regt. N. J. Vols., Inf.
(*From a Recent Photograph.*)

trophies for their gallant charge. Hazlett, by the most extraordinary exertions has succeeded in placing his battery on the summit of Little Round Top. Dragging the heavy guns by hand, skillfully surmounting the numerous obstacles in the shape of huge bowlders and fallen trees, which were met with at every step, his plucky artillerymen performed a service as remarkable as it was glorious. Training his guns upon the enemy below, he began a cannonade against the forces so fiercely attacking Ward, and as the sound of his guns was heard, a cheer went up along the Union line, and all knew that Little Round Top was safe.

The battle which raged between the contesting forces on Little Round Top, and Benning, Anderson and Robertson's rebel brigades with the troops of Ward and De Trobriand, was of the most desperate nature. The two Federal brigades supported by Smith's and Winslow's batteries resisted stubbornly, but their position became more and more perilous. Smith leaving three of his guns, went to the rear and opened that section of his battery, firing obliquely through the gully. The rebels were everywhere. They were strongly disposed behind the natural defenses of rocks and ridges and kept up an incessant musketry and artillery fire. The Sixth New Jersey Regiment, Lieutenant-Colonel J. R. Gilkyson, commanding, was sent to Ward's support, and at the same time the Fortieth New York, Colonel Egan of De Trobriand's brigade. Proceeding on a double-quick to the most exposed point in Ward's line, the Sixth New Jersey took an advanced position in the gully and near the Devil's Den, where they engaged the enemy. The Eighth New Jersey was ordered in to the right of Ward's brigade, probably by General Birney's direct order, as Colonel Burling did not know what disposition had been made of it, and the One Hundred and Fifteenth Pennsylvania Regiment took position to the left of the Eighth in like manner, thus closing a gap which existed in the line between Ward and De Trobriand. Colonel Burling's command had thus been broken up and put into action at different parts of the line, over an extent of territory reaching from the Rogers house on the Emmetsburg road, to the Devil's Den, a distance of fully one mile.

The engagement had now become general along Birney's entire front. Kershaw's brigade of McLaws' division followed by Semmes' brigade had engaged De Trobriand's line and finally attacked the apex of the angle at the Peach Orchard. Tilton's and Sweitzer's brigades of Barnes' division of the Fifth Corps moved in to the relief of De Trobriand's worn out and exhausted men, whose ranks had been fearfully thinned, and met Kershaw's attack with great vigor, but they were finally driven back, thus imperiling the entire position.

The Sixth New Jersey and the Fortieth New York, who had pushed down to the support of Ward's left, "fighting like tigers," were exposed to a galling fire. For two hours the Sixth fought the enemy in the rocky gorge, protecting themselves by the huge bowlders and ledges of rock, which are to be found everywhere at this point, and only retired from the field when ordered by General Ward to rejoin its brigade. The losses of the Sixth Regiment during the battle were as follows:

### FIELD AND STAFF.

*Wounded*—Major Theodore W. Baker.

### COMPANY A.

*Wounded* — Second Lieutenant Hart W. Bodine, Corporal Smith Applegate, Corporal Thomas V. Dougherty (killed June 18, 1864, near Petersburg, Va.), Thomas Shields, William K. Morris, William Walton.

*Missing*—Samuel Applegate, David L. Compton.

### COMPANY B.

*Wounded* — Corporal Charles B. Yearkes (died August 20, 1863), Andrew Holland (died July 26, 1864, of wounds received in Wilderness).

### COMPANY C.

*Wounded*—Corporal Frederick Boorman, John Finerty, Henry Herman.

*Missing*—Austin A. Skinner, Martin Williams.

### COMPANY D.

*Wounded* — Sergeant William D. Smith, Sergeant Eli H. Baily, Daniel P. Bendalow.

*Missing*—Sergeant Edgar Hudson (supposed dead), Samuel English.

COMPANY E.

*Wounded*—Second Lieutenant Levi E. Ayres, First Sergeant George W. Jackson, Sergeant Charles G. P. Goforth (died September 1, 1864), William Hartman, Edward Johnson.

COMPANY F.

*Wounded* — Sergeant Adam Sheppard, Samuel B. Matlack, Charles Horstman.

COMPANY G.

*Wounded*—William E. Eastlack.

COMPANY H.

*Wounded*—Corporal Stephen Hull, Ambrose Kizer, Peter Wean (died July 11).

COMPANY I.

*Wounded*—Sergeant John E. Loeb, Henry Hessel.
*Missing*—William D. Jacobs, James W. Lewis.

COMPANY K.

*Killed*—Corporal Benjamin F. Reeves.
*Wounded*— John Lane, Dennis Laughlin, John A. Smith (died of peritonitis November 30, 1863).

RECAPITULATION.

|  | Killed. | Wounded. | Missing. | Total. |
|---|---|---|---|---|
| Officers | — | 3 | — | 3 |
| Enlisted Men | 1 | 29 | 8 | 38 |
| Total | 1 | 32 | 8 | 41 |

BRIG.-GEN. WILLIAM H. PENROSE,
Colonel Comm'd'g 15th Regt. N. J. Vols., Inf.
(*From Photograph after the War.*)

The Eighth New Jersey Regiment, Colonel John Ramsey, when ordered into action advanced across the wheat-field, taking position behind a stone wall, from whence they were ordered further to the right, placing them in an exposed position, with the stone wall on their left, and a rocky hill on their right. In front of this position there was a thick brush, big timber and rising ground, beyond which was a ravine with a hill on the other side. A few fence rails that were lying about were quickly seized upon and made to form a slight protection before the coming storm of battle should strike them. The only troops in front were a few of Berdan's sharpshooters. While some of the men were gathering fence rails they discovered Kershaw's column of troops approaching in line of battle to the attack of De Trobriand's position, on the left of whose line they were, and quickly gave the alarm. In a few minutes the enemy came into full view, and then ensued a sharp, severe and bloody struggle. The Eighth fought with the gallantry and bravery which proved them worthy followers of the heroic Kearny. Their ranks were rapidly thinned, and as they fell slowly back, their colors became entangled in a tree. The remnant of brave fellows rallied around them with cheers and re-formed to meet the advancing foe. At this point the Eighth was subjected to a severe musketry fire and sustained heavy losses. Colonel Ramsey was wounded, and the command of the regiment devolved upon Captain John Langston, of Company K. A brigade of the Fifth Corps came into line at this time and the Eighth was relieved. Its losses were 49, out of about 150 men who went into action, as follows:

### FIELD AND STAFF.

*Wounded*—Colonel John Ramsey.

### COMPANY A.

*Killed*—George B. Hopwood, Anson R. Waer.

*Wounded*—First Lieutenant Leonard M. Lambert, Sergeant John M. Freeland, Corporal James Van Wickle, James M. Day, Thomas Oldham, Henry M. Shugard (died July 29).

### COMPANY B.

*Killed*—Sylvester W. Hardy, Charles Meeker.

*Wounded*—Second Lieutenant Joseph Browe, Joseph Burroughs (died July 16), David L. Shipley, James E. Jones, William Robinson, John Jackson.

### COMPANY C.

*Wounded*—Charles E. Creelan, David James, Ira J. Smith (also missing).

### COMPANY D.

*Wounded*—Second Lieutenant Andrew J. Mandeville, Harvey K. Ammerman, Anthony C. Bull, John L. Hoffman.

### COMPANY E.

*Killed*—John Classer, David Cooper.

*Wounded*—Mark Greengrove.

COMPANY F.

*Killed*—Sergeant James Riley.

*Wounded*—First Lieutenant Henry Hartford, First Sergeant Daniel M. Ford, Stephen D. Longee, Thomas Van Cleave (died July 17).

COMPANY G.

*Wounded*—Captain Edward C. Nichols, Corporal John Cahill, Edward Quigley, William Riley.

COMPANY H.

*Killed*—Jonas W. Longenhuer.

*Wounded*—Captain Andrew S. Davis (died July 29), First Sergeant William J. Donnelly, Sergeant Obadiah Evans, John H. Gustus, Ervin Wilson, J. Irwin Lake, Elisha Bowlby.

*Missing*—Corporal Andrew J. Hoppock (prisoner of war).

COMPANY I.

*Wounded*—William R. Ralph, John F. Clouser, Patrick Riley.

COMPANY K.

*Wounded*—Corporal Benjamin Murphy.

RECAPITULATION.

|  | Killed. | Wounded. | Missing. | Total. |
| --- | --- | --- | --- | --- |
| Officers | — | 7 | — | 7 |
| Enlisted Men | 8 | 34 | 1 | 43 |
| Total | 8 | 41 | 1 | 50 |

The Seventh New Jersey Regiment suffered considerably from the artillery fire of the enemy while lying in support of the batteries, a number of men being killed and wounded. A ball from one spherical caseshot exploding overhead, plunged into the neck of Corporal Eugene Pollard of Company K as he lay on his face in the ranks. His brother and file-mate picked him up for dead and carried his body back to the woods and rocks where the regiment first formed, laying him down where he might be found again, when they returned to their places.* One shell came screaming over the regiment from the left to the right and plunging into the ranks exploded, killing two or three and wounding several others, among the latter Second Lieutenant Stanley Gaines of Company K, who was detailed to the command of another company, which had no commissioned officer present.

At last when the fighting was the fiercest at Little Round Top, the Devil's Den and the wheat-field, the Seventh became exposed to a shower of flying bullets at their backs. The regiment changed front to the left by the right flank, bringing them to face the lane and moving a few hundred feet over toward the Emmetsburg road, and nearer to Trostle's lane. Just at this time the artillery, in order to escape the advancing lines of Longstreet's hosts, limbered up and came hastening to the rear from the Peach Orchard and

---

\* Corporal Pollard was only slightly wounded, and the bullet which the surgeons cut out of his neck he carried in his pocket.

from the field. One battery coming straight toward the Seventh Regiment, caused the right four companies to separate from the line, thus causing a gap, and to avoid being crushed to death by the reckless drivers of the battery, were forced across Trostle's lane. The artillery became temporarily blocked in the lane, the anxiety of the drivers caused them to lap their horses over the pieces and caissons in front of them, thus effectually preventing the right four companies of the Seventh from rejoining their colors and the other six companies on the south side of the lane. Simultaneously with this blockade in Trostle's lane, came the rebel lines into the sunken road, running from the Emmetsburg pike to Round Top, and with colors planted on this natural breastwork, they opened a galling fire upon the Seventh New Jersey and the Second New Hampshire which, falling back from its first position at the extreme angle in the Peach Orchard, had made this its last stand, in the field about midway between the two roads. The right of the Seventh, which was then the color company of the regiment commanded by Captain Hillyer, rested under a single tree that still stands on the fence line of Trostle's lane. The regiment could not return with any effect the fire of the rebel line, as nothing but the slouch hats of their men were visible; they were unable to lie down in the lane owing to the blockade of the artillery, and there was no other shelter for the gallant veterans of the Seventh, who had no thought of leaving the field without firing one shot at the enemy at least, before the guns were safely withdrawn. Colonel Francine, Lieutenant-Colonel Price and Major Cooper in a few moments saw that it would be impossible to hold the men together inactive, exposed to this concentrating and galling fire, which in a few moments would become deadly when the rebel riflemen had obtained a more accurate range. Believing that a charge on the double-quick, with hearty Yankee cheers would check the advance of the enemy's line and draw his fire from the retreating batteries, at the same time destroying his range, the order was quickly given: "Fix bayonets; forward, double-quick, charge!" and this devoted little band swept across the field with shouts of confidence. As they reached about the prolongation of the line of the Second New Hampshire—which stood like a wall, hopelessly matching its spent, feeble and almost exhausted fire against the long line of battle confronting it—the hopelessness of the Seventh's effort was apparent, and all knew that any further advance meant certain annihilation for the brave Jerseymen. A halt, a hasty adjustment of the line, and a volley at the line of dirty slouch hats in front, was the work of but a minute, and the rattle of musketry drowned all other sounds, while the smoke totally obscured the rebel hats and colors.

At this point Colonel Francine, Lieutenant Mullery, Adjutant Dougherty, and over one-third of the Seventh were quickly placed *hors du combat.* The few who were still able to get away (wounded and unhurt) fell back beyond the Trostle house where they joined the other four companies, under the command of Lieutenant-Colonel Price, who rallied the scattered fragments and made another stand near Trostle's dwelling, until he himself fell shot through the thigh when the command devolved upon Major Frederick Cooper. In falling back from its most advanced position many more were struck by the shower of balls, among them Captain Hillyer who managed to hobble from the field with a flesh wound in the calf of his leg.

The losses of the Seventh were severe, amounting to 114, killed, wounded and missing, as follows:

### FIELD AND STAFF.

*Wounded*—Colonel Louis R. Francine (died July 16, 1863), Lieutenant Colonel Francis Price, Jr.

### COMPANY A.

*Killed* — Corporal Parker S. Davis, Martin Van Houten, James Flavegar.

*Wounded*—Lieutenant Robert Allen, First Sergeant Frederick Laib (died July 7), Corporal Swain S. Reeves, William H. Kirby, Thomas Brady, Lewis Haag, Jonathan C. Stevens, Owen S. Clark (died July 20), John Geckler.

### COMPANY B.

*Killed*—First Lieutenant Charles F. Walker, George W. Berry.

*Wounded*—Corporal Daniel Collins, Corporal John W. Donnington, Sopher Powers, Wallace Waer,

Patrick Carrigan, Stephen P. Williams, Reuben Pierce, William Noonburg.

*Missing*—Thomas Flannery, Cornelius Vandervliet.

### COMPANY C.

*Killed* — Sergeant James H. Harrison, Sergeant James Brown.

*Wounded* — Corporal Robert N. Beach, Corporal George W. Major, Corporal Alfred Husk, Stephen W. Edwards, James Keene, John Norman, Charles Wilson, Garret C. Bush.

*Missing*—John Lynch.

### COMPANY D.

*Wounded*—Lieutenant James H. Onslow, First Sergeant Walter Rotherham, Sergeant John T. Pine, Corporal Martin Cook, Corporal Samuel R. Stibbins, Joseph Deighlebohr, Mahlon Hackney.

*Missing*—John Mushlee, Charles W. Guice, Charles Stibbins.

### COMPANY E.

*Wounded*—Sergeant Calvin J. Osmun, Sergeant James Roseberry, Corporal Edward Creveling, Corporal David R. Rockafellow, James McKeever (and missing), William H. Pettit, John S. Gulick, Robert Dalrymple, Joseph Weaver, Michael Barry.

### COMPANY F.

*Killed*—Henry Rourke, James Bennett, Jeremiah McNulty, Joseph Hall.

*Wounded*—Sergeant James F. Renshaw (died July

11), Sergeant Edward H. Ridgway, Charles P. Platt (died July 24), Thomas J. Labaugh.

*Missing*—Edwin F. Platt.

### COMPANY G.

*Killed*—Corporal Thomas Flannigan, Edward Mewhanney.

*Wounded*—James Fletcher (died July 8), Henry Van Riper, Thomas Walthall, Robert Dunkerley, John James.

*Missing*—William K. Willis.

### COMPANY H.

*Killed*—John A. Dempsey.

*Wounded*—Lieutenant Charles R. Dougherty, Lieutenant Thomas Clark, First Sergeant Jesse C. Morgan, Corporal William B. Davis, Corporal Lorenzo Paynter, John Armstrong, Samuel T. Beckett, Henry F. Harrold, Albert Johnson, George C. Lovejoy, Samuel H. Nelson, Joseph Wolf, Thomas W. Wyne, William J. Wallen.

*Missing*—Daniel W. Simmerman.

### COMPANY I.

*Killed*—Sergeant William A. Ezekiel.

*Wounded*—First Sergeant Edward R. Holt, Corporal Ryerson Space, Joshua Leonard, Daniel Sheldon.

*Missing*—Richard South.

### COMPANY K.

*Wounded*—Captain William R. Hillyer, Lieutenant Michael Mullery, Lieutenant Stanley Gaines, Corporal

Eugene Pollard, Corporal George W. Derrickson, Corporal John L. Denton, Lemuel Adams, George F. Bayles, Charles Y. Beers (died July 6), Abel Gruber, Jacob S. Hopping (died July 16), John H. Haley, Robert L. Jolly (died July 22), Theodore F. Searing, George Shipman.

*Missing*—Joseph Ward, John Recanio.

RECAPITULATION.

|  | Killed. | Wounded. | Missing. | Total. |
|---|---|---|---|---|
| Officers | 1 | 10 | — | 11 |
| Enlisted men | 14 | 77 | 12 | 103 |
| Total | 15 | 87 | 12 | 114 |

The Fifth New Jersey Regiment, Colonel William J. Sewell, which had been ordered to the relief of the picket line on the Emmetsburg road, moved by the right flank at a double-quick, and reached the position named by deploying as skirmishers. The right of the regiment rested at a white house, the left extending to a barn on the Emmetsburg road, the line covering the entire front of Humphreys' division. The Fifth was subjected to a severe artillery fire for full an hour, when the enemy's infantry (Barksdale's brigade) made their appearance to the left and in front of the position occupied by the regiment. Colonel Sewell at once notified General Humphreys of the enemy's appearance, and after an examination of the ground was convinced that the only place to check the attack was on the road and the crest of the hill which he held. The enemy first encountered the left of the line of battle, and pushed forward in such strong force as to drive in

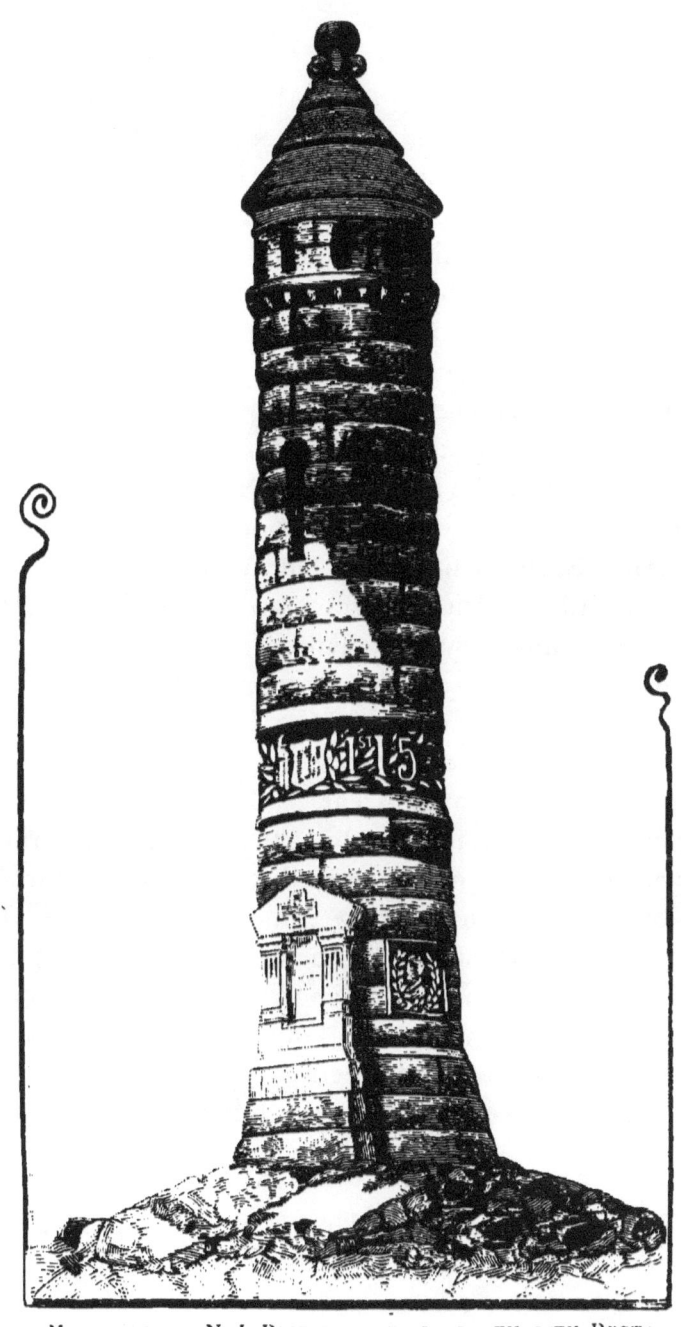

Monument 1st N. J. Brigade—1st, 2d, 3d, 4th, 15th Regts.

the troops on Sewell's left. The flank of the Fifth Regiment thus becoming exposed, the left of the line fell back and the ground thus surrendered was at once occupied by a rebel battery. Sewell held his men firmly to the position expecting an advance of the troops in his rear, but none came to his support. The Fifth was now seriously compromised. Exposed to a combined musketry and artillery fire which it was impossible to withstand, it was apparent that to remain any longer meant annihilation or capture. Rallying the regiment on the right Colonel Sewell skillfully withdrew it from its perilous position, at the same time covering Seeley's battery, which was firing in retreat. As the Fifth fell back in good order and amid a terrible fire of musketry and artillery, it was noticed that Humphreys' line was changing front to his rear and right so as to connect with the First Division, which had been compelled to vacate its position. The Fifth Regiment fought with great gallantry and confronted overwhelming numbers, but the strong and rapid advance of the enemy carried everything before it. Colonel Sewell and Acting Major Victor M. Healey were both seriously hurt, the former by a musket ball and the latter by a piece of shell. Captain E. P. Berry, acting adjutant, was so badly hurt that his leg had to be amputated, from the effects of which he died July 6. The casualties complete were as follows:

FIELD AND STAFF.

*Wounded*—Colonel William J. Sewell, Captain, and Acting Adjutant, Edward P. Berry.

## COMPANY A.

*Killed*—Second Lieutenant Henry R. Clark, Samuel W. Bradford.

*Wounded*—Corporal Thomas Hannigan, Charles H. Compton, John Haney, Michael Humphrey, John Miller, Patrick Ryan (died July 8), Henry Schweis, Patrick Tynan.

*Missing*—Augustus F. S. Singleton.

## COMPANY B.

*Killed*—Corporal Edgar S. Van Winkle.

*Wounded*—Captain Virgil M. Healy, Sergeant John McIvors (died July 16), Corporal John J. Keeney, James W. Andrews, James Bell (died July 12, 1864), Roderick Egan, Michael Fox, John H. Ibbs, Annanias H. Lynn, George W. Trauger, George T. White.

## COMPANY C.

*Killed*—John Ryan.

*Wounded* — Captain Henry H. Woolsey, Sergeant John W. Jennings, Edward Bessigkommer, David J. Huntington, Michael C. Manning, Michael McTigh, George Schriber, William Waldron.

## COMPANY D.

*Wounded*—Corporal John F. Chase, Andrew Jackson, John Coyle.

*Missing* — Corporal John H. Brady, Levi Hall, Edward Cassaday (died January 2, 1864, at Belle Isle, Va., prisoner of war), John Roaleff.

*Missing*—Lewis J. Low (supposed dead).

COMPANY E.

*Killed*—Henrich Troch.

*Wounded* — Corporal Hugh Riley, Anton Burtz, James R. Clark, Samuel Haines, Eli Hamilton, Albertus K. Hibbs, Jacob Meyers, John Melcher, William Nelson.

COMPANY F.

*Killed*—First Sergeant Theodore Sutphin.

*Wounded* — Sergeant Richard P. Ogden, George Drummond, Jacob M. Frazer, James M. Welsh, Jonathan Wentzell.

*Missing*—Corporal Samuel Ray.

COMPANY G.

*Wounded*—Sergeant Martin Doyle, John J. Irving, David McManus, David Miller.

*Missing*—Jacob Baier, John O. Heath (missing, supposed dead), David Stolter.

COMPANY H.

*Killed*—Samuel Henselman, Patrick Kelly.

*Wounded* — Sergeant Hugh Starrs (died June 29, 1864, at Andersonville, prisoner of war), Corporal John F. Lee, George Rhinecker, Howard O'Daniel, William H. Ketch (missing, supposed dead), Joseph Zahn.

*Missing*—John H. Johnson (supposed dead).

COMPANY I.

*Killed*—Captain Thomas Kelly, William L. Bennett, Edward Martin.

MONUMENT 5TH N. J. VOLS., INF.

*Wounded*—Sergeant William K. Haines, Corporal Thomas Norcross (died October 30, 1863), Benjamin O. Birch, Richard Nesbitt, George Whitney.
*Missing*—Alfred L. Britton.

#### COMPANY K.

*Killed*—Sergeant Samuel Shackleton.

*Wounded*—Captain Cyrus H. Rogers, William J. Button (died September 24, 1863), William H. Cary, Thomas Hampton, Charles B. Leonard.

*Missing*—First Sergeant Edwin G. Smith, James Brady, John Easch (supposed dead), Nehemiah Sayers.

#### RECAPITULATION.

|  | *Killed.* | *Wounded.* | *Missing.* | *Total.* |
|---|---|---|---|---|
| Officers | 2 | 5 | — | 7 |
| Enlisted Men | 11 | 60 | 16 | 87 |
| Total | 13 | 65 | 16 | 94 |

The praise bestowed upon the fighting qualities of Burling's Jersey brigade is wholly deserved. General Birney says of them: "I cannot estimate too highly the services of the regiments from Burling's brigade, Second Division—the Fifth, Sixth and Seventh New Jersey Volunteers. These regiments were sent to me during the contest and most gallantly did they sustain the glorious reputation won by them in former battles." The absence of any allusion to the heroic conduct of the Eighth Regiment is undoubtedly due to the fact—as Colonel Burling says in his report—that it was taken from him without his knowledge, and as Colonel

Ramsey, who commanded the regiment was wounded, no report of its services was ever sent in.

Of the brilliant services of the Fifth Regiment General Humphreys who commanded the Second Division of the Third Corps, says:

"Colonel Sewell, commanding the Fifth New Jersey Volunteers, of my Third Brigade, reported to me and relieved the pickets of General Graham's brigade on my left, some of which extended over a part of my front. This regiment had been posted but a short time when a most earnest request was made by a staff officer of General Sickles that another regiment should be sent to the support of General Birney. At this moment Colonel Sewell sent me word that the enemy was driving in my pickets and was about advancing in two lines to the attack. * * * * Seeley's battery had now opened upon the enemy's infantry as they began to advance. Turnbull's battery was likewise directed against them, and I was about to throw forward somewhat the left of my infantry and engage the enemy with it, when I received orders from General Birney (General Sickles having been dangerously wounded and carried from the field) to throw back my left and form a line oblique to and in rear of the one I then held, and was informed that the First Division would complete the line to Round Top ridge. This I did under a heavy fire of artillery and infantry from the enemy, who now advanced on my whole front.

"At this time Colonel Sewell's regiment returned to

the line, having maintained most gallantly its position on picket, with very heavy loss.

\* \* \* \* \* \*

"As I have already stated, my Third Brigade was ordered to the support of Major-General Birney, commanding the First Division. The accompanying report of Colonel George C. Burling, commanding that brigade, exhibits the disposition that was made of the regiments of the brigade. In succession they, with the exception of Colonel Sewell's regiment, were sent to aid the brigades of the First Division. The Seventh New Jersey, Colonel Louis R. Francine, commanding, and the Second New Hampshire, were sent to the support of General Graham's brigade, and the Eighth New Jersey, Colonel John Ramsey, commanding; the Sixth New Jersey, Lieutenant-Colonel J. R. Gilkyson, commanding, and the One Hundred and Fifteenth Pennsylvania, were sent to the support of General Ward's brigade. For the part taken in the engagement by these regiments I must refer to the reports of the commanders of these brigades. That they did their duty in a manner comporting with their high reputation is manifest from the severe loss they met with—430 killed and wounded. Colonel Sewell, Colonel Francine, Colonel Ramsey, and Lieutenant-Colonel Price, officers distinguished for their skill and gallantry, were severely wounded. Colonel Francine's wound proved to be mortal.

\* \* \* \* \* \*

"Colonel Sewell's conspicuous gallantry in the main

tenance of his post has been already mentioned by me. He was severely wounded soon after his regiment rejoined the main line."

General Ward, to whose support the Sixth and Eighth New Jersey Regiments were sent, makes no mention whatever in his report of the valuable services rendered by these splendid regiments, an oversight that appears strange indeed, in view of the profuse praise bestowed on other regiments whose services were no better, nor more greatly needed. Captain Smith of the Fourth New York Battery, is an honorable exception to both General Ward and Colonel Tipton who commanded Graham's brigade (General Graham having been wounded and fell into the hands of the enemy) in whose support the Second New Hampshire and Seventh New Jersey went. Captain Smith says: "At this time the Sixth New Jersey Volunteers, Lieutenant-Colonel Gilkyson commanding, and Fortieth New York Regiment, Colonel Egan commanding, came to our support. These regiments marched down the gully, fighting like tigers, exposed to a terrific fire of musketry, and when within one hundred yards of the rebel line the Fourth Maine, which still held the hill, were forced to retreat. Very soon afterward the Fortieth New York and Sixth New Jersey Regiments were compelled to follow."

The Eleventh New Jersey Regiment, Colonel Robert McAllister commanding, of Carr's brigade, was also heavily engaged in the dreadful conflict which followed the impetuous charge of Barksdale's brigade, as it broke through the lines at the Peach Orchard. They heroically braved the tempest of shot and shell which ploughed through their ranks, and the heavy casualty list attests their unwavering conduct during this dreadful ordeal. General McAllister, in a recent letter to the author, thus describes the scene:

"We (the Eleventh New Jersey Volunteers) were in front of the apple orchard at the Smith house, along the Emmetsburg road. During this heavy artillery firing—we not being actively engaged—I ordered my men to lie down. The shot and shell played over our heads and through the apple trees in our rear, carrying the branches through the air like chaff. The gunners and horses of our artillery were rapidly cut down. If the destruction of life could have been left out of mind I would have considered the scene grand beyond description. So exciting was it that I could not keep lying down. I had to jump up and watch the grand duel. In about half an hour the artillery ceased and the first charge of the rebel infantry was made in my front. We prepared to receive the charge. I ordered my men to 'Fire.' I was on the right of my regiment. As the rebels advanced our pickets came into our lines, and we received, the charge. I was wounded while passing from the right to the centre of my regiment—severely wounded by a minié ball passing through my left leg and a shell striking my right foot. I did not see a single man in the regiment flinch or show the least cowardice under that terrific cannonading or the fierce charge which we met."

The Eleventh was assailed on the right by Wilcox's brigade, and the charge by Barksdale at the Peach Orchard uncovered its left. To meet his attack the regiment was directed by General Carr to change front by bringing the left to the rear, which movement was as orderly and as handsomely executed under the terrible fire to which it was exposed, as though on parade. This brought the Eleventh directly in the path of Barksdale's advance. Barksdale was mounted upon a splendid horse and was conspicuous by wearing a red fez. He rode to the right and foot of his brigade, with ringing voice and waving sword urging his men on, and General Carr, recognizing the worth of this leader's example and enthusiasm sent an aide to the commanding officer of the Eleventh, directing him to bring down the mounted officer. Company H, commanded by Captain Ira W. Cory was ordered to direct its entire fire at Barksdale, and he fell pierced (as it was afterwards ascertained) by five balls.

The change of front to meet Barksdale's charge brought the Eleventh to the foot of the slope in rear of the Smith house, and there occurred its greatest loss, the casualties among the officers being unusually large. Colonel McAllister fell severely wounded just as he gave the command. Major Philip Kearney, the next in command, soon received a shot in the knee, and spinning around like a top fell, ten paces away. Captain Luther Martin, of Company D, the senior officer, was notified to take the command, but before he had time to realize the responsibility of his position, was killed. Captain D. B. Logan of Company H, who succeeded him, also fell severely wounded, and four men who were taking him to the rear were all shot down before they could reach a place of safety and Captain Logan killed. Captain Andrew H. Ackerman, of Company C, then assumed command and he, too, soon fell dead. The regiment was being cut up at a frightful rate, and began falling back. To check this movement Corporal Thomas Johnson of Company I, was ordered to take the colors—two color-bearers had already been shot—and plant them twenty paces to the front. He did so and remained there kneeling until ordered back, when the regiment moved with the line of battle to a position some distance to the rear, where it halted behind a hedge.

The casualties in the Eleventh were heavy—over fifty per cent. of the number who went into action. They were as follows:

### FIELD AND STAFF.

*Wounded*—Colonel Robert McAllister, Major Philip J. Kearney (died August 9, 1863), Adjutant John Schoonover.

### COMPANY A.

*Wounded*—Corporal Tyler L. Haring (died July 4), First Sergeant Joseph Burns, Corporal George H. Johnson, Emmet Burke, Christopher Snyder, Robert E. Mayo, William H. Weaver, Nathan E. Wappenstein, Archibald Patten, Isaac Harlow, Daniel L. Snider, Henry McMahon.

## COMPANY B.

*Wounded* — First Lieutenant William S. Provost, First Sergeant William Hand, Corporal Charles A. Voorhees (loss of both eyes), Corporal Thaddeus Doane, Corporal Andrew Webster, John H. Rue (died July 19), Benjamin F. Jackson (died July 7), Albert Oss, William H. Smith, Fidelle Haase, J. A. Lowther, Samuel Stacker, Jacob Van Pelt (died July 9), John Voorhees.

## COMPANY C.

*Killed* — Captain Andrew H. Ackerman, Sergeant Corum Righter, Joseph Cheston, John Clark, Jr.

*Wounded*—First Lieutenant John B. Fassett, Color-Sergeant David Schafer, Corporal Amos Rockhill, John Lindsey, Franklin Armstrong, Richard Howell, James K. Webb, John Crane, Charles Stevenson, Peter Cogill.

*Missing*—Charles Purdan.

## COMPANY D.

*Killed*—Captain Luther Martin, Corporal Isaac A. Hendershot, Randolph Merriman.

*Wounded*—Lieutenant Sidney M. Layton, Corporal Manuel Runyon, Richard Burtrone, Edward Spellman, Theodore Waller, David C. Keve.

*Missing*—Edward B. Nelson, James Beattie (reported died July 2), Frederick C. Tuers (reported died July 3).

## COMPANY E.

*Killed*—Thomas Tinney.

*Wounded*—Second Lieutenant Silas W. Volk, Sergeant Eliphalet Sturdevant (died July 13), Corporal Absalom Talmadge, Corporal Elisha F. Rose, Corporal Edward J. Kinney, Charles Bowman, James F. Gibson, Benjamin H. Joinier, James King, Samuel W. Morse, Thomas Scattergood, John H. Wilson, Jacob Miller (also missing), Joseph W. Walton.

*Missing*—David Daley.

### COMPANY F.

*Killed*—John L. Cozzins.

*Wounded* — Captain William H. Lloyd, First Lieutenant Edwin R. Good, First Sergeant Benjamin F. Morehouse, Sergeant Thomas D. White, Sergeant James C. White, Sergeant John F. Bartine, Corporal George W. Morton, Corporal Charles Dilks, Corporal Edward White, Corporal William H. Terhune, Edward Powers, James Thompson, Ephraim Robbins, William Collins, Miller H. Lewis.

### COMPANY G.

*Killed*—George S. Bird, George H. Bunting, Henry Elbertson, Michael Goff, Stewart Parent, Peter Robins.

*Wounded*—Sergeant O. F. Holloway, Sergeant Ferdinand W. Krug, Corporal George Holloway, Corporal Israel Nixon, Corporal Smith H. Eldredge, Charles A. Koenig, Thomas Lowry, George A. McGuire, George F. Sever, Chapman Marcellus, William Emmons (prisoner of war), Thomas Foutch, Abijah Thompson, John Lloyd, Joseph Fowler, Thomas Kelly (also missing).

## COMPANY H.

*Killed*—Captain Dorastus B. Logan, Edward Barber.

*Wounded* — Second Lieutenant William E. Axtell, Sergeant J. V. Lanterman, Joshua Barber, Joseph L. Decker, Bartley Owen, John C. Nutt, John J. Sites, Timothy K. Pruden, Patrick King, William Halsey.

## COMPANY I.

*Killed*—Corporal James P. Stryker, Silas D. Clark.

*Wounded*—Sergeant Thomas J. Thompson, Corporal Richard J. Merrill, Corporal E. M. Robinson, Corporal John W. Joline (died August 17, 1863), Corporal Michael Cooney, Francis Wassimer, William H. Luce, James Finnons, Stacey Babcock, John M. Errickson, Alfred Barcalo, Daniel J. Buckley, George Chamberlin, Henry L. Molleson, Jacob L. Chevalier.

*Missing*—John Desbrow, Hugh Downey (died at Andersonville, September 19, 1864.)

## COMPANY K.

*Killed*—Corporal Jeremiah O'Brien, Corporal W. H. Morgan, Martin Bekie, Henry Kring.

*Wounded*—First Sergeant Charles C. Reilley, Sergeant Edward Appleton, Corporal Amon J. Foote, John Ardner, William Carson, Jr., Frederick Soldner, John A. Labort, Gersham J. Froate.

### RECAPITULATION.

|  | *Killed.* | *Wounded.* | *Missing.* | *Total.* |
|---|---|---|---|---|
| Officers | 3 | 10 | — | 13 |
| Enlisted Men | 20 | 113 | 7 | 140 |
| Total | 23 | 123 | 7 | 153 |

General Joseph B. Carr, commanding the First Brigade, Second Division, Third Army Corps, in his report calls the attention of the General commanding the division to the gallant and meritorious conduct of Colonel Robert McAllister, commanding Eleventh New Jersey Volunteers, Major Philip J. Kearney, seriously wounded (since dead), Adjutant John Schoonover, who was twice wounded, but remained in command of his regiment, and to Lieutenant John Oldershaw, acting aide-de-camp, to whom his sincere thanks are extended for valuable services rendered.

The fighting had been furious. Ward, on the left at the Devil's Den, had borne the heaviest part of it for nearly two hours, and the onslaught of Benning with Anderson's brigade finally forced him back with the loss of three guns of Smith's battery, and a casualty list of frightful proportions. The attack on De Trobriand had caused his line to recede. His ranks were frightfully decimated. The artillery also fell back a short distance to get out of the way of the advancing enemy, and if Kershaw had been able to press a little stronger success would have crowned his efforts. But just at this moment, when defeat seemed certain Caldwell's splendid division of the Second Corps arrived on the field, and Ayres' Regulars of the Fifth Corps followed in front of Little Round Top. Another effort to preserve the line was to be made. Ayres detached Weed's brigade—to which the One Hundred and Fortieth New York belonged—to reinforce the exhausted band on Little Round Top, where he

MONUMENT 6TH REGIMENT N. J. VOLS., INF.

arrived just in time to learn that the gallant Vincent and the brave O'Rorke had both been killed, and their troops menaced by another assault from Hood's persistent veterans. Moving to the right Hood sought to turn the flank of the Twentieth Maine. He opened a sharp fire along the whole line, and Weed, who was standing near Hazlett's battery encouraging his men, received a mortal wound, while Hazlett in stooping down to hear his dying words, was struck by the bullet of a sharp-shooter and fell upon the dead body of his friend a corpse. The enemy moved to the right to get in Chamberlain's rear, and in so doing was compelled to weaken his line. Chamberlain noticing the fact boldly charged upon the attacking force capturing over three hundred of them and before they could recover from their surprise at this seeming piece of audacity, Chamberlain, at the point of the bayonet forced the remainder down the mountain side. It was a glorious achievement, but only one of many of like nature which characterized the battle of Gettysburg.

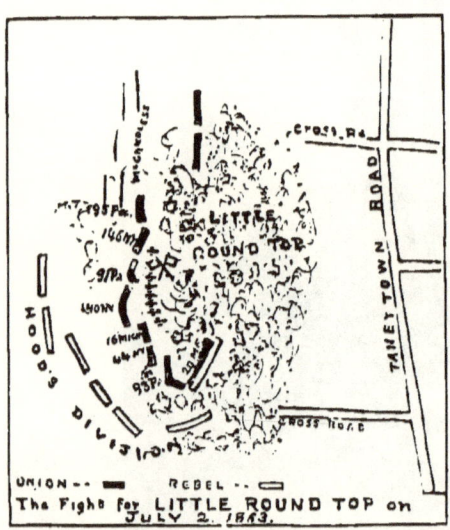

While this conflict for Little Round Top was going

on, Caldwell's division was advancing to meet the victorious troops of Anderson and Kershaw, who had driven back but had not penetrated the line of Birney and Barnes. The "Irish Brigade" commanded by Colonel Kelley, formed amid the dreadful sounds of the conflict, and before going into action, the chaplain, a Catholic priest, ascended a rocky bowlder and pronounced a general absolution for the whole brigade. At the word of command they dashed impetuously upon Anderson's line and brought his troops to a halt. Cross and Zook and Burke's brigades in turn assailed the enemy, but a movement by Wofford, who boldly dashed into the line in his eagerness to aid Barksdale, who had advanced in two lines of battle against the Peach Orchard, compelled Birney, Humphreys, Barnes and Caldwell's divisions to re-form on the main line, and relinquish the Emmetsburg road and the whole of the ground back to Little Round Top, to the enemy.

General Meade had sent for reinforcements from all parts of the battle-field, and troops from the First, Sixth and Twelfth Corps were promptly moving to the scene. Hill had begun a lively cannonade on the position of Cemetery Hill to which the batteries there responded vigorously and effectively. Meade in his great desire to preserve the left had stripped the right of his line, by ordering the whole of the Twelfth Corps to the support of Sickles, but to this movement General Slocum warmly protested. At his earnest solicitation Green's brigade of Geary's division was permitted to remain on Culp's Hill, and by extending his several regiments in a thin line along the works was able to occupy a good portion of them, but not all. At half-past seven o'clock Ruger's division took up position in line with Doubleday's division of the First Corps and Birney's of the Third Corps, forming in two lines of battle, Colgrove's brigade in front, and McDougall in rear. Lockwood's brigade, which had arrived earlier, was led by General Meade into the very jaws of the enemy, and by their successful charge, enabled the new line to become more firmly established. This movement brought the Thirteenth New Jersey Regiment, Col. Ezra A. Carman, to the scene of conflict. The Thirteenth had been massed on the southeasterly slope of Culp's Hill at an early hour in the morning, when Meade's orders to charge Ewell's line had been given, and on the abandonment of that scheme, relieved the Third Wisconsin Regiment in McAllister's wood to the south of Spangler's Run. The Twelfth Corps had thrown up a line of small breastworks along the crest of Culp's Hill, and in McAllister's woods, and when ordered to the left vacated them all except that part of the line held by Green's brigade of Geary's division on the summit of Culp's Hill.

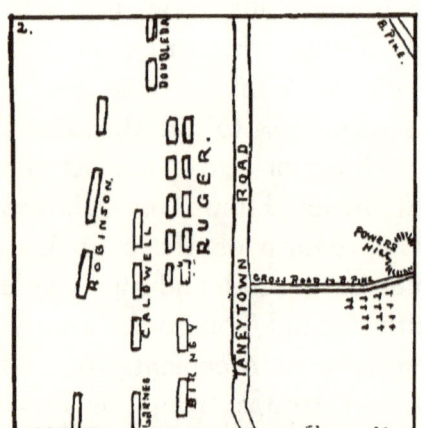

Meade had called upon every corps in the army, during the day, except the Eleventh, for reinforcements to Sickles' line, and they all moved promptly to the left, where they were put in at every exposed point. The wounding of Sickles, put Birney in temporary command of the Third Corps, but by order of General Meade, Hancock was placed in command of the corps in addition to his own. Hancock performed herculean service. His watchful eye detected every weak spot in the line and he promptly protected it. The attack culminated by the effort of Wilcox, Perry and Wright's brigades to break through Humphreys' line, and Wright succeeded in piercing the centre of the Federal position by the capture of four guns. Wilcox was almost in a line with him, but General Newton sent forward Doubleday's division of the First Corps who reached Webb's line in time to see Wright falling back, but they pursued him sharply and recaptured six guns which had been in the enemy's possession. By Hancock's own order the First Minnesota Regiment bravely attacked Wilcox, and drove him back as far as the Emmetsburg road, but with a loss of half its men.

Never before had the artillery branch of the service endured such a tremendous strain. The loss in horses and men was unusually heavy, and the abandonment of so many guns by the Federals shows with what desperation the fighting was carried on. Batteries were kept at work until there were not left enough men and horses to draw them away, and Bigelow's battery, which took position near the Trostle house,

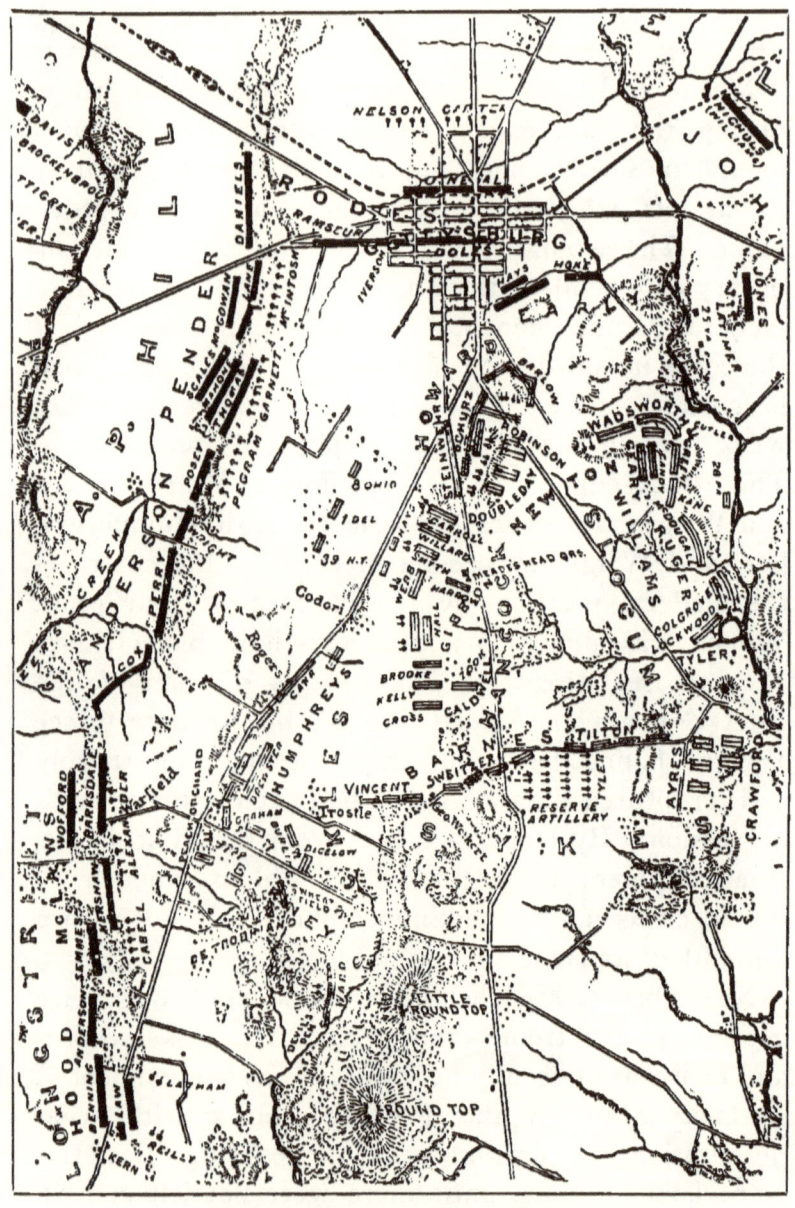

LONGSTREET IN POSITION FOR HIS ATTACK ON SICKLES.
The map on the opposite page shows the Union line after Sickles' defeat.
UNION, WHITE; CONFEDERATE, BLACK.

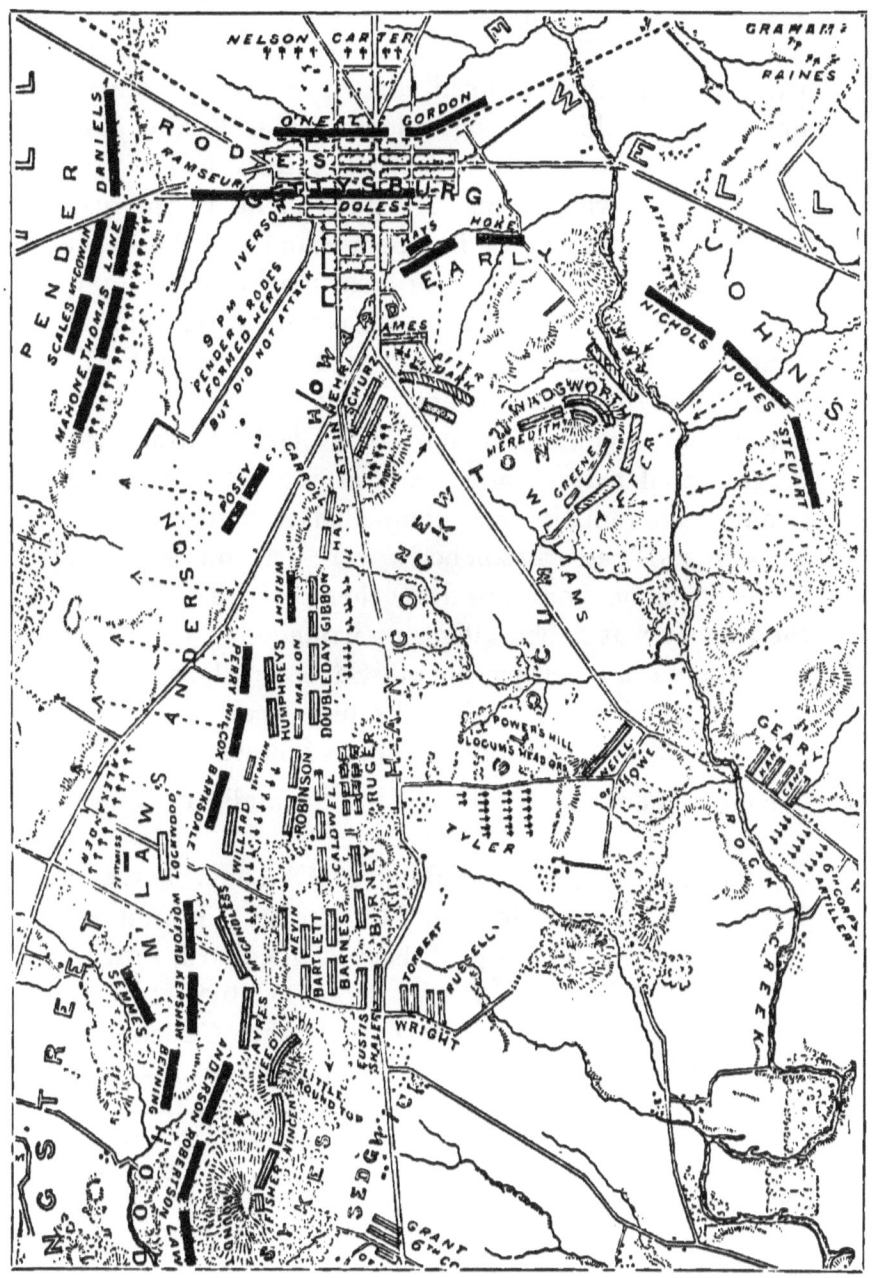

was deliberately sacrificed, the men firing canister until they could no longer load owing to the close approach of the enemy. Clark's battery ("B" First New Jersey) was in the very thickest of all this carnage. When Kershaw's line penetrated into the Peach Orchard a South Carolina regiment moved boldly up to Clark's pieces. A Pennsylvania regiment lying in the "sunken road" concealed, rose up and poured a deadly volley into their faces which caused them to retire in confusion. From 2 p. m. until 6.30 Clark's battery was in continual action, and when at the retiring of the infantry column, it was compelled to fall back, one caisson and one caisson-body were left on the field there being no horses to draw them off. The loss in the battery was 2 men killed, 15 wounded, 3 missing, 2 of whom were taken prisoners. Seventeen horses were killed and five so badly disabled that they were abandoned. The casualties were as follows:

*Killed*—Thomas N. Post, Jr., Rensallaer Casselman.—2.

*Wounded*—Sergeant Leander McChesney, Privates Richard S. Price, Joseph M. Morris, [1] Hiram A. Grover, [2] Hiram Tierney, [3] Edson E. Sheppard, Patrick F. Castello, William Riley, Robert Stuart, [4] John Truly, Anthony Collier, Joseph Baker, Chileon D. Richards, Leopold Smally, [5] Stephen McGowan.—15.

---

[1] Hiram A. Grover, [2] Hiram Tierney, of the Second Michigan Volunteers; [3] Edson E. Sheppard, [4] John Truly, of the Sixty-third Pennsylvania Volunteers; and [5] Stephen McGowan of the Ninety-ninth Pennsylvania Volunteers, were temporarily attached to the battery, and were not members of it.

*Missing*—Privates Henry C. Buffum, Henry E. Davis, Daniel W. Laws—all prisoners of war.—3.

Colonel McGilvery, who commanded the First Volunteer Brigade, Artillery Reserve, describes the artillery fighting at this part of the line:

"A New Jersey battery (Clark's "B" First New Jersey Artillery) immediately on the right of the two Massachusetts batteries, was receiving the most of the fire of two or more rebel batteries. Hart's Fifteenth New York Independent Battery reporting at that time I placed it in position in a peach orchard on the right and a little to the front of the New Jersey battery. The four batteries already mentioned presented a front at nearly right angles with the position occupied by our troops, facing toward our left, the fire of which I concentrated on single rebel batteries, and five or more were driven in succession from their positions.

"At about a quarter to six the enemy's infantry gained possession of the woods immediately on the left of my line of batteries and our infantry fell back both on the right and left, when great disorder ensued on both flanks of the line of batteries. At this period of the action all of the batteries were exposed to a warm infantry fire from both flanks and front, whereupon I ordered them to retire two hundred and fifty yards and renew their fire. The New Jersey battery was relieved, being out of ammunition, and retired to the rear. Captain Bigelow retired by prolonge, firing canister, and with Phillips and Thompson on the right.

in their new position checked the enemy for a short time."

During the fighting on Sickles' front the enemy's skirmishers kept up an annoying fire upon the Second Corps' line. Their reserves occupied an old building, known as the Bliss barn, which also commanded the line, and about five o'clock in the afternoon General Hayes directed Colonel Smyth, commanding the Second Brigade, to dislodge them. Colonel Smyth called upon the Twelfth New Jersey Regiment, whereupon the whole regiment arose to volunteer, when he indicated that a detachment of four companies would be sufficient for the work in hand. The barn mentioned was of brick, was five hundred and eighty-seven yards from the line, and it and the line of the Twelfth's advance were so completely covered by the fire of the enemy's skirmishers and artillery, that it was known that serious loss must result from the attack. Major John T. Hill detached for this service companies B, H, E and G, under command of Captain Samuel B. Jobes, the ranking officer.

The column moved out by the flank to the right of the Bryan barn; then, formed by company into line. As the rear cleared the wall the movement came under the eyes of the whole brigade and of part of Gibbons' division, and of Robinson's division of the First Corps upon the right, and now in close formation the Twelfth begins its march. The artillery of Hill's Corps opened upon the line at once, the enemy's skirmishers poured in an annoying fire, his reserve from the

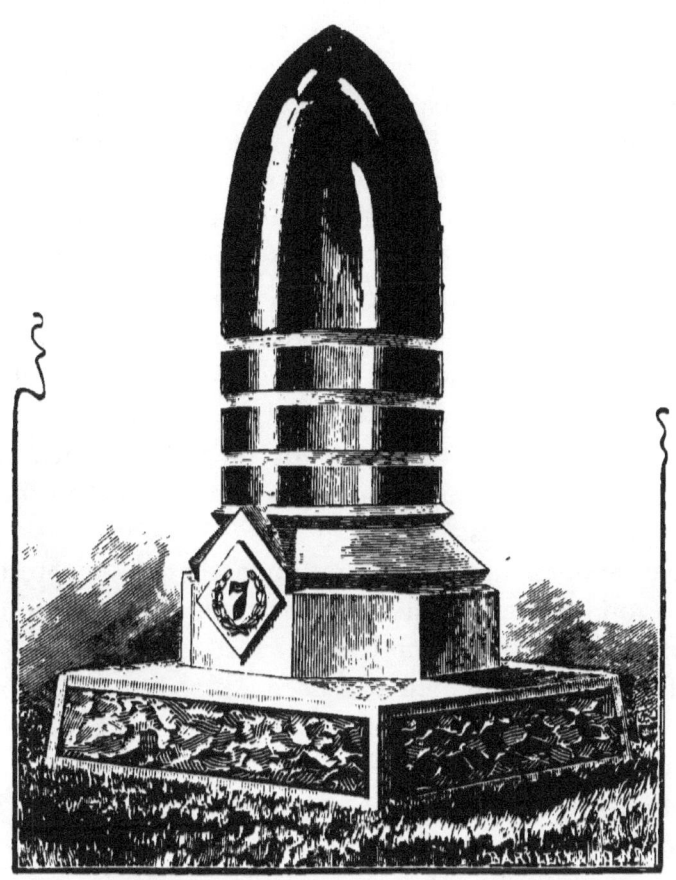

MONUMENT 7TH REGIMENT N. J. VOLS., INF.

the shelter of the barn thinned its ranks, Jobes was wounded, Captain Horsfalls, of Company E, was killed, and 40 men out of the 200 were stricken down ; but there was no wavering in that brave column of Jerseymen.

Bringing their arms to the right shoulder, and taking the double quick, with ringing cheers they burst through the enemy's skirmish line with the might of a giant, and in one bold mass closed down upon, surrounded and captured the Bliss barn, with the enemy's picket reserve of ninety-two men and seven officers, and bringing their prisoners with them, regained our lines.

No bolder attack was made upon that well-contested field, and it deservedly gave the regiment a reputation for gallantry which it never lost.

The battle on the left had been a bloody one. Longstreet's men, nerved to their work by the belief that victory would surely follow their assault and this be followed by the speedy ending of the war, fought with a valor and heroism unsurpassed; but they had not only the physical force of the Union army to contend against. Every man in it who handled a musket or wielded a sabre felt that Lee's army was in their power, and never once thought of defeat. This battle ground meant defeat for one side or the other, and no man in the Army of the Potomac believed defeat possible for them. The driving in of the First and Eleventh Corps the day before had not disheartened them ; but as the news of the rout at the first battle of Bull Run created a feeling throughout the North that the rebellion should be put down at whatever cost, so the defeat of these two corps on the first day of July made the determination of Meade's soldiers to win, all the stronger.

The fighting for the day had not been confined wholly to Sickles' front, and though Longstreet had failed to turn the left of the army, yet sufficient ground had been wrested from the Union line to give a semblance of victory to his desperate efforts. The Third Corps had been defeated, but the Union line of battle was intact. A startling report, however, came to Meade's ears from the right of the line, which he had stripped to reinforce Sickles. This was to the effect that Ewell had advanced and occupied the position vacated by the Twelfth Corps !

---

CORRECTION.—In the final revision of the casualty lists of the regiments engaged in the second day's fighting, certain changes were made which were not carried forward in the recapitulation, and this omission was not discovered until too late for correction. The following tables show the losses sustained by the several New Jersey troops on that occasion, compared with the number reported present for duty on June 30. From the latter an allowance of fifteen per cent. for detailed men should be made to get at the actual number present for action :

## CASUALTIES ON JULY 2.

|  | OFFICERS. | | | ENLISTED MEN. | | | | |
|---|---|---|---|---|---|---|---|---|
|  | Killed. | Wounded. | Total. | Killed. | Wounded. | Missing. | Total. | Aggregate. |
| Battery "B" 1st N. J. Artillery | -- | -- | -- | 2 | 15 | 3 | 20 | 20 |
| Fifth Regiment | 2 | 5 | 7 | 10 | 61 | 16 | 87 | 94 |
| Sixth Regiment | -- | 3 | 3 | 1 | 29 | 8 | 38 | 41 |
| Seventh Regiment | 1 | 9 | 10 | 14 | 77 | 12 | 103 | 113 |
| Eighth Regiment | -- | 7 | 7 | 8 | 33 | 1 | 42 | 49 |
| Eleventh Regiment | 3 | 10 | 13 | 20 | 113 | 7 | 140 | 153 |
| Total | 6 | 34 | 40 | 55 | 328 | 47 | 430 | 470 |

## PRESENT FOR DUTY JUNE 30.

|  | OFFICERS. | MEN. | TOTAL. |
|---|---|---|---|
| Battery "B" 1st N. J. Artillery | 4 | 139 | 143 |
| Fifth Regiment | 15 | 206 | 221 |
| Sixth Regiment | 13 | 233 | 246 |
| Seventh Regiment | 22 | 309 | 331 |
| Eighth Regiment | 13 | 185 | 198 |
| Eleventh Regiment | -- | ---- | 275 |
| Total | -- | ---- | 1,414 |

## CHAPTER XII.

THE SECOND DAY'S BATTLE CONCLUDED — THE TWELFTH CORPS POSITION ATTACKED BY EWELL'S TROOPS—GREEN'S HEROIC DEFENCE—THE ATTACK ON CEMETERY HILL. — A FIERCE AND DEADLY HAND-TO-HAND STRUGGLE — RETURN OF THE TWELFTH CORPS TO THE RIGHT DURING THE NIGHT.

GENERAL LEE'S orders for a simultaneous attack on the right and left of the Union line miscarried, but had they been promptly acted upon he would not have been any more successful. It would have prevented the stripping of Slocum's line, which would have made the Union position on the right still more difficult, if not impossible, to carry, and the Sixth Corps could have been utilized for the duty which called the Twelfth Corps away. Had Longstreet turned the Federal left and got in rear of the Union army, that would no doubt have made a great difference in the situation, but the left of Meade's line did not rest where Lee thought it was, and when after the most stubborn and heroic resistance ever made by any body of troops, the Third Corps was forced back, it was not upon a demoralized body of men, but to the original line of battle, to defend which Meade had more troops at command than could be used. It was really better for General Lee that the attack by Ewell was delayed, but the advantage he had gained was lost by the ignorance which caused Johnson's division to halt all night long in the vacated works of the Twelfth Corps.

It seems strange to those who have always considered General Lee, *par excellence*, the one great soldier developed by the war, that he should have left Ewell wholly dependent upon his sense of hearing to fix the precise time of his attack. The instructions to Ewell were to advance as soon as he heard the firing of Longstreet's guns. The time fixed for the latter's assault, after innumerable delays, was four o'clock, and at that hour the fighting had begun in dead earnest along Birney's front. But another providential circumstance favored the Union army. The wind blowing directly from Ewell carried the sound of Longstreet's artillery and the Union batteries replying to it, to the southwest, so that he did not hear it at all! Nearly one hundred pieces of artillery on both sides kept up a continuous and rapid firing, not two miles from Ewell's front, and the deafening roar of musketry which accompanied it, made a noise loud enough to have drowned the sound of a dozen Niagaras, but Ewell might as well have been a deaf man on that occasion. His silence led Meade into the false belief that no danger was to be apprehended from that quarter, and he had therefore stripped his right, instead of utilizing his reserves, to reinforce the threatened left.

Ruger's division of the Twelfth Corps, on it arrival at the left, formed in two lines of battle west of the Taneytown road ; while Geary, who evidently misunderstood the orders given him, moved to the extreme right and halted on the Baltimore pike, east of Rock Creek, two miles from the fighting on the left and at least a mile to the right of his position on Culp's Hill, with no enemy in his front.

About six o'clock Hill opened with his batteries in pursuance of the original plan, on the Union centre, and Ewell, hearing his guns, formed for the proposed attack. His line, it will be remembered, extended from Benner's Hill on the left which was occupied by Johnson's division, Early's division being to his right and fronting Cemetery Hill and the ridge connecting it with Culp's Hill, while Rodes' division occupied the streets of Gettysburg, and extending to the right fronted Cemetery Hill proper. It is also urged as a reason why Ewell did not sooner advance, that he had sent two of his brigades on a wild-goose chase on the York road, because of a report that a body of Federal infantry had moved in that direction, and he was waiting for their return. However, about seven o'clock, just as the Twelfth Corps was vacating its line, Johnson's division was moving down to Rock Creek, his march being concealed by the thick woods into which he entered. The nature of the ground was unfavorable for the use of artillery and Johnson left his on Benner's Hill.

The line of works constructed by the First Brigade of Ruger's division and by the One Hundred and Seventh New York and Thirteenth New Jersey Regiments of Colgrove's brigade, were practically defenceless. General Green had extended his brigade in a thin line to cover the position vacated by Geary and could furnish little more than a weak skirmish line for the defence of the entire slope. He also established a picket line along the bank of the stream, but Johnson's movements were unperceived by them.

Culp's Hill, which Johnson was ordered to assault is a thickly wooded eminence, and the approaches to the summit are obstructed by numerous rocks and immense bowlders. The troops of Williams had utilized many of these rocks as a means of defence by connecting them with a line of works made of logs, stones, branches of trees and whatever could be utilized for the purpose. This afforded ample protection against the musketry fire of·an infantry column and would have been difficult to carry.

Johnson's line advanced with Steuart on the left, Jones on his right, supported respectively by Williams' and Nichols' brigades. Rock Creek, which separated them from Culp's Hill, is a shallow stream, and easily forded. Crossing boldly they soon drove in the Union pickets, and Steuart advanced to the vacated works on the south followed by Williams. These were easily taken, but Jones who advanced to attack the left of Green met with stubborn opposition. Green, however, was hard pressed. Steuart was on a line with his works, and to prevent a flank attack, Green shortened his line and extended it obliquely to the west, and sent an urgent demand for assistance. The fighting waxed hotter and hotter. Attacked by a force three times larger than his own, he held them all at bay and inflicted severe injuries upon the enemy. Jones was badly wounded and Nichols moved promptly up to his relief. At this time a brigade from the Eleventh Corps came to Green's assistance, and Wadsworth extended his line to the right in support. Night soon settled down upon the scene and the conflict ended save by a desultory firing which continued for some time.

When Johnson's division moved down to the attack on Culp's Hill, Ewell ordered Early and Rodes to advance and attack in their front. This movement, which should have been performed in unison appears to have been affected by a misunderstanding of orders. Early moved at once with the brigades of Hays and Hoke (Avery commanding), with Gordon's brigade in reserve. The Confederate artillery on Benner's Hill opened fire upon the Union position, but the batteries on Cemetery Hill soon silenced it. As the brigades of Early advanced to the slope of the hill, their movement was aided by the houses and other buildings which concealed them from the Union line, and when they reached the ascending ground the batteries in their front were trained upon them, but the guns could not be depressed sufficiently to do effective work.

It was now eight o'clock, and Rodes ought to have

been in position on the left to assault there, but that officer had some difficulty in getting through the streets of the town to the position he desired, and lost thereby considerable time. Advancing the brigades of Iverson, Ramseur and Doles toward the western face of Cemetery Hill a short distance he halted them, evidently intending to await the result of Early's attack. When the brigades of Hays and Avery emerged on the open ground to ascend the slope, they brushed away Von Gilsa's brigade of the Eleventh Corps, and rushed for the summit. Their left flank became exposed to the Fifth Maine Battery, which poured an enfilading fire down their whole line, but without checking them. In an instant they were among the guns of Weiderick's and Rickett's batteries, capturing the former and spiking two of Rickett's guns. The order had been given to these gallant artillerists not to retreat under any circumstances, but to fight to the last moment, and right loyally they obeyed. The fighting was hand-to-hand, rammers being used as clubs, and hand-spikes and even stones, being hurled into the faces of the enemy. This movement of the enemy brought their left flank in front of Stevens' battery, which opened a terrible fire of double canister upon them, and the Thirty-third Massachusetts poured in, obliquely to their line, a destructive musketry fire, but still they fought on desperately, vainly expecting Rodes' division to attack on the other side. In fact the Federal line was prepared for just this sort of thing, and Hancock momentarily expected Rodes' line to advance,; but his trained ear heard the desperate fighting going on to the right and rear of his position, and as the enemy in his front remained stationary, he detached Carroll's brigade to the rescue of Howard's guns. Advancing with a firm tread they soon came in sight of the battle and moving rapidly over the hill plunged with cheers and shouts into the midst of the enemy, who retreated hastily. As they went flying down the slope the Federal batteries opened a raking fire upon them practically annihilating Hays' "Louisiana Tigers," which went into the fight one thousand seven hundred and fifty strong and returned with scarcely one hundred and fifty men! The Eleventh Corps' line was restored, and Carroll's brigade, which did such signal service was by the request of Howard permitted to remain on that part of the line.

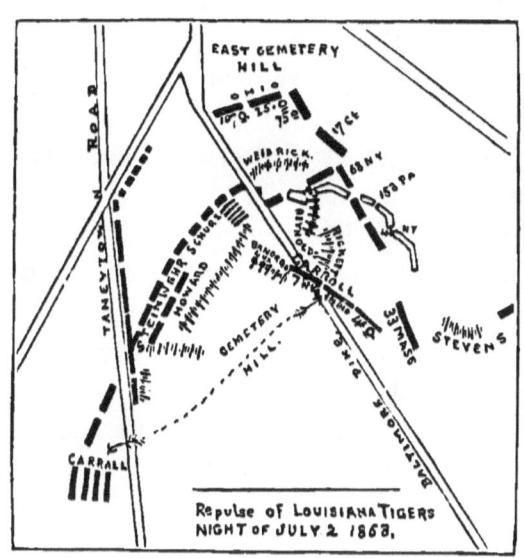

Repulse of Louisiana Tigers
NIGHT OF JULY 2 1863.

The sound of the desperate contest on the right and right centre reached the ears of the Union troops on the left as soon as the firing in that quarter ceased, and about ten o'clock an order was sent to Ruger to return to his old position on the right as the enemy were in possession on the Twelfth Corps' works. The division promptly moved, Colgrove's brigade leading, and as they neared Culp's Hill a skirmish line was sent forward to feel the position of the enemy. One man was captured in the old line of works in McAllister's woods, and Company F of the Second Massachusetts advancing across the open ground into the woods at the base of Culp's Hill and near Spangler's spring, captured twenty-three men, with whom they returned. From these it was ascertained that Steuart's and Jones' brigades held the position. Filing into McAllister's woods the brigade sought their old works, but as it was discovered that the position of the Third Wisconsin, which had been occupied by the Thirteenth New Jersey, and the line along Rock Creek, would be enfiladed by the fire of the enemy,\* the brigade was formed on a line about fifty yards to the rear. In taking this position two companies

---

\* Extract from Colonel Hawley's report: " Darkness coming on I received orders from you, sir, (Colonel Colgrove) to move out as we had marched in, and following the regiment on my right flank was marched back to the position which I had spent the day in fortifying, and there rested under arms. It then being ascertained that the enemy had advanced over our breastworks and occupied a rocky, wooded hill on my left, thus enfilading my position and severing our line, by your order I took position perpendicular to my former line, so as to face the enemy's advance in this position, and there lay under arms for the remainder of the night."

of the Thirteenth New Jersey, Company C, Captain David A. Ryerson, and Company I, Captain Ambrose M. Matthews, were refused, to connect with the right of the Second Massachusetts, the rest of the line of the Thirteenth running along the edge of the woods on a rising piece of ground fronting Rock Creek. The line as thus formed was as follows: Thirteenth New Jersey on the right, Second Massachusetts centre, Third Wisconsin on the left, Twenty-seventh Indiana in reserve. The First Brigade, McDougall's, formed on the left of Colgrove. During the night also Geary's troops returned from their isolated position on the Baltimore pike, and joined with Green's forces on Culp's Hill.

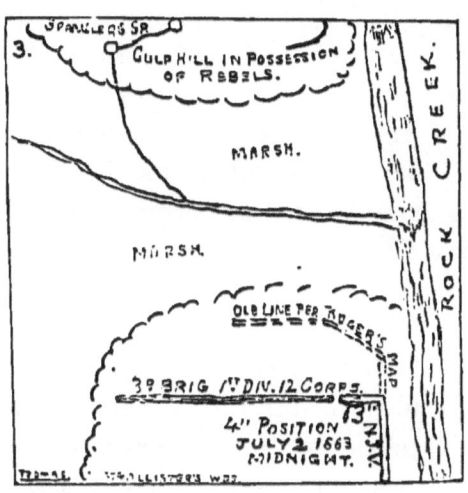

The prisoners brought in by the Second Massachusetts were turned over to the Thirteenth New Jersey Regiment and Company D was detailed by order of acting Lieutenant-Colonel Beardsley, to conduct them to the Provost Marshal of the corps near Two Taverns.

At midnight the Twelfth Corps had all arrived and lay in line awaiting the approach of daylight to advance upon and drive the enemy from their position on Culp's Hill.

## CHAPTER XIII.

THE THIRD DAY'S BATTLE — THE TWELFTH CORPS CHARGE THE ENEMY AT CULP'S HILL AND REGAIN THEIR WORKS—THE SECOND MASSACHUSETTS AND TWENTY-SEVENTH INDIANA REGIMENTS CHARGE THE ENEMY SUPPORTED BY THE THIRTEENTH NEW JERSEY REGIMENT—LEE FOILED IN HIS ATTACK ON THE FEDERAL RIGHT.

THE Confederates seem to have had little knowledge of the topography of the country about Gettysburg, otherwise the failure of Ewell to follow up the great advantage he had so fortunately gained on the night of July 2d must be classed as a stupendous blunder. The left of Steuart's line was within one hundred yards of the Baltimore pike, the road over which Meade's army would be compelled to retreat in the event of defeat. The reserve artillery of the Army of the Potomac lay parked back of Powers' Hill on the slope of which General Slocum had his headquarters, while Meade's headquarters were but a short distance off. Furthermore, the presence of the rebel army in force on the pike would have created consternation in the Federal army. Unquestionably Ewell was ignorant of the advantage he had gained, and conversation with some of the survivors shows

MONUMENT 8TH REGT. N. J. VOLS., INF.

that the rebels were greatly surprised at the ease with which they got possession of the vacated works, and feared that some Yankee trick was being played upon them. Of the great blunder Meade had committed, of course they knew nothing, and this was only compensated for by the rapid approach of darkness, which caused Johnson to exercise great caution in his movements. He only knew the enemy was in his front, and he determined to attack at daylight. The men whom he commanded were "Stonewall" Jackson's veterans, who had won many hard-fought battles, and they were not easily to be disposed of.

During the night a conference was held in McAllister's woods, at which General Hunt, chief of artillery, Generals Slocum, Williams and Ruger were present. The artillery, twenty-six guns in all, had been posted on every commanding eminence to cover the enemy's position on Culp's Hill, and only awaited the appearance of daylight to open upon it.

As early as three o'clock Johnson began to form his men for attack, and Geary noting that some movement was contemplated by the enemy determined to assume the offensive. At day-break the crash of musketry was heard. Geary opened a fierce fire along his whole front and with deadly effect. The First Brigade sent forward the Twentieth Connecticut to penetrate the woods at the southern base of the hill and the Second Massachusetts and Twenty-seventh Indiana of the Third Brigade were ordered to charge the enemy in flank by Colonel Colgrove. The Union artillery opened along the whole line, and from this time until ten o'clock a fierce, stubborn and desperate battle was waged. On the success of the Twelfth Corps now depended the safety of the army. Reinforcements were sent to Culp's Hill, Lockwood's brigade of the Twelfth and Shaler's brigade of the Sixth Corps both going to the support of Geary. The continued roll of musketry, the deafening roar of the artillery were listened to by the waiting army with apprehension. The long lines of wounded men being carried to the rear gave evidence of the severity of the struggle. The Reserve Artillery back of Power's Hill had harnessed and was made ready for any call upon it. The cavalry to the right were all mounted and drawn up ready for action. The Sixth Corps in reserve were under orders for an advance at a moment's notice. There was plenty of support for the right, should further help be needed. Still the battle raged. The enemy were driven back repeatedly and they as often returned to the charge. They were now able to note where they were and as they caught glimpses of the Federal wagon trains and ambulances moving down the Baltimore pike it seemed to drive them to desperation. Too late they realized what had been lost by the night's delay. They fought madly, heroically and with a bravery which only Jackson's men could show, but they were at a disadvantage. The Union line sheltered by the rocks and immense bowlders up to the face of which the rebels charged again and again, enabled them to inflict serious injury upon their assailants, and heavy as the Union loss was that of the enemy was treble.

When the order was given at dawn for the Second Massachusetts and Twenty-seventh Indiana of Colgrove's brigade to advance and attack the enemy, there was thought to be a mistake in the meaning of it. Lieutenant Snow who brought the order from General Ruger was asked a second and third time as to the intent of it, and he repeated, the order is to advance. Colonel Mudge of the Second Massachusetts, when he received the order, said, "It is murder, but must be obeyed! forward!" and the brave Mudge with as gallant a body of men as ever lived moved out to swift and certain death.

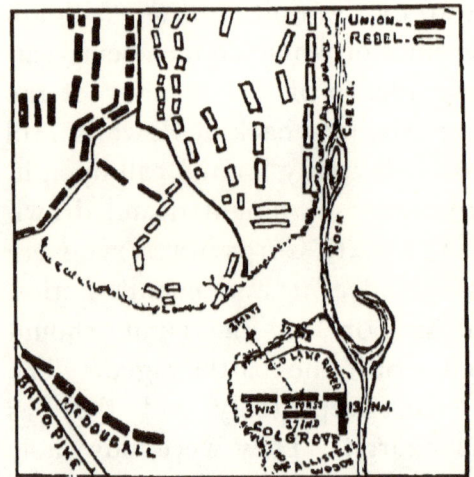

The Twenty-seventh Indiana were to advance and join the right of the Second Massachusetts, but Colonel Mudge when he reached the open ground moved at once against the enemy driving them ahead of him, and though exposed to a deadly fire the Second reached the shelter of the woods on the other side. The brave Mudge was killed, and the casualties in the regiment were severe. The Twenty-seventh Indiana

Regiment advanced gallantly, and the right companies of the Thirteenth New Jersey changed front and occupied the breastworks vacated by the Second Massachusetts. As the Twenty-seventh reached the open ground they encountered a terrible musketry fire which checked them where they were. The left wing of the regiment extended to the open ground the right resting in the wood, the line facing northeasterly. This regiment fought gallantly but was compelled to fall back,

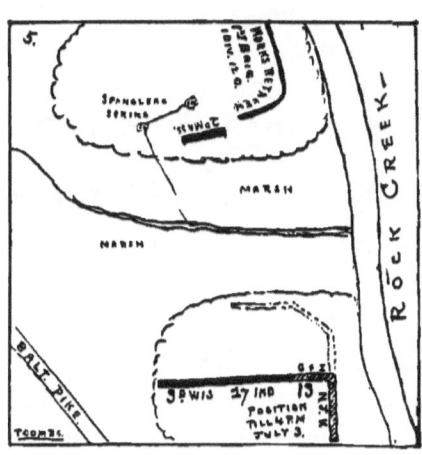

when the Thirteenth New Jersey returned to its former line and the Twenty-seventh occupied the position thus vacated. The fighting continued with great stubbornness. The enemy seeing the Twenty-seventh fall back formed for a counter-charge and advanced across the open ground to the marshy banks of Spangler's Run, where they encountered the fire of the Third Wisconsin, Twenty-seventh Indiana, and such portions of the Thirteenth New Jersey as could reach them. The two left companies, C and I, were in the direct front of the advancing enemy, and for a short time a sharp engagement ensued, in which the rebels were repulsed. The Second Massachusetts from its position on the opposite side of the swale had an enfilading fire down their line which precipitated their retreat. During this engagement Captain David A. Ryerson, of Company C, Thirteenth New Jersey, was wounded, the command of the left companies thus devolving upon Captain Ambrose M. Matthews, of Company I; James Parliament, of the same company, was struck in the breast from which wound he died a few days later, and Henry Damig, of Company G, was killed.

Walker's brigade of the enemy had been sent to the extreme left of the line to watch the movements of the regiments of Colgrove's brigade in McAllister's woods. A strong line of skirmishers appeared on the crest of the hill east of Rock Creek, and they took position behind the rocks and trees and thus picked off officers and men at their leisure. A small stone house seemed to be filled with them, and whenever a head was projected above the breastworks a bullet was sure to come unpleasantly near it. The Thirteenth New Jersey and the Twenty-seventh Indiana suffered most severely from this fire. A stretcher-bearer of the latter regiment went to the front, carrying a white stretcher with him, to look after some of the wounded lying in the edge of the woods, whose cries for water and help were agonizing. Just as he had scaled the works and before he had gone thirty feet to the front a rebel sharpshooter sent a bullet through his head and he fell lifeless at the foot of a tree. This uncalled-for act exasperated the men, and they demanded that the stone house should be demolished. Captain Winegar of

Battery "M" First New York Artillery, came down to the line, and after examining the position returned to his battery, which soon opened fire upon the building. The first shot penetrated the house and as the men saw the dust and splinters flying about they gave a prolonged cheer. No further annoyance came from that quarter.

The engagement with Johnson's division lasted until ten o'clock, when a ringing cheer broke from the men on Culp's Hill and it was known that the enemy were falling back. The Third Wisconsin, of Colgrove's brigade, advanced a picket line across the open ground in the front capturing a few men, and the regiment advanced up to the position formerly held by Colgrove's regiments on the right of the First Brigade. Geary and McDougall also advanced and reoccupied their old position and the lines of the Union right were once more intact.

The battle had been a hard one. For three hours of the previous evening Green, with his little brigade, had made a stalwart defense of the position he held, and to the valor of his men is due the safety of the Union army on the third of July. From the first break of day to ten o'clock on the morning of the third—full seven hours—the battle continued. The trees were mangled and torn with the shells and the solid shot which was hurled among them, and the effect of this dreadful day's work was noticed a year later when one part of this immense forest, where the fighting was fiercest, was found to have been killed. The trees were leafless.

The sight, after the battle, in the Union front was frightful. The fighting had been waged at such close quarters and with such desperation, that there were as many dead rebels on the ground as there were men who fought them. They lay in many instances close up to the front of the Union line of works, and the bayonet thrusts in several of the bodies testified too plainly the terrible manner of their death and the ferocity of the contest. With the recapture of the position on Culp's Hill, the fighting ceased on the right, save by skirmishers and sharpshooters posted along the Rock Creek ridge. The casualties in the Thirteenth New Jersey Regiment were twenty-one as follows:

*Killed*—Henry Damig, Company G.

*Wounded*—Company A—Edward S. Smith.

Company B—Thomas Ferris.

Company C—Captain David A. Ryerson, Alexander Barnes, James Winter, James Parliament (died July 27th), William Remington.

Company D—James P. Howatt.

Company E—Corporal Thomas H. Williams (leg amputated), John Van Winkle.

Company F—Cornelius Clark.

Company G—Captain John H. Arey, Corporal Cyrus Williams, John Welsch, drummer.

Company H—David Latourette.

Company I—Lieutenant Charles W. Johnson (acting Adjutant), Aaron Chamberlain, Smith P. Brown.

*Recapitulation*—Killed, 1. Wounded—Officers, 3: enlisted men, 17; total, 21.

## CHAPTER XIV.

THE THIRD DAY'S BATTLE CONCLUDED—LONGSTREET'S CHARGE ON CEMETERY RIDGE — DISASTROUS REPULSE OF PICKETT'S AND HETH'S DIVISIONS— DREADFUL EXECUTION WITH "BUCK AND BALL" BY THE TWELFTH NEW JERSEY—HEXAMER'S OLD BATTERY ("A" FIRST NEW JERSEY) ENGAGED—THE FIRST NEW JERSEY CAVALRY WIN NEW LAURELS.

GENERAL LEE had now unsuccesfully attacked both the right and left positions of the Union army, but with a fatuity which seems incomprehensible, he determined upon one more assault. He seems to have believed that the defeat of Sickles had seriously crippled Meade's whole army, and Johnson's success in getting possession of the vacated works of the Twelfth Corps gave him a foretaste of victory, if promptly followed up. The repulse of Hood at Round Top, of Hays and Avery at Cemetery Hill, and the failure of Wilcox and Wright to reap any substantial benefit from their advance almost into the Union lines on the second of July, were regarded as mere episodes of the battle, not worthy of serious thought. The time had come, according to General Lee's reasoning for the one great decisive blow which should end the war in his favor. But on this third day of July the entire Army of the Potomac was on the field, and so disposed that reinforcements could be sent to any point on short notice. Further the Union army felt that they had gained quite as much for their cause as Lee considered he had accomplished for himself, and though the stragglers, who poured down the roads to the rear spread dismal tales of defeat for the Army of the Potomac, the men at the front had no such feeling.

When the final charge by the Twelfth Corps was made upon the enemy's lines, and they were forced back to the opposite side of Rock Creek, it stimulated the tone of the whole army. Confident of success before they were sanguine now, and the further movements of Lee were awaited with impatience. The deep stillness which settled upon the battle-field after the cessation of the fighting on the right soon became oppressive. It was the prevalent belief that Lee intended a more desperate move than any yet planned but where the blow would fall could only be conjectured. As the centre of the line had so far escaped a direct assault the feeling grew that there the blow would fall, and the intuition which thus selected the point of attack was confirmed a few hours later.

General Lee had determined the night before to assault the centre of Meade's line, and to Longstreet's corps he assigned the task. These troops had borne the brunt of the fighting the day before, and their ranks were terribly decimated. It was impossible that they could successfully accomplish the work Lee had

MONUMENT 11TH REGT. N. J. VOLS., INF.

in hand, and further they could not well be spared from the positions they then occupied. The only division that had not participated in the battle at any time was Pickett's, and he was accordingly selected to lead the charge. Pickett had arrived within a short distance of the battle-field the night before, after a forced march from Chambersburg, and at seven o'clock on the morning of the third he reported to General Longstreet. The interviews between Longstreet and Lee were frequent. The former was opposed to the contemplated movement and interposed every possible objection to the determination of Lee to make the assault. But the rebel chieftain was immovable. He saw no reason for depression, but believed everything was favorable for success. He construed the capture of Sickles' advanced line as a victory, and in his official report uses this language:

"After a severe struggle Longstreet succeeded in gaining possession of and holding the desired ground. Ewell also carried some of the strong positions which he assailed, and the result was such as to lead to the belief that he would ultimately be able to dislodge the enemy. The battle ceased at dark. These partial successes determined me to continue the assault the next day."

Argument and protestation could not move the man who thus summed up the results of the previous day's fighting, and Longstreet was compelled to notify Pickett of the work that had been assigned him to do.

General Lee's line of battle at daylight on the third,

was much the same as when night closed in and ended the conflict of the second day. Laws' and Robertson's brigades were in front of the Round Tops, Wofford in the centre west of the wheat-field, and Kershaw on the left, occupying the Peach Orchard. The rest of Longstreet's corps stretched along the line of Seminary Ridge, and Hill occupied his former position on the left of Longstreet. Ewell was at that moment engaged in a death struggle on the extreme left, but the result was not to be awaited—victory there was confidently anticipated. It was ten o'clock before Lee gave the final order to form for the attack. With Longstreet he had fully reconnoitred the ground, and that officer again tried to dissuade him from the proposed movement. Longstreet scented defeat. He was opposed to an offensive movement and desired to turn the flank of Meade, and compel him to attack the southern army. But all in vain. It was finally determined to assail the Union line with a strong column, under cover of a heavy artillery fire, and the orders were given. Colonel Alexander posted the Confederate artillery along the ridge which Humphreys had vainly tried to hold the day before, extending from the Peach Orchard on the right to the Codori house on the left. A battery on the right of the Peach Orchard, and the Washington Artillery with Dearing and Cabell's batteries stationed on the left were to aid in the attack. This vast congregation of batteries comprised one hundred and thirty-eight pieces of cannon, and behind this wall of iron the division of Pickett, with the troops that were to support him, formed for the impending collision. Pickett's division was composed of five brigades, three only of which were upon the field—Garnett's, Armistead's and Kemper's—comprising in all about four thousand five hundred men. They formed behind the rising surface of the ground, Kemper and Garnett in the advance, Armistead in rear, and lay down to await the order for the charge to be made. A battery of light artillery was detailed to accompany them. To support Pickett, Hill contributed the brigades of Wilcox, Perry and Wright, and Heth's division, composed of the brigades of Archer, Pettigrew, Davis and Brockenborough, with the brigades of Scales and Lane added, made up a total attacking force of fully fifteen thousand men. This mighty host, supported by the concentrated fire of the largest artillery force ever gathered together, was to launch itself upon the front of the Second Corps and break the Union line in two.

The position of the Second Corps which was to be the scene of the coming conflict was an admirable one for defence. In its entire length from Zeigler's Grove—which separates Cemetery Hill from Cemetery Ridge — to the copse of trees, where the left of Pickett's line halted, is considerably less than a mile. In the advanced edge of the wood known as Zeigler's Grove—the extreme right of the Second Corps' line — Woodruff's battery (" I " First United States Artillery) was stationed, supported by the One Hundred and Eighth New York. On the left of this position, a natural out-

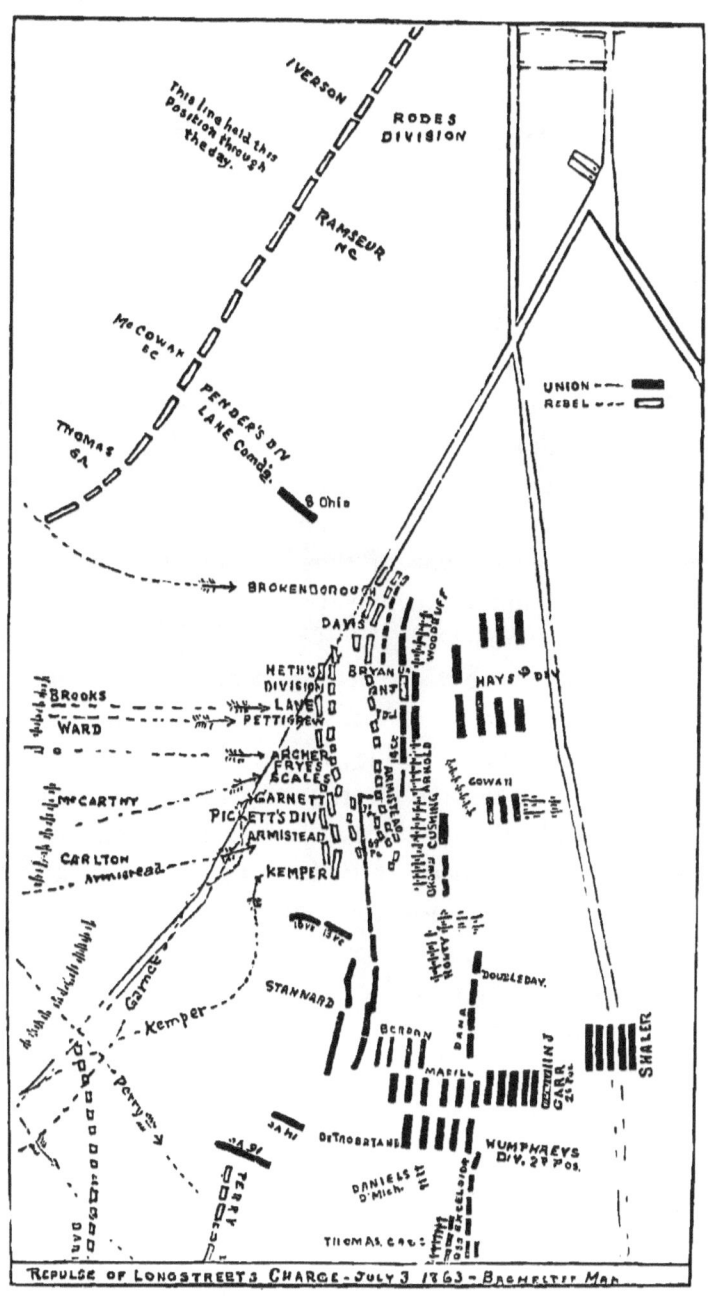

cropping of rock forms a low wall, and at a distance of fifty yards from the grove, near Bryan's well, a stone wall had been constructed on the natural rock, and continued for about three hundred and fifty yards. Hays' division of the Second Corps occupied this position being formed in two lines of battle. The left consisted of Smyth's brigade, posted in the following order: The Twelfth New Jersey on the right, the First Delaware on the left of the Twelfth, the Fourteenth Connecticut next. The One Hundred and Eleventh New York and One Hundred and Twenty-fifth New York of the Third Brigade were immediately in the rear of these regiments, on higher ground which enabled them to fire over the front line. The other regiments of the Third Brigade and Carroll's brigade were also in the rear of the line of battle for a time, but subsequently became hotly engaged. Arnold's Rhode Island battery occupied a position on the left of Smyth, and in front of Arnold the stone wall runs due west, where it connects with a post and rail fence, thus forming a sharp angle. Gibbon's division connected with Hays, Webb's brigade, on whose line Cushing's battery was posted, formed the right, and Hall's brigade with Brown's Rhode Island battery, the centre, and Harrow's brigade with Rorty's New York battery, the left. The rail fence which skirted the natural rock surface before these brigades, was thrown down and the rails used as a slight protection from musketry fire. Doubleday's division of the First Corps were to the left of Gibbon, Stannard's Vermont brigade being in a clump of bushes and trees a short distance in advance, concealed from the enemy's view. This small space of territory was destined to become the scene of one of the fiercest conflicts of modern times. The lines of men thus grouped together were to be subjected to a rain of missiles that no body of men ever before experienced, and their courage and valor was to be put to the severest test known in the annals of modern warfare. The Union line as continued to the left, comprised the following: To the left of Doubleday was Caldwell's gallant division of the Second Corps, which suffered so severely the day before in trying to repair Sickles' broken line. Birney's division of the Third Corps continued the line southward and the Fifth Corps, whose line now extended to the summit of Round Top itself, completed this front, with the Sixth Corps mainly in reserve. At every point where artillery could be used a battery was posted. McGilvery had stationed forty guns along this line in addition to the thirty guns of the Second Corps which were commanded by Captain John G. Hazzard.

During the time Lee was preparing his column for attack, General Hunt, chief of artillery, was examining the batteries along the Union line. He made the best disposition possible of the artillery at his command, and stationed the Reserve Artillery within easy supporting distance. Sharp skirmish firing broke out occasionally along the Union front.

and early in the day while the heavy firing on the right was going on, the enemy in front of the Second Corps reoccupied the Bliss barn and the Twelfth New Jersey was again called upon to dispossess them. Companies K, F, D, C and A were selected, and under command of Captain Richard S. Thompson of Company K, the charge was successfully made and a number of prisoners taken. The barn was finally burned by the Fourteenth Connecticut.

The minutes grew into hours and the Federals waited impatiently for some sign to show what the enemy intended to do. With the cessation of the firing on the right the stillness grew oppressive. The same feeling of impatience prevailed among Pickett's men. They had been formed in line for their charge ever since ten o'clock and the delay was growing tedious. Finally the word passed that all was ready. Longstreet dreaded the ordeal. Pickett was anxious to begin. Longstreet sought to impose upon Colonel Alexander the duty of notifying Pickett what to do, that officer bluntly refused, saying that unless the charge was to be made he should not order the artillery to fire. Suddenly, at one o'clock, two shots were fired by the Washington Artillery—the signal for the cannonade to begin. At once, as though the gunners had impatiently waited for the signal, there was vomited from the deep throats of the one hundred and thirty-eight cannon along the Emmetsburg road a volume of flame, and the air was filled with flying missiles on their death-dealing mission. For fifteen minutes the Federal batteries remained silent, and then from eighty guns along the Union line, all that could be brought to bear on the position, an answering refrain went up, which, combined with the volume of sound proceeding from the enemy, created an *ensemble* that was terrifying even to ears that had endured the dreadful sound of artillery warfare for months. But never before, nor since, had those who listened to the sharp detonation of those two hundred and eighteen guns passed through a more harrowing experience. The ground was ploughed into furrows. Exploding shells endangered everything within their range; the house used by General Meade for his headquarters was in the very line of this terrible, dreadful and merciless storm of iron nail. Horses tied to the fences were killed by scores or, badly wounded, filled the air with their shrieks of terror and fright. It was chaos come again. General Meade abandoned his headquarters and sought refuge with General Slocum at Powers' Hill. Caisson after caisson, being struck by the enemy's shells, exploded, but the line of infantry remained as stationary and immovable as the rocks behind which they sought shelter. A shell would penetrate their front occasionally and lessen their number, but none moved from their places. The artillerists, more exposed suffered greatly; horses were killed in large numbers, and the destruction of gun carriages, caissons and limbers was unusually heavy. For one hour and a-half this terrific duel had been kept up, when, at half-past two General Hunt ordered the firing to be gradually slackened, and in a few minutes nothing could be heard but the firing of the rebel guns. Replacing the disabled batteries with others from the Artillery Reserve and replenishing the ammunition boxes for the infantry attack which all knew would follow, the Union artillery line was reëstablished.

The accuracy of the fire from the Federal batteries had inflicted serious damage on the enemy's artillery, and had also caused much destruction of life among the infantry. Armistead's brigade was compelled to change its position three different times to get out of the range of the Union guns and with sighs of relief they noted the slackening fire from Meade's line. It was now three o'clock. Pickett formed his men for the charge and reporting to Longstreet asked for the word of command. He would not give it, and Pickett, with a gleam of fire in his eyes said, " I shall go forward, sir," to which Longstreet simply nodded his head, and the impetuous and brave southerner returned to his division. Just as the rebel line proceeded on its march, Hunt ordered up to the threatened point of attack Fitzhugh's, Weir's, Cowan's, and Parson's ("A" First New Jersey Artillery) batteries, which advanced rapidly into position.

Pickett impatiently awaited the opportunity to advance. In a short time it came in a message from Colonel Alexander to the effect that the Federal battery had been silenced. The line was formed— Kemper on the right, Garnett in the centre, Armistead on the left—and as it swept through the artillery and came into full view of the Federals, a thrill of admiration went through the breast of every man gazing upon the magnificent spectacle. Marching in close order, with measured steps, as though on parade, it moved forward deliberately, solidly. With flags unfurled, guns aligned, obeying every word of command, the line moved steadily onward. Leaving Wilcox behind, Pickett made a half-wheel to the left, the movement being finely performed, but it presented its right flank to the Union line and McGilvery concentrated the fire of all his guns upon it. The accuracy of McGilvery's fire tore great gaps in the ranks, but they were promptly closed up, and on the assailing column came across the fields, scaling strong fences, until it reached the base of the ridge Pickett was directed to assault. Here he changed direction by a half-wheel to the right, and halted his column under the heavy fire which confronted him, to rectify his line. Wilcox in the mean time moved forward to the right of Pickett, but the wheeling of Pickett's line separated them, and left a wide gap between, while Pettigrew, who with Heth's division was to support the movement on the left, was not able to get into line as soon as desired, by having a longer distance to traverse. When Pickett again advanced he was met by a terrific fire of musketry and canister from the men in his front, and McGilvery ploughed his line with shot and shell.

    The Twelfth New Jersey Regiment from its commanding position on the right of the Second Corps, had withstood the shock of the dreadful cannonade with heroic fortitude, and watched the splendid advance of the assaulting column with eagerness and expectancy. Major Hill, who was in command, encouraged the men by his own coolness and intrepidity, and cautioned them to reserve their fire until each shot could be made to tell. The men obeyed, and emptying their cartridge boxes and placing their ammunition on the ledges of stone in front of them where they could the more easily use it, they confidently awaited the approach of the attacking forces. The regiment was armed with the smooth bore musket, and they used the buck and ball cartridge, calibre sixty-nine, enabling them to give a deadly fire at short range.

The unfortunate misunderstandings which had separated Pickett from his supports on the right and left placed him in a perilous position. The ridge he now essayed to reach was held by a line of men as determined as himself and his brave Virginians. The advocates of State Rights and Human Slavery, and the defenders of National Unity and Freedom, were neither disposed to flinch now that the contest had narrowed to the space of a hundred yards. As Pickett moved up the slope the men in blue shouted "Fredericksburg." Ominous word. The slaughter at the heights of St. Marye had not been forgotten, and the fate that there befell Burnside's brave men in blue now awaited the brave men in gray. Pickett's right flank exposed itself as he advanced, to Stannard's Vermonters concealed in the copse of trees, and Hancock at once

MARKER 12TH REGT. N. J. VOLS.
(At Bliss Barn.)

ordered them to move upon it. Stannard's men poured a destructive fire into Armistead's ranks, and disorganized, the brigade surged to the rear of Pickett, which for a moment moved in the direction of Hays' division. Armistead pushed his way through the mass to the front, and then with a plunge Armistead, Kemper and Garnett's men, all in one confused crowd fell upon the brigades of Hall and Harrow, and finally concentrated upon Webb, where the mass swayed from side to side like a huge wave seeking an outlet through an opening too small for it. The fighting was now at close quarters. Webb, heroic soldier that he was, gallantly sought to stem the tide, but in vain. The enemy pierced the centre, the artillery opened with canister at point blank range, Hancock and Gibbon pushed forward all their reserves, and Webb, Hall and Harrow, had a desperate encounter with the enemy. Cushing, of Battery A, Fourth United States Artillery, advanced with his guns into the very midst of the enemy, and Armistead rushing boldly up urged his men to capture the battery. Inspired by the force of his brave example a crowd broke through the lines of Federals, and the gallant Cushing fired his last round into their faces and himself expired from a mortal wound previously received. Armistead had time only to place his hands upon the guns when he fell dead by Cushing's side. The loss of life had been dreadful on the Confederate side. Armistead and Garnett had been killed, Kemper badly wounded, and of the whole number of field officers of the splendid division which advanced so proudly and in such magnificent array across the intervening fields, Pickett and a lieutenant-colonel alone remained. Pickett was a most conspicuous figure, and was in the fiercest of the fight. His escape from death seems miraculous.

Pettigrew's command which moved out to take position on Pickett's left, comprised the brigades of Archer, Marshall, Davis and Brokenborough; these were followed by the brigades of Scales and Lane under Trimble, who took position in rear of the right. As Pickett made his left half-wheel, by which he separated himself from Wilcox, his left was brought nearer to Trimble, who hastened forward to close up the interval while the left of the line slackened its pace, thus changing the position of the attacking force from a single line of battle, supported by the two brigades of Scales and Lane, to a movement *en echelon*, in the order of Archer, Marshall, Davis and Brokenborough, with Scales and Lane in rear of Archer and in line with Marshall, the right of Scales extending beyond Archer's right. This part of the attacking force bore directly toward Smyth's brigade of Hays' division of the Second Corps, posted behind the stone wall previously described. Colonel William E. Potter, of the Twelfth Regiment New Jersey Volunteers, in his masterly address at the dedication of the monument of that regiment on the 26th of May, 1886, thus describes the advance and repulse of Pettigrew's division:

"The brigade of Smyth, now about to receive this

tremendous attack, was still posted as I have heretofore stated. Our own regiment (the Twelfth New Jersey) was its proper right. The strength of the latter, as shown at the muster of June 30th, three days before, was twenty-five officers and five hundred and seven enlisted men present for duty, or a total of five hundred and thirty-two. Despite the casualties thus far it probably then had in line four hundred men. It was armed with the Springfield smooth-bore musket, calibre 69—a terrible weapon at close range. The usual cartridge carried a large ball and three buckshot, but many of the men, while awaiting the enemy's advance, had opened their boxes and prepared special cartridges of from ten to twenty-five buckshot alone. It was the only regiment in the division bearing the arm mentioned, and I doubt whether anywhere upon that field a more destructive fire was encountered than at the proper time blazed forth from its front.

"The men were young, well disciplined, of respectable parentage, in comfortable circumstances and almost solely of native birth. In the entire regiment, as originally mustered, there were but seventy-two men of foreign nativity, and these were almost without exception faithful soldiers. The men had the confidence of their officers, who were in turn very generally trusted and respected by their men. Of very much the same stock were the One Hundred and Eighth New York, Fourteenth Connecticut and First Delaware, as they then stood.

BVT. LIEUTENANT-COLONEL WILLIAM E. POTTER,
Second Lieut. Company K, 12th Regt., N. J. Vols., Inf.
*(From a Recent Photograph.)*

"The skirmishers along our front fell back before the enemy's advance, and taking position in the Emmetsburg road, fire with destructive effect; they are, however, soon driven in.

"The enemy's column first comes in contact with the Eighth Ohio Volunteers, under command of Lieutenant-Colonel Franklin Sawyer, who, with four companies, deployed as skirmishers, supported them with the remainder of the regiment as a reserve, to the front of and somewhat to the right of Woodruff's battery. Under the stringent orders of Colonel Carroll to hold their position to the last man, they had maintained their post without relief since 4 p. m., of the second of July; having lost from their small numbers, up to noon of the third, 4 men killed, and 1 Captain, 1 Lieutenant, the Sergeant-Major and 38 men wounded.

"As the enemy's column came on, according to Colonel Sawyer's report, now ployed in mass with a regiment in line upon its flank, that officer exhibits brilliant soldiership. Instead of retiring his skirmishers, he advances his reserve to their support, and dispersing the enemy's regiment advancing in line, he changes front forward upon his tenth company, closes down upon the column itself, and opens a fierce fire directly upon its flank. Though smitten deep, the force of Sawyer was too light to stay the progress of the heavy column, which swept onward with majestic impetus to attack Smyth's brigade. The Eighth Ohio, however, captured a large number of prisoners and three stands of colors, and its total loss during the action was 101 killed and wounded; including 1 officer killed, and 9 officers, the sergeant-major, 2 orderly sergeants and 2 duty sergeants wounded.

"In our main line, to use the language of the official report of General Hancock, the 'men evinced a striking disposition to withhold their fire.' In our own regiment they did so under the orders of Major Hill, enforced by their company officers. The enemy now reached the Emmetsburg road, the fences fall before their pressure, and as they emerge into the broad turnpike, Smyth's brigade rising to its feet pours a terrific sheet of musketry into the column, before which the whole front line seems to go down. The masses in rear press on, but vainly strive to pass the line of death marked by the road. The blazing line of Smyth's brigade is in their front; the Eighth Ohio presses upon their left; the guns of Woodruff firing double charges of canister upon their flank, sweep down whole ranks at once. To advance is annihilation, to retreat is death. In vain do they make the most strenuous exertions to regain their lost momentum; in vain do their leaders, officers, color-bearers, strong men, spring to the front and endeavor to move the column forward or cause it to deploy to fire. These are instantly shot down; and in less time than I have taken to tell the story the whole of the six brigades to the left of Pickett are either prone upon the ground, or fleeing in disordered groups northward and westward to escape the fire and to regain Seminary Ridge.

"Just at the critical moment General Hays brought forward from the rear the Third Brigade and formed it in rear of the Twelfth New Jersey. These troops did not, however, open fire, though they suffered considerable loss, and one shell, it is said, exploding near the colors of the One Hundred and Eleventh New York, killed 7 men.

"In the height of the fight Lieutenant Richard H. Townsend, of Cape May county, fell shot through the heart. Promoted from the Tenth Regiment New Jersey Volunteers, he had been able to join his new command only three days before, and thus died in his first battle.

"At least 2,000 prisoners and fifteen colors were taken by Hays' division. Of the latter Smyth's brigade took nine; the Fourteenth Connecticut capturing four, the First Delaware three, and the Twelfth New Jersey two. The aggregate loss of the brigade in the action was 366. The loss of the Twelfth New Jersey was: killed, 2 officers and 21 men; wounded, 4 officers and 79 men; missing, 9 men; an aggregate of 115, about one-fourth of its total strength. The total loss of the division in killed, wounded and missing was 1,291.

"If I have made myself clear, it will thus be perceived that Smyth's brigade, with Woodruff's battery, not only checked the enemy's advance, but practically destroyed his column. No portion of the enemy's troops reached our line. One smooth-cheeked lad, indeed, the leader of thousands, ran forward through all that fire to fall dead and covered with wounds within twenty feet of our colors. Another reached the Byran barn, and from behind it, firing one shot down our line, was killed by Color-Sergeant Charles E. Cheeseman, a brave soldier, who, shot through the body himself, died by my side at the field hospital of the Wilderness, in May of 1864. These two men, like spray driven from a wave, marked the farthest limit of the enemy's advance in our front."

The disastrous fire from Hays' front threw the attacking forces into the utmost confusion and disorder, and the troops of Scales and Archer who withstood the shock united with Pickett, but it was too late, the force of the attacking column was spent, its power broken, and those who could get back to Seminary Ridge went there. Pickett's division was practically annihilated. Out of the four thousand five hundred men who advanced with him, not more than one thousand returned.

Wilcox, on the right of Pickett who had become separated from him on the advance, reached a position in front of Birney's division of the Third Corps. Without any knowledge of the disaster which had befallen Pickett on the left, he deployed his men; but Stannard who had returned to his place in the wood observed Wilcox's position, and repeating the movement by which he threw Armistead's line into confusion he advanced two of his regiments on Wilcox's flank and

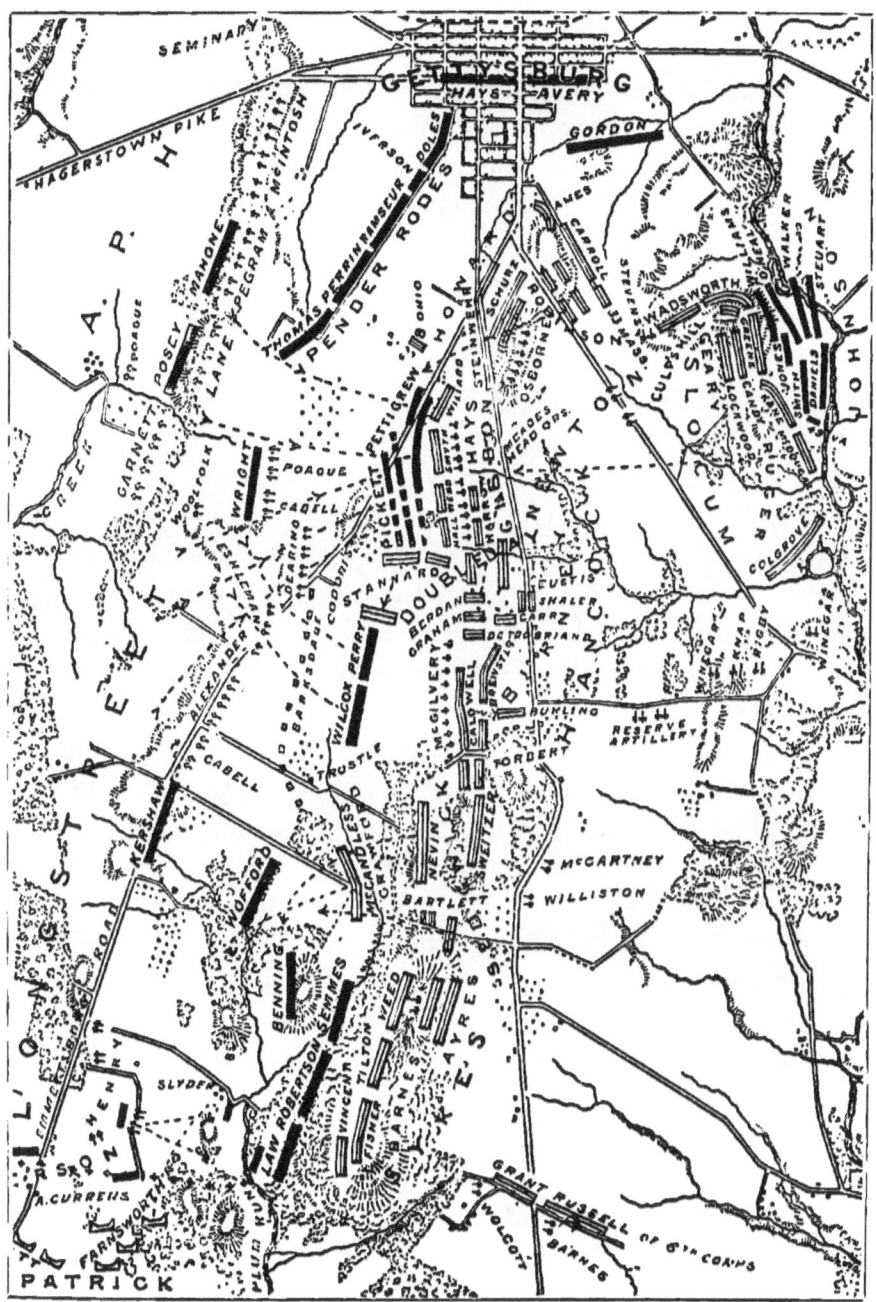

THE GENERAL LINE OF BATTLE AT THE TIME OF PICKETT'S CHARGE.

poured an enfilading fire down his line. The suddenness of this attack caused Wilcox to halt, and finding himself assailed by Stannard on the left and by artillery in front, he hastily departed with a loss of 200 of his men.

When the enemy was forming for their charge Battery "A," First New Jersey Artillery, Lieutenant Augustin N. Parsons commanding, was ordered by General Tyler, commanding the Artillery Reserve, to advance to the support of the Second Corps, in accordance with the instructions of General Hunt, chief of artillery. Promptly at the word Parsons, and his brave Germans who had distinguished themselves in many fields of action with their beloved commander Hexamer, moved into position along the Taneytown road and by order of Captain R. H. Fitzhugh was posted near the stone fence in front of General Webb's position, on the left of Fitzhugh's battery (K, First New York Artillery). "At this time," reported Fitzhugh, "the enemy were making a strong effort to break the Second Corps line, their infantry having charged up to the stone fence near a small wooded knoll about seventy-five yards on my right, while their artillery fire swept the ground occupied by the two batteries. Just then there were no other batteries at that point and there seemed to be a good deal of confusion. The rebel artillery fire, from near a house and barn, about one thousand yards on my left and front, was especially severe, but soon materially slackened and became very wild under a fire of percussion and time-shell from Battery 'K.' In the mean time Lieutenant Parsons poured forty rounds of shrapnel into the flank of the rebel infantry charging the Second Corps, and in about half or three-quarters of an hour the enemy abandoned the attack on that point altogether.

"After a pause of about an hour the rebel infantry began forming on the right of the house and barn before spoken of while from the same quarter their artillery opened upon us a brisk but poorly directed and inefficient fire, to which, by direction of General Hunt, I made no reply, but awaited the attack of their infantry (Wilcox and Perry's brigades), who soon charged over the open field toward some broken ground, about five hundred yards on my left, as they did so giving the two batteries an opportunity to pour in an enfilading fire, which they did with great effect, for the enemy did not reach the point but broke and gave way in all directions when about the middle of the field.

"Of the conduct of officers and men, both of Battery 'A' First New Jersey Artillery, Lieutenant A. N. Parsons commanding, and of 'K' First New York Artillery, with Eleventh New York Battery attached, I cannot speak too highly. Coming into position at a critical point of the rebel charge on our centre and under a galling fire, the guns were worked with great deliberation and a most decided effect."

Battery "A" sustained a loss of 2 killed and 7 wounded; 5 horses were killed and 200 rounds of ammunition expended, of which 120 rounds were shrapnel and 80 shell.

The conduct of the Twelfth New Jersey Infantry was also of the most exemplary character, and the reports of all the superior officers, mention specifically their brilliant achievements and the coolness and bravery exhibited under the most trying ordeal human nature had ever been subjected to. Colonel Thomas A. Smyth, commanding the brigade says: " The officers and men behaved with the greatest coolness, and endured this terrible fire with much fortitude. As the fire of the enemy's batteries slackened their infantry moved upon our position in three lines preceded by skirmishers. * * * * Major John T. Hill, commanding Twelfth New Jersey Volunteers, directed his men to retain their fire during the charge of the enemy until they were within twenty yards, when, at his command, so tremendous a fire of buck and ball was poured into their ranks as to render it impossible that one of them could reach the breastworks."

The report of Lieutenant William E. Potter of the Twelfth, whose duties as ordnance officer received the warm commendation of General Hays, shows that two thousand five hundred stand of arms were collected, and that fully one thousand more were left upon the field for want of time to gather them. The number of prisoners General Hays estimates at 2,000.

The casualties of the Twelfth Regiment during the two days were heavy. The loss sustained in charging the Bliss barn was severe, the total for the two days being 115, as follows:

### COMPANY A.

*Killed*—Private George H. Martin.

*Wounded*—Privates John S. Adams, James S. Butler, Joseph S. Fletcher, Benjamin F. Guant, Isaac D. Jones, Ira Knowlton, Joseph Morgan, Jr., David W. Scott, Daniel Smalley, Adam Stormes, Thomas Whitzell.

### COMPANY B.

*Killed*—Corporal Joseph B. Spachius; Privates John Bishop, Edward W. Coward, Samuel Platt, William H. Spencer.

*Wounded*—First Sergeant Henry P. Reed; Privates William L. Carty, Joseph H. Danley, Michael C. Donegan, Samuel McCulloch, George H. Rhubart, Edward Thomas, Charles D. F. Wilkie.

*Missing*—Privates Clark S. Champion (returned and discharged), John Elliott (died at Annapolis, Maryland, December 9, 1863), William G. Leak (returned and discharged).

### COMPANY C.

*Killed*—Second Lieutenant Richard H. Townsend.

*Wounded*—Privates Thomas Huttom, Charles Lex, George H. Wood, William S. Woodward.

### COMPANY D.

*Wounded* — Captain James McComb; Privates George W. Crumback, Enos Garrison, Robert Gant (died at Field Hospital, July 3, 1863), Samuel Green, Samuel L. Latcham.

COMPANY E.

*Killed* — Captain Charles K. Horsfall; Privates George Anderson, Isaac H. Copeland, James A. Riley.

*Wounded*—Second Lieutenant Stephen G. Eastwick; Corporal Thomas E. Prickett; Privates Jacob Asay, Matthew Cavanagh, Francis Haggerty, Joseph Meyers, Seth C. Southard, Charles Sullivan, William Tozer.

COMPANY F.

*Killed*—Corporal William H. H. Stratton; Privates George W. Adams, John Albright, William H. Johnson.

*Wounded*—First Lieutenant John J. Trimble; Corporal Abel K. Shute (died at Hospital, Baltimore, Maryland, July 31, 1863); Privates Alfred Eastburn, Joseph T. Garwood, John Grice, Joseph Jones, William H. Park, James K. Russell.

COMPANY G.

*Killed*—Privates John Conley, Thomas R. Middleton, Thomas J. Rudrow.

*Wounded*—Sergeant Hiram Smith; Corporal Charles Mayhew; Privates Edward L. Brick, Isaiah Groff, Thomas M. Harrison, William Herring (died at home, May 20, 1864), Charles D. Husbands, Adam Jordan, John H. Lamar, Aaron Parker, Nathan Parker, Richard F. Plum.

*Missing*— Privates Edward H. Pancoast (returned

and discharged April 5, 1865), John L. Severns (returned and transferred to V. R. C., March 31, 1864).

### COMPANY H.

*Killed*—Privates William S. Harker, Daniel Kiernan.

*Wounded*—Sergeants Alfred H. Brick, Clarkson Jennings; Corporals George A. Cobb, Edmund C. Tier; Privates David H. Atkinson, David Ballinger, Richard Barnes, Isaac A. Dubois, James Lippincott, James Magee, John Neusteal, Samuel L. Seran, James Stretch, Charles String.

*Missing*—Private William L. Seran (returned and commissioned in One Hundred and Twenty-first United States Colored Troops).

### COMPANY I.

*Wounded*—Captain Henry F. Chew; Privates Jacob Adams, Richard V. Fithian, John J. Hoffman, James Horner, John Miller (3rd), John W. Niblick.

### COMPANY K.

*Killed* — Privates Simon W. Creamer, Henry S. Sockwell.

*Wounded*—Privates Daniel H. Carman (died at Field Hospital July 3, 1863), William H. Dickeson, Charles H. Simpkins, Bloomfield Spencer, Samuel Tomlinson.

*Missing*—Sergeant Aaron Terry (died at Andersonville, Georgia, March 24, 1864); Privates Thomas C. Galloway (died at Andersonville, Georgia, August 28, 1864), Theophilus Sutton (died at Andersonville, Georgia, October 28, 1864).

RECAPITULATION.

|  | Killed. | Wounded. | Missing. | Total. |
|---|---|---|---|---|
| Officers | 2 | 4 | — | 6 |
| Enlisted Men | 20 | 80 | 9 | 109 |
| Total | 22 | 84 | 9 | 115 |

The following figures show the strength of the Twelfth New Jersey Infantry Volunteers on the dates named.

|  | Officers. | Men. | Total. |
|---|---|---|---|
| *June 30, 1863:* | | | |
| For duty | 25 | 507 | 532 |
| Total present | 27 | 569 | 596 |
| *July 13, 1863:* | | | |
| For duty | 18 | 383 | 401 |
| Total present | 22 | 441 | 463 |

None of the other New Jersey regiments were engaged in this defense of Cemetery Ridge. The Eleventh with Carr's brigade had been ordered up to the support of the line, but their services were not called in requisition. The First New Jersey Brigade was in reserve occupying a commanding position watching the contest. They were under the orders of General Newton* of the First Corps to whom they

---

* General John Newton, commanding First Army Corps, to whom the First New Jersey Brigade was sent, reports as to the formation of the line:

"The dawn of day (July 3) found the position of the First Corps as follows: First Division on Culp's Hill; Second Division on Cemetery Hill to support the Eleventh or Second Army Corps; the Third Division on the left centre adjoining Hancock. Between the left of the Third Division and Sykes on the left—an interval of half a mile—there

had been sent as a reinforcement and ready for any service.

The exhausted regiments of the Second New Jersey Brigade were in reserve in rear of Caldwell's division, and Clark's battery (" B " First New Jersey Artillery) did not become engaged. The Thirteenth Regiment lay in line of battle in McAllister's woods, and at five o'clock with the One Hundred and Seventh New York and two other regiments, all under command of Colonel Carman of the Thirteenth proceeded at a rapid pace to Rummel's farm to support Gregg's cavalry in the fierce conflict there going on. With the brilliant services of the First New Jersey Cavalry in the contest with Stuart's proud horsemen, New Jersey's record in the glories achieved on that historic field will be completed.

On the second of July Pleasonton so distributed his cavalry that Sickles was left dependent wholly upon his own skirmish line for a knowledge of what was going on upon his flank. Fortunately on the third Kilpatrick took up position on the Union left with the brigades of Farnsworth and Merritt, and moved

---

were no troops in position. I reported this fact to General Meade, who authorized me to go to General Sedgwick and obtain troops from him. While proceeding on this mission I encountered Caldwell's division of the Second Corps, which I put in position on the left of the Third Division, First Corps. General Sedgwick could only spare me the First New Jersey Brigade, General Torbert, which was placed in position on the left of Caldwell." General Newton also highly compliments Lieutenant H. W. Jackson of the Fourth New Jersey, who was acting aide-de-camp on his staff.

toward the Emmetsburg road, on which the Confederate trains were moving. This demonstration commanded the attention of Law, who succeeded Hood in command of his division, and he despatched Robertson's brigade to intercept the movement. Farnsworth charged the rebel infantry with great bold-

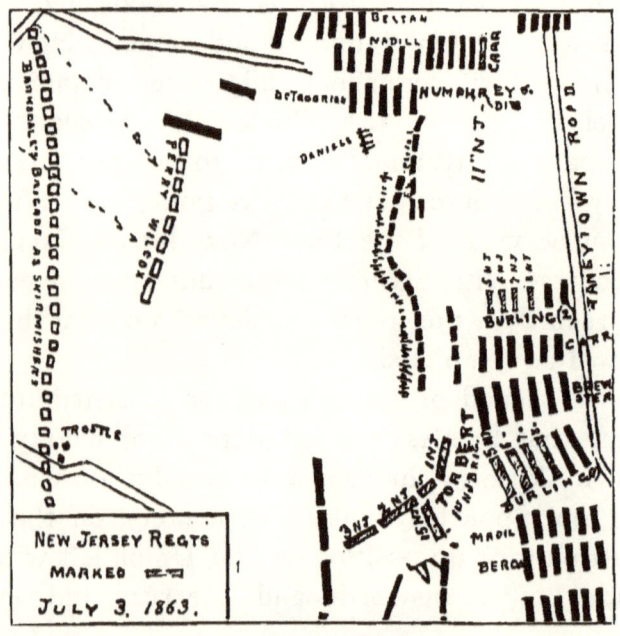

ness, but the nature of the country with its numerous fences furnished so many obstacles that he was driven to bay, and suffered heavy loss. Farnsworth was killed. Merritt on the Emmetsburg road encountered Anderson's brigade, and he was also repulsed. The cavalry was then re-united and posted to closely watch the further movements of the enemy. This by-play

MONUMENT 12TH REGT. N. J. VOLS., INF.

was productive of one good result. It called from Lee's army two brigades of infantry that otherwise could have been of service in strengthening Pickett when the attack upon the Union centre was ordered.

Stuart after receiving his instructions from Lee on the afternoon of July 1, ordered the concentration of all his cavalry on the right of the Union army. Lee's confidence in a victorious assault upon Meade's line is clearly shown in the orders he gave to Stuart which were to get around the Federal right, and take position so as to strike their column in flank, in the event of their retiring by way of Westminster. Stuart's movement was discovered by General Howard who reported to Meade that the enemy's cavalry in strong force was moving to the right of the Federal line, and General Gregg started with his cavalry to meet him. The disposition by Stuart of his troopers was such that Gregg saw his intentions, and posting the First New Jersey Cavalry as mounted skirmishers to the right and front in a wood, near the Bonaughtown road, the Third Pennsylvania was deployed as dismounted skirmishers to the left and front in the open fields, and the First Maryland on the Hanover turnpike to protect the right of his line. Stuart's force was much larger than Gregg's, and he advanced in strong force upon the latter. The firing of the skirmishers grew in volume like that of a line of battle, and both sides brought their artillery into play. Finally the rebel horsemen mounted for the charge appeared, and they galloped briskly forward, being met by the

Seventh Michigan who were driven back. The First Michigan in turn charged the victorious enemy and drove them back to their original position. Charges and counter-charges were made the enemy in every instance being foiled, and as they withdrew from the field to their left, the First New Jersey, posted in the wood, gallantly and successfully charged the flank of the column, driving them from the field. Chaplain Pyne relates the following incident which occurred during the fight:

"Sent forward as a forlorn hope, to give time for the rest of the division to come up with unblown horses, this little band of one hundred and fifty men, by their undaunted bearing and steady fire, staggered the troops that by a single charge could have ridden over them. Refusing to dismount in spite of the storm of bullets constantly whistling over our men, Janeway rode from end to end of his line of skirmishers, encouraging, warning and directing its every portion—showing here as on many another field a coolness and bravery that made him a marked man among men. Advancing from point to point, heralding each charge by a cheer which shook the enemy worse than the bullets of their carbines, for more than a hundred yards the First Jersey pushed their little line; and at last, with ammunition exhausted, they still held their ground facing the rebels with their revolvers. Then Janeway rode back to the reserve and reported to Major Beaumont the condition of his men, requesting ammunition and reinforcements. At

Major Beaumont's request, Colonel McIntosh ordered another regiment to take the place of the First Jersey. That regiment halted a hundred yards to the rear of the line where the Jerseymen were stationed, and would not advance any further, while the latter resisted every effort to move them back. Presently Colonel McIntosh rode up to Major Beaumont saying, 'Major, where is your regiment?' 'On the skirmish line, sir!' 'But I ordered them to be relieved.' 'The other regiment cannot be got to relieve them!' 'I will see about that,' said the Colonel; 'recall your men!' I have recalled them,' replied the Major, 'and' they won't come.' Even Colonel McIntosh failed to get the relieving regiment up through the tremendous fire to the position of the First Jersey; old soldiers as they were they could not calmly face it. At length, however, the Third Pennsylvania came upon the line, and the First Jersey was at liberty to retire from the action. But no! they sought every method to avoid falling back. Borrowing ammunition from the Pennsylvanians, they kept their boldly won position, and cheering like mad, defied the efforts of the enemy— only a handful retiring, casting reluctant looks behind as they went."

The charge by the New Jersey Cavalry—which the historian of the regiment strangely omits all mention of—was one of the most brilliant and effective exploits during the day. General Gregg, commanding the division, and General Pleasanton, of the Cavalry Corps, both speak of it in their reports. There is no official report from the officers of the regiment of its services at Gettysburg, and none by the commander of the brigade previous to July 4. The regiment sustained a loss of 7 men wounded during the battle.

About eleven o'clock at night the brigade of infantry from the Twelfth Corps under command of Colonel Carman, appeared on the Hanover road, but their aid was not required. The battle was over. Lee had been defeated at every point, and sorrowfully he prepared for the southward march, his men never more to appear on Northern soil, except as men of peace, and all American citizens under one flag and one government.

The total casualties in New Jersey Regiments during the two days they were engaged are given in the following table:

|  | OFFICERS. | | | ENLISTED MEN. | | | | | Total present for duty June 30. | Per centage of loss. |
| --- | --- | --- | --- | --- | --- | --- | --- | --- | --- | --- |
|  | Killed. | Wounded. | Total. | Killed. | Wounded. | Missing. | Total. | Aggregate. | | |
| First New Jersey Cavalry........ | .... | .... | .... | .... | 7 | .... | 7 | 7 | 234 | 3 |
| First New Jersey Artillery Bat. A.. | .... | .... | .... | 2 | 7 | .... | 9 | 9 | 116 | 8 |
| First New Jersey Artillery Bat. B.. | .... | .... | .... | 2 | 15 | 3 | 20 | 20 | 143 | 14 |
| Fifth New Jersey Infantry......... | 2 | 5 | 7 | 10 | 61 | 16 | 87 | 94 | 221 | 42 |
| Sixth New Jersey Infantry......... | .... | 3 | 3 | 1 | 29 | 8 | 38 | 41 | 246 | 17 |
| Seventh New Jersey Infantry...... | 1 | 9 | 10 | 14 | 77 | 12 | 103 | 113 | 331 | 34 |
| Eighth New Jersey Infantry....... | .... | 7 | 7 | 8 | 33 | 1 | 42 | 49 | 198 | 24 |
| Eleventh New Jersey Infantry..... | 3 | 10 | 13 | 20 | 113 | 7 | 140 | 153 | 275 | 55 |
| Twelfth New Jersey Infantry...... | 2 | 4 | 6 | 20 | 80 | 9 | 109 | 115 | 532 | 21 |
| Thirteenth New Jersey Infantry.... | .... | 3 | 3 | 1 | 17 | .... | 18 | 21 | 360 | 6 |
| Total...................... | 8 | 41 | 49 | 78 | 439 | 56 | 573 | 622 | 2656 | 22 |

The First New Jersey Brigade though not at any time engaged in the battle sustained a few losses from stray bullets and shells, and its detailed skirmishers also suffered somewhat. On the march back to Virginia there were several skirmishes with the enemy, the total casualties in the several regiments being reported on July 18th as follows:

SECOND REGIMENT NEW JERSEY VOLUNTEERS.

*Wounded*—July 3d, 1863, at Gettysburg—Sergeant William Duffy, Company C; Charles Lenz, Gottfried Schraitman, William Krauss, Frederick Imhaff, Company D; Wallingsen Van Houten, Company I. On skirmish line near Hagerstown, July 11, 1863—Second Lieutenant Johan J. G. Schmaltz, Corporal Ernest Fischer. Total 8 wounded.

THIRD REGIMENT NEW JERSEY VOLUNTEERS.

*Killed*—Corporal Daniel Schuh, Company H, July 5, 1863, near Fairfield, Pa.

*Wounded*—Captain John Frantz, Company B, July 12, 1863, near Funkstown, Md.; John C. Martin, Company E, and Corporal Matthew H. Ivory, Company H, both on July 3, near Gettysburg.

Total—1 killed, 3 wounded.

FIFTEENTH REGIMENT NEW JERSEY VOLUNTEERS.

*Wounded*—At Gettysburg, July 3—Isaac Cathrell, Company A (died July 13th); Jacob B. Hendershot, Company B; John C. Conklin, Company K; near Funkstown, July 12—Jacob O. Burdett and John Ackerson, Company D. Total, 5 wounded.

Total losses for the First New Jersey Brigade— killed, 1; wounded, 16.

## CHAPTER XV.

AFTER THE BATTLE—SCENES ON THE FIELD—THE CARE OF THE WOUNDED—EFFECT OF GENERAL MEADE'S ORDER SENDING ALL WAGONS TO THE REAR—PROMPT AND EFFECTIVE SERVICE AT THE TWELFTH CORPS HOSPITAL—RETREAT OF LEE'S ARMY AND THE PURSUIT.

THE battle of Gettysburg was a complete and decisive victory for the Federal army. The news of Lee's defeat was flashed across the continent the next morning—July 4th—and a few hours later a dispatch from General Grant announcing the capitulation of Vicksburg, filled the whole North with rejoicing. Bells were rung, salutes fired, enthusiastic greetings exchanged, public meetings held, and it is safe to say that never before was there such a celebration of the Nation's birthday as that of July 4th, 1863.

The scenes on the field of battle defy description. Beginning on the right of the Union line, the dead bodies of the enemy which lined Culp's Hill from its summit to the banks of Rock Creek presented a harrowing sight. They were so close together that it was impossible to walk over the ground without carefully selecting a spot for each step, and the broken muskets, straps, belts, clothing and implements of warfare which go to make up the debris of a battle-field, presented a demoralizing spectacle. Behind the rocks and trees along the creek, and in the stone house from which the enemy's sharpshooters did such effective work in the ranks of the Thirteenth New Jersey and Twenty-seventh Indiana regiments, the dead bodies of several rebels were found, showing that the fire from these regiments had done severe execution. The rebel battery on Benner's Hill had met with disaster. The dead bodies of the horses which were killed by the fire of the batteries on Cemetery Hill, lay where they fell, while the newly-made graves to the rear marked the last resting places of the brave men who manned the guns. Two disabled caissons remained, further evidences of the destructive and accurate fire of the Union batteries. In front of the ridge which connects Culp with Cemetery Hill, where the Louisiana Tigers made their heroic but fatal charge similar scenes were witnessed, but across the open country in front of the line of the Second and Third Corps, the sights beggared description. Dead and bloated horses, the disfigured bodies of hundreds of brave soldiers, abandoned material of every kind conceivable met the eye in all directions. Along Sickles' angle, in the Peach Orchard and beyond, over the wheat-field and among the rocks of the Devil's Den, blue bodies and gray were intermingled. Under the porches—and even under the houses themselves— wounded men had crawled to escape the dreadful hail

of leaden missiles, only to die of neglect. It was such a sight as only the destroying angel could reproduce, and it told of the horrors of war, as only a battle-field can tell it. But these mortifying bodies could not be permitted to remain. Details of men, with shovels and picks were seen moving over the field. Wide trenches were at first dug and the dead placed side by side and covered up, a board with the number of bodies buried, being placed at the head of the mound. In the case of Union men who were buried by details from their own regiments, the board would be marked with the name and company of the dead soldier, but it happened in many cases that the dead of one regiment were buried by details from other regiments, and thus came about the long list of "Unknown" dead, whose bodies were afterward transferred to the National Cemetery. The number of bodies to be buried was so large that trenches could not be dug for all, and as a matter of sanitary policy, it became necessary to simply cover them where they lay with earth, and in that manner hundreds were disposed of.

The care of the wounded was however the most important duty. The Medical Director of the army had made ample and complete arrangements for the establishment of field hospitals, but the trains with the necessary supplies were not permitted to come nearer the battle-field than Taneytown, and on July 2d all trains were ordered by General Meade still farther to the rear—to Westminster—twenty-five miles from the battle-field. *The effect of this order was to deprive the Medical Department of the means for taking proper care of the wounded until the result of the engagement of the second and third days of July was fully known.  In most of the corps the wagons exclusively used for medicines moved with the ambulances, so that the medical officers had a sufficient supply of dressings, chloroform, and such articles until the wagons could come up, but the tents and other appliances were not available until July 5th, and though this was a disobedience of orders, yet it produced such excellent results that the Medical Director of the army quotes approvingly from the report of Medical Director McNulty of the Twelfth Corps, who says: "It is with extreme satisfaction that I can assure you that it enabled me to remove the wounded from the field, shelter, feed them, and dress their wounds within six hours after the battle ended, and to have every capital operation performed within twenty-four hours after the injury was received." Medical Director Letterman says of this: "I can, I think, safely say that such would have been the result in other corps had the same facilities been allowed—a result not to have been surpassed, if equaled, in any battle of magnitude that has ever taken place."

The following interesting account of the hospital work of the Twelfth Corps, is from one of the prominent surgeons of the First Division:

---

*Report of Jonathan A. Letterman, Medical Director.

"The Twelfth Corps Field Hospital was first located in the rear of Power's Hill, but after being shelled out on the afternoon of July second was permanently located (by Surgeon J. McNulty, medical director of the corps, and Surgeon A. Chapel, chief medical officer of the First Division), on a farm owned, I think, by G. Bushman, situated or lying on Rock Creek, near a cross road running from the Baltimore pike to the Taneytown road, some two or two and one-half miles from the town of Gettysburg. The farm house was used as a dining place for the surgeons and attendants, and the female portion of the farmer's family were kept busy in the preparation and serving of food. The large barn was utilized for shelter for as many of the wounded as it would hold, and hospital tents were put up in rows on each side of an imaginary street running up in the field north from the barn. The tents on the west side of the street were alloted to the Second Division, and those on the east side to the First Division. Surgeon H. E. Goodman, Twenty-eighth Pennsylvania, was placed in charge of the Second Division, and Surgeon J. J. H. Love, Thirteenth New Jersey Volunteers, had the care of the First Division. In the First Division the chief operators were Surgeons W. C. Rodgers, Forty-sixth Pennsylvania; W. C. Burnett, Fifth Connecticut, and W. H. Twiford, Twenty-seventh Indiana. While in the Second Division Surgeons J. A. Ball, Fifth Ohio; A. K. Fifield, Seventh Ohio, and E. L. Dunn, One Hundred and Ninth Pennsylvania, were assigned to similar

John J. H. Love,
Surgeon-in-Chief 3d Brigade, 1st Division, 12th Corps.
Surgeon 13th Regiment, N. J. Vols., Inf.
*(From a War-Time Photograph.)*

duty. To keep the records, provide shelter and food was assigned to Surgeons R. T. Paine, Twenty-eighth New York; J. A. Freeman, Thirteenth New Jersey; Geo. W. Burke, Forty-sixth Pennsylvania; E. L. Bessell, Fifth Connecticut; W. T. Tibbals, Fifth Ohio, and C. H. Lord, One Hundred and Seventh New York.

"During the evening of July second the wounded began to arrive, and all that night and the next day until afternoon late the ambulances were constantly bringing in loads of wounded men. First Lieutenant George M. Hard, Thirteenth New Jersey Volunteers, had charge of the ambulance train of the First Division. My records state that about six hundred (600) wounded were brought to the hospital. These were sheltered, their wounds dressed, all necessary operations performed, and everything fixed up in good condition by Sunday afternoon, July fourth. Then the army having left the vicinity, Surgeon H. E. Goodman with twelve assistant surgeons and the necessary number of hospital stewards and nurses were detailed to take charge of the hospital, and the balance of the surgeons mounting their horses took a hasty gallop over the battlefield and rejoined their respective commands late that night at Littlestown, Pennsylvania. Surgeon Freeman and Hospital Steward Albert Delano, of the Thirteenth New Jersey Volunteers, were among those left behind to assist in caring for the wounded.

"The facility and despatch shown by the surgeons of the Twelfth Corps in caring for their wounded at this battle, was the result of a disobedience of or a neglect to obey an order issued by General Meade on July first, reducing the medical transportation and sending all trains, except ammunition wagons and ambulances, to the rear, somewhere between Union Mills and Westminster. The medical department of the Twelfth Corps had its full allowance of supplies on hand ready for use, and was the only corps in the Army of the Potomac that had.

"During the memorable cannonade on the afternoon of July third, the surgeons and attendants became so excited that all, for a time, left their work and crowded the top of a knoll in rear of the hospital, from which a view could be had toward our line of battle. The roar was terrific; the ground under us trembled; all knew that the great crisis in the history of the Army of the Potomac and that of Northern Virginia had come; that one or the other must conquer or be defeated, and all understood what the consequences would be in either event. The bursting shell comes nearer. Look! there falls one in the field across the road from us. The roar increases. The shell rain on that ploughed field, hurling its loose dirt in great masses skyward. The enemy must be driving our troops, or else secured a more favorable position for one of their batteries. See, there! the Second Corps Hospital, between us and Little Round Top, is under fire, and they must move, and that quickly. Men, wounded and otherwise, ambulances, hospital wagons, mules, led horses, servants, surgeons, all come hurrying through the fields under that shell fire. How soon will our turn come? The cannonade begins to slacken and die out, and in a little while come the rattle and steady roar of musketry. Which side holds its own? No ambulances come in; no messengers from the front; no stragglers can be seen pouring over the hill, as on the previous afternoon when the Third Corps was fighting its great battle. The minutes seem hours. Presently an orderly is seen hurrying across the fields. We call him to us and eagerly ask what news from the front. 'The Union lines stand firm,' he shouts. Each man breathes a silent prayer of thanks to God, and then with three cheers for General Meade and the Army of the Potomac all return to their work."

The number of wounded who were cared for by the medical director of the Army of the Potomac was 14,193, and Confederates 6,802—a total of 20,995. These figures include the Federal wounded of July 1, who fell into Union hands on the 4th.

The wounded from other corps suffered dreadfully. During the morning of July 4th a heavy rain fell—an occurrence which seemed to succeed every great battle, and hundreds of disabled soldiers were without shelter, and unable to reach any. The water in Rock Creek rose to a considerable height and in immense volume rushed southward with great force, in several instances carrying down with it the wounded men along its banks who were unable to move to higher ground, and some were drowned. The effect of the rain upon the dead bodies of men and horses lying on the field was ghastly—but it would be painful to particularize.

The town of Gettysburg had not suffered much in a material sense. The enemy occupied it, and this saved it from the terrible effects of a cannonade from that side. Its residents were Union people and no attempt therefore to shell the rebel lines there was made by Meade. But occasionally a cannon ball penetrated the town and in two instances houses were pierced, the balls remaining imbedded in the brick walls where they can now be seen.

On the morning of July fourth about eight o'clock the Thirteenth New Jersey Regiment rejoined its corps and with them went on a reconnoissance over the enemy's position on the Union right. They found no signs of Ewell's troops, that officer having retired the night before, and passing through Gettysburg formed a new line with Lee's army, along the ridge of Seminary Hill. Meade did not attempt a countercharge after the fight on the third. General Hancock, when wounded, had suggested it, but Lee had been given too much time to prepare for defence. On the evening of the third of July Meade sent forward a body of troops to feel the enemy, who speedily withdrew, and at a council of his corps commanders that night it was decided not to atattack Lee, nor to follow the same route, if he retired. It was not at all clear to Meade's mind that Lee was so badly punished that he was not able to outnumber him, and taking the benefit of the doubt, he waited to ascertain what Lee intended doing. That officer however was preparing for his march back to Virginia, and taking advantage of Meade's inaction had covered a long distance before the Army of the Potomac moved. Lee had the shorter and more direct route to the Potomac and his advance had reached the river several days ahead of his pursuers, but the heavy rains had so swollen the stream that he could not replace the bridges that had been swept away. It was the twelfth of July before Meade confronted him in line of battle and on the night of the thirteenth unmolested Lee crossed over into Virginia. A few of his rear guard were captured the next morning by Union cavalry, but Lee, with all his plunder, had escaped. The Army of the Potomac recrossed into Virginia and no engagement of any importance took place between the two armies. There was a good deal of lively skirmishing between the cavalry. On the fifth of July the First New Jersey had a sharp engagement in the mountain passes north of Emmetsburg, and again on the sixth, Lieutenant Thomas S. Cox receiving a bad wound. On the fourteenth the regiment had an encounter with the Twelfth Virginia and captured its colonel. Affairs of this kind occupied the attention of the cavalry daily, but aside from these nothing of moment occurred on the march.

The Comte de Paris who has made an exhaustive research among the figures presented by both armies sums up the effective strength during the battle to be:

For the Army of the Potomac from eighty-two to eighty-four thousand men; army of Northern Virginia from sixty-eight to sixty-nine thousand men, actually upon the field of battle. The losses were enormous for the number of combatants engaged, amounting to twenty-seven per cent. for the Union army and thirty-six per cent. for the Confederates.

The losses in officers in both armies were heavy. On the Union side were Major-General Reynolds, and Brigadier-Generals Vincent and Weed, killed; Major-Generals Sickles, Hancock, Doubleday, Gibbon, Barlow, Warren and Butterfield, and Brigadier-Generals Graham, Paul, Barnes, Brooke and Webb, wounded.

The rebels lost in killed Generals Armistead, Barksdale, Garnett, Pender, Semmes and Pettigrew (during the retreat); and Generals Anderson, Hampton, Hood, Jenkins, Jones, Kemper and Scales, wounded. The rebel General Archer was captured on July 1st.

The list of officers of lower rank would fill a page. The death of Hazlett and Cushing of the artillery service, and of Colonels Rorty, Sherrill, Zook, Cross and Willard, of the infantry each signify especially heroic services rendered most opportunely, and under circumstances of the most exalting nature.

The success of the Union arms at Gettysburg did for the cause of humanity precisely what the Declaration of Independence did for mankind in 1776. The latter was the protest of a misgoverned people against the encroachments of kingly rule upon their rights and privileges; the battle of Gettysburg proclaimed the dawn of liberty to an enslaved race and exhibited to the world the sublime spectacle of a nation of freemen determined that every one within its borders should have that liberty which the Declaration of Independence proclaimed to be the inalienable right of all men. The war for the Union, first begun by the slaves States of the South, was waged on the part of the government for national preservation, but when President Lincoln issued his Proclamation of Emancipation, the contest took on a new phase, and slavery was doomed to eternal destruction by the success of the national arms. How eloquently President Lincoln drew the picture in his dedicatory address at Gettysburg—a speech immortalized as a masterpiece of English composition, in the breadth of thought as well as in the beauty of expression which characterizes it:

"Fourscore and seven years ago, our fathers brought forth on this continent a new nation, conceived in liberty, and dedicated to the proposition that all men are created equal. Now, we are engaged in a great civil war, testing whether that nation, or any nation, so conceived and so dedicated, can long endure. We are met on a great battle-field of that war. We have come to dedicate a portion of that field, as a final resting-place for those who here gave their lives that the nation might live. It is altogether fitting and proper that we should do this. But, in a larger sense, we cannot dedicate—we cannot consecrate—we cannot hallow this ground. The brave men, living and dead, who struggled here, have consecrated it far above our poor power to add or detract. The world will little note nor long remember what we say here, but it never can forget what they did here. It is for us the living, rather, to be dedicated here to the unfinished work which they who fought here have thus far so nobly carried on. It is rather for us to be here dedicated to the great task remaining before us—that from these honored dead we take increased devotion to that cause for which they gave the last full measure of devotion. That we here highly resolve that these dead shall not have died in vain; that this nation, under God, shall have a new birth of freedom; and that the government of the people, by the people, and for the people, shall not perish from the earth."

## CHAPTER XVI.

ORGANIZATION OF THE GETTYSBURG BATTLE-FIELD COMMISSION—A RECORD OF ITS WORK—DESCRIPTION OF THE MONUMENTS.

FOR several years efforts had been made to enlist the sympathies of the survivors of New Jersey regiments for the purpose of securing the erection of monuments to mark the position occupied by each of them on Gettysburg battle-field. For a long time little progress was made, until at a meeting of the Eighth Regiment Association a bill was prepared and presented to the Legislature for State aid in the work of erecting monuments, which was enacted into a law. The Twelfth New Jersey Regiment previous to this with commendable promptness and energy went voluntarily to work to procure a monument for themselves and were the first New Jersey organization to erect and dedicate a monument on the battle-field.

In 1885 the Legislature passed the bill entitled "An act to provide for the erection of suitable monuments to mark the position of New Jersey regiments upon the battle-field of Gettysburg," which provided for the appointment by the Governor of three commissioners, to be known as " the Gettysburg Battle-field Commission of New Jersey," and empowering them to call to their aid one officer or enlisted man who was present at the battle of Gettysburg, from each New Jersey regiment and battery there engaged, to assist them in locating the lines and positions occupied by their respective regiments and batteries. This bill became a law on May 27, 1886, and the Governor subsequently appointed the following Commissioners: Colonel James N. Duffy of Newark, Honorable William H. Corbin of Elizabeth and Honorable Gottfried Kreuger of Newark. The Commissioners organized by the selection of Colonel Duffy for president and Honorable William H. Corbin as Secretary. In accordance with that provision of the law which authorized the selection of representatives of the several regiments and batteries engaged at Gettysburg, to aid in locating the sites of their respective commands, the following were selected by the commission:

First Infantry—First Sergeant William Brant.
Second Infantry—Surgeon Lewis W. Oakley, Lieutenant Joseph Donovan.
Third Infantry—First Sergeant A. W. Cattell.
Fourth Infantry—John P. Beech.
Fifteenth Infantry—Corporal Jacob Reidinger.
Fifth Infantry—Colonel William J. Sewell.
Sixth Infantry—Joseph Smith.
Seventh Infantry—First Sergeant W. H. H. Condit, Theodore Searing.
Eighth Infantry—Sergeant Benjamin Murphy.

GETTYSBURG BATTLE-FIELD COMMISSION OF NEW JERSEY.

COL. JAMES N. DUFFY, *President.*

HON. WILLIAM H. CORBIN, *Secretary.*  HON. GOTTFRIED KRUEGER.

Eleventh Infantry—Frank P. Mulcahy.
Twelfth Infantry—Sergeant James White.
Thirteenth Infantry—Samuel Toombs.
First Cavalry—Lieutenant George A. Bowne.
Battery "B," First Artillery—Captain A. Judson Clark.

The Commission, with these representatives, visited the Gettysburg battle-field on the first of July following and selected the positions for the monuments to the several regiments. When the expenses of the trip were defrayed and the payment to the Gettysburg Battle-field Memorial Association of $3,000 was made, it was found that but $370 remained for each regiment and battery with which to erect a monument.

The Thirteenth New Jersey Regiment held its first reunion since the war at Orange on October 13th following, and appointed a committee on monument which promptly organized and submitted a design for the approval of the Commission. As the cost was to be two thousand dollars, and the State appropriation was only three hundred and seventy dollars, the Commission approved the design, the committee of the Thirteenth Regiment becoming responsible for the balance of the money. This was the first monument erected and dedicated by the State Commission.

In 1886 and 1887 the act creating the Commission was amended by increasing the amount to be appropriated to each regiment and battery to nine hundred and fifty dollars each, and this sum was increased to one thousand dollars by voluntary subscriptions from a few public-spirited and patriotic gentlemen.

The Commission presented its first report to the Legislature of 1887, wherein is set forth the several locations as agreed upon, and which will be found marked on the map accompanying this book.

The work of the Commission has been most admirably performed, and the greatest care has been exercised that in every particular, the foundations, material and workmanship shall be of the very best, and the most durable in quality. These stones are not erected for a day but for all time and they will stand for centuries silent monitors of the greatest battle of modern times; and coming generations will read the inscriptions engraved on them with mingled feelings of curiosity and respect for the valor of the men who so stubbornly fought on that bloody field for the integrity of the Republic and the rights of mankind.

## THE MONUMENTS.

### TWELFTH NEW JERSEY INFANTRY.

The handsome stone which commemorates the services of the members of this regiment in their gallant defense of Cemetery Ridge on the third day of July, was erected by private subscription among the members of the regiment and their friends, and was the first of the New Jersey monuments put up. As early as 1882, members of the regiment interested themselves in the work, and at the annual meeting of the Society of the Twelfth Regiment New Jersey Volunteers in 1883, a monument committee, comprising Comrades Joseph Burroughs, Frank M. Acton and James S. Kiger, was appointed. At the next meeting in 1884, the committee was enlarged by the appointment of Comrades H. F. Chew and George Danenhower. Under the active surpervision of this committee the necessary funds were raised and on the 26th of May, 1886, the monument was formally dedicated. Captain F. M. Riley of Bridgeton, the President of the Association presented the monument to the Gettysburg Battle-Field Memorial Association and it was accepted by the Secretary, J. M. Krauth, Esq. Colonel William E. Potter, who was Second Lieutenant of Company K at the time of the battle, delivered the oration.

The monument is constructed of Richmond granite, a very durable stone, and is twelve feet six inches in height.* It is located in the centre of the position occupied by the regiment, and is one of the most prominent in the whole line. The base of the monument is four feet eight inches square, and two feet high with sides rustic-dressed. The sub-base is three feet eight inches square and eighteen inches high, fine hammered, and containing this inscription: "2d Brig. 3d Div. 2d Corps," on three of its sides. The die is two feet eight inches square by four feet ten inches in height, polished on the two faces fronting Round Top avenue and inscribed as follows: On first face:

"In memory of the men of the Twelfth Regiment New Jersey Infantry Volunteers, who fell upon this field July 2d and 3d 1863, and who elsewhere died under the flag, this monument is dedicated by their surviving comrades as an example to future generations."

On the second face:

"Buck and Ball
calibre 69."

"This regiment made two separate charges on the Bliss barn and captured it."

The capstone is three feet two inches square by two feet high, upon each face of which has been placed the badge of the Second Corps, the Trefoil, raised and polished.

The capstone is surmounted by a pedestal upon which is a representation of the missiles so effectively used by the regiment in repelling the charge of the enemy — buck and ball. The monument was constructed by Mr. Michael Reilly of Camden, N. J., and cost entire $1,000.00.

TWELFTH REGIMENT MARKER.

Under the provisions of the law by which the New Jersey Gettysburg Battle-Field Commission are governed, the Twelfth Regiment was entitled to a monument by the State, and the Commission very wisely determined to place a substantial marker on the site of the Bliss barn, in the capture of which the Twelfth had performed one of the most daring and heroic acts which characterized the battle. The site of the Bliss barn had been purchased by the Fourteenth Connecticut Regiment, who also charged upon the enemy secreted there, and burned it, but they generously accorded to the State Commission the right to put a marker there for the Twelfth Regiment. This marker or tablet is one massive piece of Quincy granite, ten feet three inches long, three feet nine inches wide and two feet thick, extending into the ground five feet, and weighs about eight tons, and was constructed by Messrs. Frederick & Field, of Quincy, Mass. The part above the ground measures five feet three inches in height. The stone is in the form of a tablet and base combined, cut solid, and the upper part is polished front and back and suitably inscribed. On the slant, or top, are two crossed bayonets, carved, and corps badge laid on top, face of same polished. Also "12th N. J. Vols," in raised and bold face letters. On front is the following inscription:

"Erected by the State of New Jersey, 1888, in honor of the 12th Regiment of Volunteers, a detachment of which in the afternoon of July 2, 1863, charged the Bliss house and barn here, capturing the enemy's skirmish reserve of 7 officers and 85 men stationed therein."

On the rear of the tablet is the following:

"On the morning of July 3 another detachment of the regiment charged, capturing the buildings, one officer and one man, and driving back the skirmish reserve. The regiment lost in their charges 60 officers and men."

THIRTEENTH NEW JERSEY INFANTRY.

The beautiful memorial stone of the Thirteenth Regiment was the second New Jersey monument erected on the battle-field, and the first in which the State Commission was officially interested. This regiment manifested a very marked interest in the work of the Commission, and in the erection of its monument. At a meeting of the Regimental Association in September, 1886, a monument committee, comprising the following members of the association was appointed: F. H. Harris, A. M. Matthews, J. J. H. Love, Albert Delano, Samuel Toombs, John Grimes, W. S. Clarke, M. Conners, Charles Webber, D. A. Ryerson, G. W. Lawrence, W. B. Jacobus, William H. Pridham, Andrew Jackson, Jacob White, Joseph E. Crowell, Ogden Foxcroft, Charles A. Hopkins. The committee worked so faithfully and diligently that by the next July—but ten months from the time of their appointment—they had secured enough funds which, added to the State appropriation, enabled them to dedicate the monument with appropriate ceremonies on July 1, 1887, addresses being made by Major-General Henry W. Slocum, His Excellency Governor Robert S. Green, Honorable William H. Corbin, Adjutant-General W. S. Stryker, Captain A. M. Matthews and Dr. J. J. H. Love.

The monument stands on a knoll in an open space in McAllister's woods, directly overlooking Rock Creek, the site being, as near as could be determined, exactly where the colors of the regiment stood on the third day of July, 1863. The monument is a tablet-shaped

bowlder, seven feet high, five feet nine inches across
the face, two feet ten inches thick at bottom, tapering
to two feet in thickness at the top, and was constructed
by the Smith Granite Company of Boston, Mass. This
tablet rests on a granite support six feet six inches
broad at the base, three feet in height and four feet
thick, all supported by a rock foundation made of
broken stone and Portland cement. The excavation
for the foundation is six feet in depth below the
original ground surface, and the stone work has been
carried up four feet above the ground line. This pro-
tects it absolutely from frost, and as there are but two
immense stones in the monument itself it will require
an extraordinary revulsion of nature to disturb it.
The four feet of foundation above the ground surface
has been concealed from view by mounding it over and
sodding it carefully. The entire height of monument
above original ground line is fourteen feet. The height
of monument proper ten feet. On the easterly face of
the stone is carved a figure, life-size, of a soldier kneeling and in the act of firing. He is represented as in
the woods, his haversack and canteen at the foot of a
tree, and all the detail of uniform and equipments faithfully portrayed. Across the stone is the legend:
"13 New Jersey Vols." The inscription on the
western face is as follows:

13TH REGIMENT, N. J. VOLUNTEERS,
3D BRIGADE, 1ST DIVISION, 12TH CORPS.

Thirteenth Regiment, N. J. Volunteers, reached this
battle-field 5 P. M. July 1, 1863, and with the brigade

went into position on the north side of Wolf Hill. During the night occupied a position in support of Battery M., First N. Y. Artillery. July 2, in morning, held position near Culp's Hill; in afternoon marched to relief of Third Corps near Round Top; at night returned to right of the army. July 3d occupied position marked by this monument, supporting Second Massachusetts and Twenty-seventh Indiana in their charge on Confederate flank. In evening moved to extreme right to support Gregg's Cavalry.

Killed and mortally wounded, 2; wounded, 19.

Mustered in August 25, 1862. Discharged June 8, 1865.

### ENGAGEMENTS:

Antietam, 1862.
Chancellorsville, 1863.
Gettysburg, 1863.
Resaca, 1864.
Cassville, 1864.
Dallas, 1864.
Kulp's Farm, 1864.

Nancy's Creek, 1864.
Peach-Tree Creek, 1864.
Siege of Atlanta, 1864.
March to the Sea, 1864.
Siege of Savannah, 1864.
Averysboro, 1865.
Bentonville, 1865.

Total losses during the war: Killed or Died of Wounds, 75. Died of Disease and in Prison, 43. Wounded, 244. Total, 362.

### FIRST BRIGADE MONUMENT.

*(First, Second, Third, Fourth and Fifteenth Regiments Infantry.)*

The monument erected to the First New Jersey Brigade is one of the most conspicuous objects on the battle-field. It represents a watch-tower and is forty feet in height, being constructed mainly of battle-field granite—a dark colored and exceedingly hard stone—the trimmings being of light granite. At the base the monument is eight feet thick and in the entablature in front the inscription is placed. The Sixth Corps badge—a Greek cross—is cut in the stone above and the fluted columns on each side give it the appearance of being an entrance way to the interior. Bronze medallions of General Philip Kearny, who organized the brigade, and of General A. T. A. Torbert, who commanded it at Gettysburg, are conspicuously placed, one on each side. A carved stone, weighing several tons, containing the State arms and the number by which each regiment was known, the figures being interlaced with leaves and vines, is one of the attractive features of this handsome design. While this tower marks the position of the brigade on the third day of July, each regiment has separate markers designating their position, the marker for the Fourth Regiment being placed a little south of Power's Hill, that regiment having been on duty with the division trains during the battle. The brigade monument was designed by, and the contract awarded to, the New England Monument Company of 1321 Broadway, New York. The monument bears the following inscriptions:

*Front:*

First Brigade, New Jersey Volunteers.
Brig.-Gen. Alfred T. A. Torbert.
(1st 2d 3d 4th and 15th Regiments Infantry).
1st Brig. 1st Div. 6th Corps.

July 2 in reserve. July 3 and 4, detached from the Corps, held this position.

Erected by the State of New Jersey, A. D. 1888, in testimony of the patriotism, courage and patient endurance of her volunteer soldiers.

*Rear:*

"Kearny's New Jersey Brigade"
Fought in all the important battles of the Army of the Potomac from May 1861 to the end of the war at Apommattox Court House in 1865.

Total Strength 13,805, including 10th, 23d and 40th Regiments of New Jersey Volunteers which were attached to the Brigade.

### FIFTH NEW JERSEY INFANTRY.

This monument located on the west side of the Emmetsburg road, just south of the Rogers house is a massive and enduring structure, and is made of Hallowell, Me., granite. The base is six feet square, and the total height fifteen feet six inches, and weighs about fifteen tons. The die or lettered piece of monument rests on two bases and contains the following inscriptions:

*Front:*

5 New Jersey Vols.
Col. William J. Sewell.
3d Brig. 2d Div. 3d Corps.
July 2, 1863.

*Left side:*

The Regiment first held the skirmish line 400 yards to the front and left of this spot, and afterwards to position in the line of battle here.

*Right side:*

Losses—Killed, 18; wounded, 60; missing, 16; total, 94, being one-half the number engaged.

On a polished band on front of second base or plinth in raised letters the legend:

Erected by the State of New Jersey, 1888.

*Back:*

Mustered in August 22, 1861.
Consolidated with 7th Regiment N. J. Vols.
Nov. 6. 1864.
Engaged in 32 battles.

The shaft has an emblem carved in high relief, consisting of two muskets, cartridge box and belt, with a laurel wreath at the stocks, enclosing a large figure 5 in centre. These military accoutrements are full size and modeled from the actual implements, being correct in every detail. The neck of the shaft has a band of thirteen polished face stars raised above the surface. The monument is finished with an appropriate cap, and is an imposing and handsome structure. The design and the work is by Messrs. Frederick & Field of Quincy, Mass.

SIXTH NEW JERSEY REGIMENT.

This monument, erected near the Devil's Den, is of the obelisk style and is composed of four pieces. It measures five feet six inches square at the bottom and stands nineteen feet high. On front of the second base or plinth is carved on the stone the corps badge, the face of which is highly polished. On this rests the die piece each side of which is polished, and contains the following inscriptions:

*Front:*

6th New Jersey Volunteers.
Lieut. Col. S. R. Gilkyson.
3d Brig. (Burling's)
2d Div. 3d Corps.
Erected by State of New Jersey 1888.

*Right:*

Engaged here July 2, 1863, being detached from the Brigade.
Supported batteries on Cemetery Ridge, July 3.
Losses—Killed, 5; wounded, 29; missing, 7. Total, 41.

*Left:*

Mustered in Aug. 19, 1861.
Consolidated with 8th Regt. N. J. V. Oct. 12, 1864.
Engaged in 30 battles.

The top of the die is heavily moulded and on front is a finely carved United States shield. Around the top of the die under the moulding is a row of carved rifle balls. On the die rests the obelisk having on its front two crossed muskets and a wreath of laurel finely carved in bold relief. The monument is constructed of the best quality of selected Barre granite and weighs about twelve tons. Messrs. Frederick & Field are the contractors and makers.

MONUMENT BATTERY B, 1ST N. J. ART.
(Clark's Battery.)

## SEVENTH NEW JERSEY INFANTRY.

The stone which marks the heroic services of this regiment is unique in character and different from anything else on the field. It is a correct representation of a minié ball, and is of mammoth proportions, and mounted on two bases. These bases are of light Quincy granite finely dressed, and the rifle ball is of dark Quincy highly polished. The dark color of the polished surface of the ball makes a fine contrast with the light color of the cut surfaces of the bases, and the effect is decidedly novel and pleasing. The first base measures six square feet chamfered on top to receive another octagon base. On the front side is raised a large Third Corps badge on which appears the figure 7 enclosed by a carved laurel wreath. The other seven sides contain the inscriptions on polished surfaces as follows:

    No. 1—7th New Jersey Vols. July 2, 1863.
    No. 2—*Killed 24, wounded 77, missing 13, total 114.
    No. 3—Here Colonel Francine fell.
    No. 4—First Position 300 yards N. E. of this. Heavily engaged there. Moved here to reinforce Graham's brigade.
    No. 5—Erected by the State of New Jersey 1888.
    No. 6—Mustered in Sept. 3, 1861. Mustered out July 17, 1865. Engaged in 38 battles.
    No. 7—3d Brig. 2d Div. 3d Corps.

---

* This is an error. The casualties will be found on page 258 of this book.

The rifle ball measures three feet two inches in diameter, and the whole monument will stand ten feet six inches high above foundation, and will weigh about twelve tons. The foundation being raised about two and a-half feet from the ground surface, with a symmetrical mound of earth and grass at the base makes it one of the most attractive objects on the ground. Messrs. Frederick & Field of Quincy, Mass., are the designers and makers.

EIGHTH REGIMENT NEW JERSEY VOLUNTEERS.

This monument, situated beyond the famous wheat-field, is a graceful shaft, surmounted by a cap, the crowning feature of which is the Third Corps badge. The base measures five feet four inches square, on which rests a second base or plinth, which supports the die or lettered piece of the monument. This die measures three feet one inch square, and is four feet three inches high. On the front appears the figure 8 encircled by a finely carved laurel wreath. The shaft rests upon the die, and is handsomely embellished, having in front two crossed muskets and flag carved in high relief. The cap surmounting the shaft is finely moulded and carved. The monument was made by Messrs. Frederick & Field of Quincy, Mass., and is constructed of the best quality of light Quincy granite, and weighs thirteen tons. The following are the inscriptions on the stone:

*Front:*

8th New Jersey Volunteers.
Col. John Ramsey.
3d Brig. (Burling's).
2d Div. 3d Corps.
Erected by the State of New Jersey 1888.

*Right:*

Engaged here July 2, 1863, being detached from the Brigade.
Supported batteries on Cemetery Ridge July 3d.
Took into action 170.
Killed 7; wounded 7 officers, 31 men; missing 2.
Total 47.

*Left:*

Mustered in Sept. 14, 1861.
Mustered out July 17, 1865.
Engaged in 38 Battles.
Casualties — Killed 8 officers, 125 men; wounded 38 officers, 583 men. Died 2 officers, 149 men. Total 905.

ELEVENTH NEW JERSEY INFANTRY.

The handsome design for the monument to this regiment is by The Smith Granite Company of Boston, Mass., and represents an open book, mounted on a pedestal of rock work. It stands about ten feet in height and is finely proportioned. It stands near the Smith or Essex house on the Emmetsburg road, and shows the most advanced position held by the regiment during its fierce struggle with superior numbers of the enemy. The following are the inscriptions:

11th New Jersey Vols.
Col. Robert McAllister.
1st Brig. 2d Div. 3d Corps.
July 2, 1863.
Mustered in August 18, 1862.
Mustered out July 1865.
Engaged in 29 Battles.
Erected by the State of New Jersey, 1888.

This stone marks the spot reached by the right of the regiment, the left extending toward the southeast. The position was held under a severe fire which killed or disabled nearly three-fifths of the regiment, including every officer present above the rank of lieutenant.

Number engaged 275. Killed 31, wounded 109, missing 13. Total 153. Of the missing six are supposed to have been killed.

BATTERY "A" FIRST NEW JERSEY ARTILLERY.

The monument for this battery is of symmetrical proportions and beautiful in design. Its general dimensions are as follows: Base five feet square and total height ten feet. It is hexagonal in design and surmounted by a counterfeit cannon ball which adds to the attractiveness of its appearance, and the whole is made of granite from the quarries at Barre, Vt. The design and workmanship are by George Brown & Co., of Newark, N. J. The following inscriptions are cut in square sunken letters:

*Front:*

Battery A 1. N. J. Art., from its position in reserve S. W. of Powers' Hill, galloped into action at 3 P. M. July 3, 1863. Fired 120 rounds shrapnel at Pickett's column, and 80 shell at a battery in left front.

Erected by the State of New Jersey, 1888.

*South side:*

Served August 12, 1861, to June 22, 1865. Engaged in 30 battles.

*North side:*

Losses—Killed 2, wounded 7. Position in action 45 yards E. of this stone.

CLARK'S BATTERY "B" FIRST NEW JERSEY ARTILLERY.

This monument is a large massive structure, measuring at bottom six feet three inches long and five feet three inches wide. Its height is twelve feet six inches and weighs thirteen tons. It consists of but four pieces and is constructed throughout of the best dark Quincy granite. The die or lettered piece of monument measures four feet long, three feet wide and is five feet eight inches high. On each end is carved a representation of a cannon and two rammers which are faithful reproductions of the guns actually used by this battery at Gettysburg. The finial or cap has a band of thirteen stars and terminates with an enlarged representation of a cannon ball which is cut solid on the stone, and is highly polished. The style of the monument is pleasing and eminently suitable for the brave battery for whose services it is erected by a grateful State. The polished ball crowning the monument is especially suitable and is well calculated to show the beauty of the Quincy granite. The die piece contains the following inscriptions:

*Front :*

Clark's Battery.

Battery B, 1st New Jersey Artillery fought here from 2 until 7 o'clock on July 2, 1863, firing 300 rounds of ammunition. Losses — Killed 1 ; wounded 16 ; missing 3.

Erected by State of New Jersey, 1888.

*Rear :*

Mustered in September 3, 1861.

Mustered out June 16, 1865.

Engaged in 26 battles, including all the important actions on the Peninsula, Fredericksburg, Chancellorsville, Wilderness, Spottsylvania, Cold Harbor, Petersburg, Appomattox.

FIRST NEW JERSEY CAVALRY.

The position of this regiment near Rummel's farm, about three miles from the battle-field proper, is marked by a handsome stone. The monument is a massive structure consisting of six pieces, and is six feet square at bottom and fifteen feet high. It is surmounted by an elaborate emblem, carved in the best manner representing saddle, uniform, carbine, sabre, bugle, and in fact all the implements used by cavalry. This emblem is two feet four inches by two feet four by three feet four inches in height, and is a fine piece of artistic carving in Westerly granite, all the rest of the monument being of dark Quincy granite. The die piece on which the lettering is put is two feet nine inches by two feet nine, and six feet high. At the top is a band of raised polished face stars. The die is polished on all four sides. The cap is three feet five inches square by one foot ten inches, and on the front is the cavalry corps badge raised on a pediment the face of which is highly polished. The weight of this monument is about fourteen tons, and Messrs. Frederick & Field are the designers. The following are the inscriptions on the stone:

*North Front:*

First New Jersey Cavalry.
Maj. Myron H. Beaumont.
1st Brigade, 2d Cavalry Division.
July 3, 1863.
Erected by the State of New Jersey 1888.

*West Side:*

Organized in September, 1861, and served to the end of the War. Participated in 97 Engagements.
Lost—Killed in Action, 79; Died of Wounds, etc., 170; Died prisoners of war, 34; Missing (supposed dead), 12.

MONUMENT FIRST N. J. CAVALRY.

*East Side:*

Fought here July 3, 1863, both mounted and dismounted, holding this position several hours. Assisted in repelling the charges of the Enemy's Cavalry.

*South Side:*

OFFICERS KILLED IN BATTLE DURING THE WAR.

| | |
|---|---|
| Col. Hugh H. Janeway. | Capt. Moses H. Malesbury. |
| Lt.-Col. Virgil Broderick. | Lieut. Alexander Stewart. |
| Maj. John H. Shellmire. | " Edward E. Jemison. |
| " James H. Hart. | " John W. Bellis. |
| " John H. Lucas. | " Voorhees Dye. |
| Capt. Thomas R. Haines. | " Alanson Austin. |

## THE DEDICATION.

The formal dedication of the New Jersey monuments took place on Saturday, June 30th, under the direction of the Governor, Comptroller and Adjutant-General, in connection with the Gettysburg Commission of the State. A provisional regiment from the National Guard, commanded by Colonel Campbell of the First Regiment, survivors of New Jersey regiments present at the battle, and a large number of citizens and public men were present by invitation of the State. His Excellency Governor Robert S. Green was the orator of the occasion and five-minute addresses were made by representatives of the several regiments who participated in the battle.

# Biographical Sketches.

### MAJOR-GENERAL JOSEPH HOOKER.

Joseph Hooker was born in Hadley, Mass., November 13, 1814; graduated at West Point July 1, 1837; served on frontier and garrison duty till 1846, and 1846-48, in the war with Mexico on the staff of Generals Persifer Smith, Hamer and Butler; in 1847 appointed assistant adjutant-general; brevetted captain, major and lieutenant-colonel for gallantry at Monterey, the National Bridge, and Chepultepec. In February, 1853, he resigned from the army and engaged in farming in California, also as superintendent of military roads in Oregon. On the outbreak of the civil war (1861) he tendered his services to the government and was appointed (May 17, 1861,) brigadier-general of volunteers, serving in the defences of Washington and on the lower Potomac until March, 1862, when he was assigned to the command of a division of the Third Corps, Army of the Potomac; in the Peninsular campaign, 1862, was engaged in the siege of Yorktown, April-May; battle of Williamsburg, May 5; Fair Oaks (second day), Frazier's Farm and Malvern Hill. Promoted to be major-general of volunteers, to date from the battle of Williamsburg, continuing in command of a division and engaged at the battle of Manassas, August 29-30, and Chantilly, September 1; appointed to command the First Corps, September 6, 1862, he displayed great bravery at South Mountain and Antietam, being severely wounded at the latter battle and disabled until November when he returned to the field, having in the mean time (September

20) been appointed brigadier-general in the regular army, and on Burnside's succession to the command of the Army of the Potomac was assigned to command the centre grand division (Third and Fifth Corps) in the new organization of that army. In January, 1863, succeeded Burnside in command of the Army of the Potomac, and in May following fought the battle of Chancellorsville. At the time of the invasion of Pennsylvania, the Army of the Potomac had reached the vicinity of Frederick, Md., when, owing to the refusal of General Halleck to place the troops at Harper's Ferry at the disposal of Hooker, the latter requested to be (June 27), and was, relieved from the command of the army the next morning. For the skill and energy by which he first covered Washington and Baltimore from the meditated blow of the advancing enemy, General Hooker received the thanks of Congress. In September, 1863, he was assigned to the command of the Eleventh and Twelfth Corps, and accompanied them west where they were consolidated into the Twentieth Corps, Army of the Cumberland; was distinguished at the capture of Lookout Mountain, battle of Missionary Ridge (November 24-25), the pursuit of the Confederate army, and the action of Ringgold, Ga., November 27, 1863. In the invasion of Georgia by the army of General Sherman, Hooker led his corps in the almost constant fighting up to and including the siege of Atlanta, until July 30, 1864, when on a question of command he was relieved at his own request. He subsequently commanded the Northern Department, the Department of the East, and that of the Lakes; brevetted major-general United States Army for gallantry at Chattanooga, and October, 1868, retired upon full rank of major-general. General Hooker died October 31, 1879, at his home in Garden City, L. I.

## MAJOR-GENERAL GEORGE G. MEADE, U. S. A.

George Gordon Meade was born in Cadiz, Spain, December 31, 1815, during the consulship of his father, Richard W. Meade. On the return of the family to the United States, George was sent to the famous school for boys in Washington, D. C., then kept by the late Chief Justice Salmon P. Chase. In 1831 he entered the United States Military Academy at West Point, where he was graduated four years later, and commissioned a brevet second lieutenant of the Third United States Artillery. He received the full rank the same year, and took part in the Seminole Indian War in Florida. In 1836 he resigned his commission and engaged in civil engineering. In 1842 he returned to the artillery under appointment as second lieutenant of topographical engineers. During the Mexican War he served as engineer on the staffs of Generals Taylor and Scott, distinguishing himself in the battles of Palo-Alto, Resaca-de-la-Palma and Monterey, and receiving as an acknowledgement of his gallantry a brevet of first lieutenant. He was promoted to a full first lieutenancy in August, 1851, and to a captaincy of engineers in May, 1855.

Upon the first call of the National Government for volunteers in 1861, Meade was summoned to Washington, appointed a brigadier-general of volunteers, and assigned to the command of the Second Brigade of the Pennsylvania Reserve Corps. Soon after the Corps was attached to the Army of the Potomac, and was engaged in the advance on Richmond.

During the Peninsula campaign General Meade took an active part in the battles of Mechanicsville, Gaines' Mill and Glendale, being severely wounded in the latter. He speedily recovered, however, and in September, 1862, was assigned to the command of a division in the First

Army Corps. He again distinguished himself in the battles of South Mountain and Antietam, and when General Hooker was wounded in the latter engagement, General Meade was placed in command of the Corps, sustaining a slight wound and having two horses killed beneath him. For his services in this emergency he was promoted to be major-general of volunteers in November, 1862. On General Hooker's recovery, General Meade returned to the command of his division, and with it led the attack, in December, 1862, at Fredericksburg. During the same month he was placed in command of the Fifth Corps, and with it proceeded to Chancellorsville, where it covered the retreat of the army.

On June 28, 1863, the Army of the Potomac being at Frederick, Md., President Lincoln appointed General Meade commander-in-chief, as successor to General Hooker, who had resigned. About the middle of July General Meade recrossed into Virginia, where he had several encounters with the enemy in October and November, 1863. He was second in command during the operations against Richmond in 1864, his immediate army fighting the battles of the Wilderness, Spottsylvania Court House and Cold Harbor, and being engaged in the siege of Petersburg. Beyond the honors conferred upon him, already mentioned, he was promoted to the rank of major of engineers in the Regular Army June 18, 1862; advanced, by the several grades of lieutenant-colonel and colonel, to the brigadier-generalship in the Regular Army July 3, 1863; received the thanks of Congress during the session of 1863–64; and was promoted to the rank of major-general in the Regular Army, to date from August 18, 1864, on Febuary 1, 1865. When, on July 1, 1865, the army was reorganized on a peace basis, he was assigned to the command of the Military Division of the Atlantic, with headquarters at Philadelphia, where he resided in a dwelling presented his wife by the citizens until his death on November 6, 1872.

## MAJOR-GENERAL HUGH JUDSON KILPATRICK.

Hugh Judson Kilpatrick, major-general United States Volunteers, was born near Deckertown, N. J., January 14, 1836. He entered the United States Military Academy at West Point on June 20, 1856, and, with a number of advanced students, was graduated in April, 1861, by special permission of the War Department on the proffered pledge that they would, as young officers, complete their education on the field of battle. The day he was graduated he was also married and mustered into the military service. He was appointed a second lieutenant of artillery on May 6, and commissioned captain in the Fifth Regiment of New York Volunteers, better known as Duryea's Zouaves, three days later. This regiment was then encamped at Fortress Monroe. During a battle on June 10 he was wounded in the right thigh with a grape shot.

Kilpatrick resumed the field in September following, and was commissioned lieutenant-colonel of the Second Regiment of New York Cavalry Volunteers, the "Harris Light Cavalry," of which he became colonel in December, 1862, and was also promoted to be first lieutenant in the Regular Army. In addition to these promotions he was appointed a member of the board for examining the cavalry officers of the volunteer service, and inspector-general of General McDowell's division. In July and August he made a series of raids for the purpose of breaking up the Confederate General Jackson's communication with Richmond, striking the Virginia Central Railroad at Beaver Dam, Frederick Hall and Hanover Junction, inflicting all the damage possible. He participated in the Rappahannock campaign, in the second battle of Bull Run and many minor actions in the Maryland campaign, and in General Stoneman's raid to the rear of General Lee's army, commanded a brigade of cavalry. His boldness as a cavalry officer was a marvel alike to friend and foe. He was promoted to be a brigadier-general of volunteers in June, 1863, and at the memorable battle of Gettysburg he commanded both a brigade and a division.

In April, 1864, at General Sherman's request, Kilpatrick was ordered to duty with that army in the West, and sustained a severe wound in the battle of Resaca in the following month. He was forced by his suffering to return to the North; but as soon as he heard of General Sherman's intentions toward Atlanta, he hastened to join his old chief. During the March to the Sea and the subsequent passage through the Carolinas, he commanded the cavalry and was actively engaged, although obliged to avail himself of the use of a carriage that his officers fitted up for him.

In June, 1865, he was promoted to be a major general of volunteers; in the following December he resigned his commission in the Regular Army, and in January, 1866, his commission in the volunteer army. These resignations were prompted by his appointment, in November, 1865, as United States Minister to Chili, an office he held till 1868, when he was recalled. While residing at Santiago, the Chilian capital, he was married to the niece of the Roman Catholic Archbishop, who subsequently accompanied him to his Deckertown home. In the Spring of 1881, he was re-appointed Minister to Chili, and died at his post on December 6 of that year. His remains were brought to the United States, reaching New York on October 13, 1887, and, after lying in state in the Governor's Room of the City Hall, were taken to West Point and buried in the military cemetery on the 18th, with the honors due his courage, his skill and his rank.

## MAJOR-GENERAL ALFRED T. A. TORBERT.

Alfred T. A. Torbert, major-general United States Volunteers, was a native of Delaware, born in July, 1833. He was graduated at the United States Military Academy at West Point in 1855; commissioned a brevet second lieutenant, and assigned to the Fifth United States Infantry. On reporting for duty he was first engaged in conducting recruits to Fort McIntosh, Texas ; then in scouting against the Lipan Indians in the hostilities against the Seminoles in Florida ; again on frontier duty with the Utah expedition ; and in 1860 in the march to New Mexico. At the outbreak of the civil war, Lieutenant Torbert was sent to New Jersey, where he was employed in mustering volunteers into the service from April till September, 1861. In the latter month he was appointed Colonel of the First New Jersey Volunteers, and, with his regiment, participated in the Peninsula campaign in Virginia, being engaged in the siege of Yorktown and the actions at West Point, Gaines' Mills, and Charles City Cross Roads.

On August 28, 1862, he was given command of a brigade in the Sixth Army Corps, and fought in the second battle of Bull Run, at South Mountain, where he was wounded, and at Antietam. His distinguished services in these actions gained for him promotion to the rank of brigadier-general of volunteers, his commission bearing the date of November 29, 1862. In June, 1863, he returned from his sick leave, was assigned to duty with his old corps, and took part in its operations during the winter of 1863-64. During the Richmond campaign he won high encomiums by his dashing and discreet conduct as a cavalry officer, being in command of the cavalry through General Sheridan's notable raid. He assumed command of the First Division on General Sheridan's return, and was in many actions in the summer of 1864, Hawes' Shop and Cold Harbor being among them. As chief of cavalry of the Middle Military Division, he was an active participant in all the operations in the Shenandoah Valley, and was subsequently in command of the Army of the Shenandoah and of various districts in Virginia, till January 15, 1866, when he was mustered out of the volunteer service. He was successively brevetted major, lieutenant-colonel, colonel, and brigadier-general, for his gallantry at Hawes' Shop, Winchester, and Cedar Creek, and major-general for gallant and meritorious services in the field during the war.

On being mustered out of the service he retired to his home in Milford, Del., but had been scarcely three years in private life when President Grant appointed him United States Minister to the Central American States. Two years later he was sent to Havana as consul-general, and thence to Paris in the same capacity. He entered upon his duties in the French capital in the latter part of 1873, and held the office till May, 1878. On August 25, 1880, General Torbert sailed from New York city in the Havana steamship "City of Vera Cruz," and was drowned in the foundering of that vessel off the Florida coast on Sunday morning following (29th). His body was washed ashore, and recovered and reverently buried by some of the saved seamen who were attracted by his handsome appearance and stalwart figure. It was subsequently disinterred and and brought north under a military escort detailed by the Secretary of War.

## COLONEL SAMUEL L. BUCK.

Colonel Samuel L. Buck, who commanded the Second Regiment New Jersey Volunteers at Gettysburg, was born of revolutionary stock at Bethel, Vt., June 8, 1820. In infancy he was taken to Montreal, Province of Quebec, and at the breaking out of the first Canadian rebellion enlisted in the Montreal Rifle Battalion which was detailed for garrison duty during the absence of the regular troops. A short time after this he was living in the city of New York, and in the year 1838 enlisted in the Sixth Regiment National Guard of New York. From there Colonel Buck removed to Newark, N. J., and his love of military life caused him in 1850 to join the " Union Blues," which was afterward incorporated with the Newark City Battalion, New Jersey State Militia, and was commissioned first lieutenant and adjutant.

In response to the call for seventy-five thousand three months' men about sixty or seventy men of the City Battalion organized at once and elected Adjutant Buck captain. Active measures were taken to organize a regiment, which was speedily effected, and at the election for field officers Captain Buck was elected major. Mustered in the United States service at Trenton as the Second Regiment New Jersey Volunteers, it was ordered to Washington, D. C. After a week or more delay in Washington the regiment was ordered to report to General Runyon at Alexandria, Va. Shortly after the first Bull Run battle the regiment was brigaded with the First and Third regiments under General Kearny as the First New Jersey Brigade. On the 31st of December, 1861, Colonel McLean resigned and Major Buck was promoted lieutenant-colonel. At the battle of Gaines' Mills (or Farms) Colonel Tucker was killed and Major Ryerson wounded and captured. From that time up to and after the battle of Antietam Lieutenant-Colonel Buck was the only field officer in the regiment. At New Baltimore, Md., July 1, 1862, he received his commission as colonel. At the battle of Salem Heights, while in command of the brigade, Colonel Buck had his shoulder dislocated by his horse falling under him, and being ordered to Washington for medical treatment was placed on court-martial duty, where the second invasion of Maryland found him. By special order of the Secretary of War Colonel Buck was granted leave to join his regiment, which he did and continued with it to the close of the campaign, when he returned to Washington for medical treatment. During the Wilderness campaign under General Grant until the regiment reached White House Colonel Buck commanded the regiment. As the three years for which it enlisted had expired some time previous to this the regiment was ordered home for muster out, and on July 21, 1864, Colonel Buck received his honorable discharge.

## COLONEL HENRY W. BROWN.

Colonel Henry W. Brown of the Third Regiment, is a native of Boston, Mass., and at the beginning of the Civil War, resided in Philadelphia. He was engaged in recruiting a company in that city and was invited to take charge of a full company in Woodbury, N. J., which he accepted, turning over his Philadelphia men to H. G. Sickell, who was at that time organizing a company in Philadelphia. On the 29th day of April he received his commission as captain of Company A, Third New Jersey Regiment and was mustered in May 22, 1861. On the 31st of the same month he was promoted lieutenant-colonel of the regiment and on May 15, 1862, was promoted colonel to succeed Colonel Taylor, who had been promoted brigadier-general. Colonel Brown served faithfully with his regiment and performed distinguished and gallant services. At Salem Heights, Va., on May 3, 1863, he was wounded, while commanding the brigade, and again at Spottsylvania, Va., on May 12, 1864, he was severely injured by a shot from the enemy. Colonel Brown remained in the service until the close of the war and was mustered out at Trenton, June 23, 1864.

## LIEUTENANT-COLONEL CHARLES EWING.

Lieutenant-Colonel Charles Ewing was born in the city of Trenton, N. J., Sunday, June 6, 1841. He was the son of Francis A. Ewing, M. D., and grandson of the Chief Justice of New Jersey whose name he bore. In August, 1859, he sailed as master's mate in the United States Steamer Sumter for the African Coast, and on that station was transferred to the United States Frigate San Jacinto. He was sent home (to Norfolk, Va.) as one of the officers in charge of a slaver captured by the latter vessel, arriving in January, 1861, just before the outbreak of the rebellion. In April of that year he went out as ensign of Company A, Third Regiment, under the President's call for three months' troops, being then not quite twenty years of age. On their return in July he went to recruiting for the Sixth Regiment New Jersey Volunteers, three years' troops, and on September 9, 1861, was commissioned captain of Company B. He served with this regiment until January 8, 1863, when he was promoted major and transferred to the Fourth Regiment New Jersey Volunteers. He was in command of this regiment during the Gettysburg campaign and on September 11, 1863, was commissioned lieutenant-colonel. Colonel Ewing was constantly in service in the field, and was several times wounded, once at Second Bull Run, again at Fredericksburg Heights, and again while on picket duty. At the expiration of the term of service of the regiment, they reënlisted for the war and Colonel Ewing went with them. At Spottsylvania Court House he received a serious and nearly fatal wound, being shot through the body, which kept him an invalid for a long time and finally caused his honorable discharge. He regained ordinary health, but never fully recovered from the effects of his wound. Colonel Ewing died in Trenton March 14, 1872, in the thirty-first year of his age.

## BREVET MAJOR-GENERAL WILLIAM J. SEWELL.

In the list of casualties at Gettysburg, every field officer of the five New Jersey regiments engaged on the second of July—except in the case of Lieutenant-Colonel Gilkyson of the Sixth Regiment—was wounded, some of them mortally. On this roll of honor appears the name of Colonel William J. Sewell, of the Fifth New Jersey. Colonel Sewell was born in Ireland in 1835, and coming to the United States at an early age, developed a strong love for his adopted country as he advanced in years. When the call for troops to serve for three years was issued, Sewell recruited a company for the Fifth New Jersey Volunteers, and on the 28th of August, 1861, received his commission as Captain of Company C. On the 7th of July, 1862, he was promoted to be lieutenant-colonel of the regiment, and on the recalling of Colonel Starr, to his post in the regular army, Sewell was on October 21, 1862, commissioned Colonel of the Fifth Regiment. In all the trying emergencies of army life Sewell was never found wanting. Always watchful for the interests of his men he exacted from them a faithful performance of duty, and so well did each come to know the other that the regiment was noted for its steadiness and bravery under the most trying circumstances. This faculty, possessed by few men, exhibited itself most conspicuously at the battle of Chancellorsville, when Sewell led the whole brigade into a charge, and accomplished a signal and valuable service. The brigade, under General Mott, had heroically defended its position on the Plank road against superior numbers of the enemy. General Mott was wounded, and Colonel Sewell assumed command. The men were exhausted from their severe labors, and had expended almost all their ammunition. As no relief came to them they withdrew. The enemy at this time grew bold in the prospect of victory, and taking possession of some works which had been thrown up for the protection of artillery, they defiantly opened fire upon the Federal lines. Colonel Sewell seeing the importance of retaking the position gallantly led the brigade to the charge and drove the rebels from the works. But that fatality which seemed to accompany every daring movement at Chancellorsville, was experienced by Sewell—the brigade was not supported and the brave Jerseymen were compelled to fall back exposed to a terrible fire and suffering great loss.

Colonel Sewell's wounds at Gettysburg were severe, and prevented his doing active service in the field for some time. He recovered, however, but during the Wilderness campaign he was prostrated by exposure. On the second of July, 1864, he resigned owing to ill-health, but in September following he accepted the colonelcy of the Thirty-eighth Regiment and remained with it until its term of service expired—October, 1864. He was brevetted brigadier-general for gallantry and distinguished services at Chancellorsville, and major-general of United States Volunteers, for meritorious services during the war.

At the time of the railroad strikes in 1877 General Sewell was appointed by Governor Parker provisional commander of the State forces at Phillipsburg, and to his well-known reputation for military ability and personal bravery, is largely due the subsidence of the trouble.

In public affairs General Sewell has occupied a prominent place. He represented Camden county in the State Senate for three successive terms, and in 1880 was president of that body. He was elected to the United States Senate in 1881, succeeding ex-Governor Theodore F. Randolph, and served until March 4, 1887, when his term expired.

### BRIGADIER-GENERAL GEORGE C. BURLING.

General George C. Burling, the commander of the Second New Jersey Brigade, which did such heroic service on the second day of July at Gettysburg, was born on the 17th day of February, 1834, in Burlington county, New Jersey, a few miles from the city of Burlington. He was reared on his father's farm and educated at a private school conducted by Mr. Aaron at Norristown, Montgomery county, Pa. He entered into business life in Burlington at an early age, and at the breaking out of the war was engaged in the retail coal business. He was a public-spirited young man and identified himself with various measures in which his neighbors and friends were interested, being at this time captain of the "Marion Rifles" of Burlington—Company K, Fourth New Jersey Militia. He promptly offered his services with his company to Governor Olden, and was accepted and mustered in for three months' service on the 27th of April, 1861. On their return home and muster out in July, 1861, Captain Burling immediately recruited his original command, and with it, a company of over one hundred men, was mustered in for three years' service on September 9, 1861, and was designated as Company F, Sixth Regiment New Jersey

Volunteers. On March 19, 1862, he was promoted major and on May 7, 1862, received his commission as lieutenant-colonel. On the promotion of Colonel Mott to brigadier-general of United States Volunteers, Burling was promoted colonel of the Sixth Regiment, and, as the senior officer, commanded the brigade at Gettysburg, a position he held until October of the same year, when ill-health caused him to relinquish it, and compelled him to resign on March 4, 1864. He was brevetted brigadier-general on March 13, 1865.

On the 15th of October, 1862, while colonel commanding the Sixth New Jersey Volunteers, Colonel Burling married Miss J. T. Reckless of Abingdon township, Montgomery county, Pa. (formerly of Philadelphia), and their wedding tour extended to Colonel Burling's headquarters at Alexandria, Va., where the bride remained until the command was ordered away. After the close of the war, with his health greatly broken he went with his family to reside on a farm near Byberry (Twenty-third ward of Philadelphia). Subsequently he became connected with the Pennsylvania Railroad, at their main office, Fourth street below Walnut, Philadelphia. General Burling died at his residence 1842 North Eighteenth street, Philadelphia, on December 24, 1885, from a pulmonary cancer, the result of a contused wound received at the battle of Chancellorsville. He had been wounded twice previous to this—at Williamsburg, May 5, 1863, and at Second Bull Run, August 29-30.

## COLONEL LOUIS R. FRANCINE.

Colonel Louis R. Francine, of the Seventh Regiment New Jersey Volunteers, was born, one account says, at Dillerville, Lancaster county, Pennsylvania, March 26, 1838. Another account says he was born in Philadelphia in 1839. He was by profession a civil engineer, graduated from the Polytechnic College at Philadelphia in 1855, then went to Europe in 1856 and was graduated from the L'Ecole Polytechnique at Paris. At the outbreak of hostilities Francine was about entering upon the practice of his profession, but when the call for three year troops was issued he recruited Company A of the Seventh Regiment and was commissioned its captain on September 18, 1861. He was senior captain and acted as field officer during the greater part of the Peninsula campaign. July 8, 1862, he was promoted lieutenant-colonel, and on December 9th of the same year was commissioned colonel, succeeding Colonel Revere who had been promoted brigadier-general United States Volunteers. Colonel Francine was a brave and fearless officer and was engaged in rallying his men when he received the wound at Gettysburg from the effects of which he died on July 16, 1863. He was buried from one of the churches in Philadelphia with military honors, Major-General A. A. Pleasonton commanding the funeral escort. His remains are interred at Laurel Hill Cemetery. For his gallant services at Gettysburg Colonel Francine was brevetted brigadier-general of volunteers on July 2, 1863.

## BREVET MAJOR-GENERAL JOHN RAMSEY.

General John Ramsey, who commanded the Eighth Regiment New Jersey Volunteers at Gettysburg and was wounded there, was one of the young soldiers of the army, and became noted for his daring and energy. He was born in the city of New York October 7, 1838, and was in his twenty-third year when hostilities began. On the 17th of April, 1861, he enlisted in Company G, Second Regiment New Jersey Volunteers for three months, as a private, and was subsequently elected first-lieutenant by his company, being mustered in April 25th. On the election of Captain H. M. Baker to the colonelcy Ramsey was made captain on May 1, 1861. He was mustered out with his regiment at the expiration of its term of service, July 31, 1861. The command participated in no battles and Ramsey, who had little relish for that sort of soldiering, reëntered the service on August 17, 1861, as captain of Company B, Fifth Regiment New Jersey Volunteers, and remained in the army until the war was fought out, being mustered out July 17, 1865. On the 7th of May, 1862, he was promoted major of the Fifth for distinguished gallantry at the battle of Williamsburg, and on October 21, 1862, was commissioned lieutenant-colonel of his regiment. In April, 1863, he was promoted Colonel of the Eighth Regiment.

Colonel Ramsey took an active part in all the campaigns of the Army of the Potomac, from the Peninsula, under McClellan, to the surrender of Lee at Appomattox on April 9, 1865—on which day his command formed part of the advance line. The only important battle in which he was not a participant was Antietam, caused by the detention of the Third Corps in the vicinity of Washington after the defeat of Pope at the second battle of Bull Run This corps had been sent from Harrison's Landing to join Pope at Warrenton with all possible despatch, and reached there only to be ordered back. On the way back to Centreville they engaged the enemy in numerous skirmishes, and receiving orders to proceed to the front again encountered Jackson at Bristoe, whom they compelled to retire, and reached Pope a day or two before the second battle of Bull Run, in which Ramsey's command took part, as also in the battle of Chantilly. The Third Corps then proceeded to Alexandria, and the Second New Jersey Brigade was ordered to move in light marching order. To make all possible speed in reaching their destination, their effects were put on board the cars, and these being burned, all was lost. The men were used up, many of them without shoes, and other articles of clothing, and were in no condition for the Maryland campaign, which they were thus prevented participating in. For distinguished services in the campaign before Richmond, Colonel Ramsey was brevetted brigadier-general and by a special order of President Lincoln, he was assigned to duty with that rank. On June 5, 1864, General Ramsey was assigned to the command of the Second Brigade, Second Division, Second Army Corps, known as the Corcoran Legion, and was one of the commands that was ordered to attack Petersburg on the night of June 16, 1864, in which engagement General Ramsey was wounded. When able for duty he was given the command of the First Brigade, First Division, Second Army Corps, and remained with it until he assumed command of the First Division, Second Army Corps. General Ramsey was five times wounded—at Second Bull Run, Chancellorsville, Wilderness, Gettysburg and Petersburg. On March 13, 1865, he was brevetted major-general of United States Volunteers for gallant and meritorious services during the war.

## MAJOR-GENERAL ROBERT McALLISTER.

The subject of this sketch was born in Juniata county, Pennsylvania, on June 1, 1813, in which State he spent the early years of his life, but his war record belongs to New Jersey, with whose troops he served during the continuance of the conflict. He was one of the very first to take up arms in defence of the Union, and he was present in the field when General Lee surrendered at Appomattox. When the First Regiment, three years' volunteers, was being recruited, McAllister was, on May 21, 1861, commissioned its lieutenant-colonel, and with it proceeded to the Capital. He was a quiet, steady, fearless man, of even temperament and thoroughly self-possessed. Lieutenant-Colonel McAllister remained with the First New Jersey Regiment until June 30, 1862, when he was commissioned colonel of the Eleventh New Jersey Regiment, then being recruited. This regiment was mustered into the United States service August 18, 1862, and was assigned to the First Brigade, Second Division, Third Army Corps. At Fredericksburg and Chancellorsville Colonel McAllister displayed marked heroism. At Gettysburg he was wounded during the second day's fighting in the left leg with a minié ball, and in the right foot with a fragment of shell. For three months he was unable to take the field, but with this exception he served continuously through the war, from the first battle of Bull Run to the surrender of Lee at Appomattox. Colonel McAllister was brevetted brigadier-general for his glorious behavior at the first "Bull Pen," as the tremendous fight on Boydton Plank road, October 27, 1864, was styled, and major-general for meritorious conduct throughout the war. Since the war he has been engaged as general manager of the Ironton Railroad Company, in mining and shipping ore to the furnaces in Lehigh Valley.

## LIEUTENANT-COLONEL JOHN SCHOONOVER.

John Schoonover was born at Bushkill, Pa., August 12, 1839. He received his education from the common schools of his native place, and the instructions of the Rev. J. K. Davis, of Smithville, Pa. At the age of sixteen he began the work of teaching and preparation for college. The outbreak of the rebellion found him thus employed at Oxford, Warren county, N. J. Soon after the proclamation of President Lincoln calling for seventy-five thousand men to serve for three months, Schoonover joined a company raised by Captain Campbell at Belvidere. The company reported at Trenton, but so quickly had the State's quota been filled—the four regiments being completed in seven days—that they reached the Capital too late for acceptance. As the company was about to return to Belvidere, Captain Campbell stepped to the front and asked all who were willing to go with him for three years to do likewise; but seven responded—Schoonover being one of the seven—the number of three year patriots being so small all returned to their homes. But Schoonover's patriotism was not of the kind that could rest content with the acquisition of such laurels as these, and we soon find him again at Trenton as a private in Company D (Captain Valentine Mutchler) First New Jersey Regiment for three years. This regiment left the State June 28, 1861. The following September Schoonover was made corporal. The ensuing winter, Colonel Torbert, then commanding the First Regiment, issued an order directing each captain to select a sergeant to prepare for examination, the one standing the highest to receive a commission as second-lieutenant of Company D. No sergeant of D being willing to stand the trial, the subject of this sketch was selected to represent that company. Four only appeared for examination, the successful one being Commissary Sergeant S. G. Blythe. Schoonover, standing second, was promoted commissary sergeant, dating from March 24, 1862. He served in that position until August 2, 1862, when he received a commission as adjutant of the Eleventh New Jersey Volunteers, then organizing at Trenton. The Eleventh left the State on August 25, 1862, and was first engaged in Burnside's attack upon Fredericksburg. This first engagement proved to the men of the Eleventh that their adjutant was one on whom they could depend. During the desperate fighting of the regiment in the woods at Chancellorsville on May 3 and 4, 1862, Adjutant Schoonover was conspicuous for his bravery and coolness, and received honorable mention therefor. On the second of July at Gettysburg he received two wounds and six bullet holes through his clothing, and on the third his horse was shot under him. He again received slight wounds at Spottsylvania and at Barker's Mills, but he never thought his wounds sufficiently severe to necessitate going to the rear. He was commissioned lieutenant-colonel in 1863 and brevetted colonel March 13, 1865, for conspicuous gallantry.

## MAJOR JOHN T. HILL.

Major John T. Hill was born in New Brunswick, N. J., July, 1836, and he was therefore twenty-five years of age when the war broke out, at which time he was a clerk in the Park Bank of New York City. He had no previous military training and took but little interest in military affairs, but his patriotism was of the most practical sort. When hostilities opened he joined a militia company in his native city, passing through all the grades from a private in the ranks to captain of the company. When recruiting began for the Eleventh New Jersey Volunteers Major Charles Herbert, private secretary for Governor Olden, sought to obtain for Captain Hill the adjutancy, but recruiting for the command was so slow that the officers became very much discouraged. Company "I" had enrolled about thirty men, and it seemed impossible to rise beyond that number. Major Herbert sent word to Captain Hill that if he would take the company as it was and fill it up to the required number he should have the captaincy. Notwithstanding the discouragements which had operated against enlistments Captain Hill consented, resigning his position in the bank, and at once began the work of recruiting, in a comparatively short time securing the enrollment of one hundred and three names. He was at once commissioned and became second in order of seniority, Captain Martin having been mustered in one week before. The Eleventh Regiment, under Colonel McAllister, went to Washington in August, 1862, and just before the battle of Fredericksburg was assigned to the Third Army Corps, taking part in that desperate engagement. The following April Captain Hill received a commission as major of the Twelfth New Jersey Infantry, and joined that command in the latter part of the same month, a short time before the beginning of the Chancellorsville campaign. The Twelfth Regiment was in the Second Brigade, Third Division, Second Army Corps, and was closely engaged with the enemy. After the rout of the Eleventh Corps, Colonel Willets being badly wounded in the early part of the fight, the command devolved upon Major Hill, owing to the absence of the lieutenant-colonel, who was sick. The Twelfth sustained severe losses in this engagement, and did heroic work under the command of Major Hill. At Gettysburg the regiment was also under his command, and its splendid achievements on that battle-field are fully recorded in the preceding pages. After the battle Major Hill remained in command until the return of Lieutenant-Colonel Davis the latter part of the Summer of 1863, and was soon after stricken down with inflammatory rheumatism, which prostrated him for two years. He was discharged from the hospital at Annapolis in 1864, much against his will, but the board of army surgeons exercised the arbitrary power conferred upon them and compelled him to take an involuntary, though honorable discharge. Major Hill's military record throughout was that of a brave and faithful officer, a trusted and honored commander, and his enforced withdrawal from service was regretted by all his comrades in arms. He still resides in the city of New Brunswick, and is President of the Ninth National Bank, New York City.

## COLONEL WILLIAM E. POTTER.

William Elmer Potter, the youngest son of James Boyd and Jane Barron Potter, was born June 13, 1840, in Bridgeton, Cumberland county, New Jersey. His grandfather, Colonel David Potter, was a soldier of the Revolution, and saw considerable service. He was first colonel of the second battalion of Cumberland, and, as such, was in command of his regiment forming a part of the brigade of Brigadier-General Hugh Mercer, at Perth Amboy in the Autumn of 1776. He was elected brigadier-general by the Legislature of New Jersey, February 21, 1777, but declined the appointment. He again entered active service as colonel of a battalion of State troops. On the twentieth of September, 1777, by order of Governor Livingston, he was detached in command of the effective troops of the brigade of Brigadier-General Silas Newcomb to reinforce the main army under General Washington, then retreating after the disastrous battle of the Brandywine. He crossed the Delaware with his command, and in some one of the skirmishes preliminary to the battle of Germantown, or in that battle itself, it is not now known which, he was taken prisoner by the enemy. He was confined for a long time upon the prison hulks in Long Island Sound, and was afterward released upon parole, and was not exchanged, at least as late as 1781. He was afterward marshal of the Admiralty Court of New Jersey, sheriff of the County of Cumberland, and one of the commissioners to ratify the Constitution of the United States.

The subject of this sketch having determined upon the

law as a profession, entered the office of Honorable John T. Nixon, as a student, in October, 1857. He remained until September, 1859, and the same month became a student at the law school of Harvard University. From this school he graduated in January, 1861, with the degree of LL. B., and in September of the same year entered the junior class of Princeton College. Under the spur of patriotic ardor he abandoned his collegiate studies, and in July of the following year enlisted in Company K, Twelfth Regiment New Jersey Volunteers. He was commissioned second lieutenant of the same company August 14, 1862, and mustered into the service of the United States as such September 4, 1862. He was promoted to a first lieutenancy of the same company and regiment August 6, 1863, and to the captaincy of Company G February 4, 1864. Captain Potter became brevet-major United States Volunteers for meritorious services, May 1, 1865, by promotion of the President of the United States, and was, in 1866, commissioned aide-de-camp to Governor Marcus L. Ward, of New Jersey, with the rank of lieutenant-colonel, upon whose staff he served for three years.

While in the field with his regiment he was detailed as ordnance officer of the Third Division, Second Army Corps, and acted as such in the campaigns of Chancellorsville and Gettysburg, on the staff of Major-General William H. French, and with Brigadier-General Alexander Hays. He served in that capacity until October 1, 1863, and was then appointed judge-advocate of the division on the staff of General Hays, continuing thus until he rejoined his regiment and took command of his company. He was wounded at the battle of the Wilderness while in command of his company on the sixth of May, 1864, and reported again for duty at Cold Harbor, Va., June 4, of the same year. On the first of July, 1864, he was detailed as aide-de-camp to Colonel Thomas A. Smyth, commanding Third Brigade, Second Division of the Second Army Corps. On the first of August, 1864, he was made judge-advocate on the staff of Major-General John Gibbon, commanding the Second Division, Second Army Corps, and served thus until January 15, 1865, when he was detailed as aide to Major-General John Gibbon, commanding the Twenty-fourth Army Corps, Army of the James, and as acting judge-advocate of the corps. He remained on duty in the latter capacity until mustered out of service, June 4, 1865. During this period Colonel Potter was present in the following engagements: Chancellorsville, Gettysburg, Auburn, Bristoe Station, Blackburn's Ford, Locust Grove, campaign of Mine Run, Morton's Ford, Wilderness, Cold Harbor, the entire campaign of Petersburg, Deep Bottom (first and second engagements), Reams' Station, Hatcher's Run, Boydton Road, assault and capture of Petersburg, Rice's Station and Appomattox Court House. By an order from headquarters, Twenty-fourth Army Corps, in company with five other officers, he was detailed to deliver the colors, surrendered by General Lee's army, seventy-six in number, to Honorable Edward M. Stanton of the War Department, which ceremony occurred on May 1, 1865. He was the only New Jersey officer present on this occasion.

Colonel Potter, during his military career, displayed gallantry and judgment, which won for him the highest encomiums from his superior officers. Colonel Potter received from Princeton College his degree of A. B. in 1863 and of A. M. in 1866. He was admitted as an attorney at law in 1865, and as a counselor in 1869. Having begun practice in Bridgeton, he, in 1870, formed a co-partnership with J. Boyd Nixon, with whom he has since continued his professional labors, and attained a prominent position at the bar of New Jersey.

He was a delegate to the Republican National Convention at Chicago in 1868, as also to the convention held at Cincinnati in 1876, and an elector on the Garfield ticket in 1880. He was elected an honorary member of the Society of the Cincinnati of New Jersey, July 4, 1874, and president of the New Jersey Officers' Association for 1880. The colonel was, on the 27th of May, 1869, married to Alice, daughter of the late Alfred Eddy, D. D., of Niles, Mich. Their children are Alfred E., James Boyd, David, Alice, and Francis Delavan.

## BREVET BRIGADIER-GENERAL EZRA A. CARMAN.

Ezra A. Carman, colonel of the Thirteenth Regiment New Jersey Volunteers, entered the service in 1861, being commissioned on September 14th of that year lieutenant-colonel of the Seventh Regiment. He was wounded in the battle of Williamsburg, Va., May 5, 1862, and was commissioned colonel July 8, 1862. He organized the Thirteenth Regiment, which he commanded, and with it proceeded to Washington on August 31st. He was disabled at Antietam and Chancellorsville, and at Gettysburg was placed in command of a provisional brigade, which was sent to support Gregg's cavalry, on the evening of July 3d. At the close of the Gettysburg campaign three regiments of the brigade to which the Thirteenth belonged were sent to New York to aid in quelling the riots which had been in progress there and Colonel Carman commanded the brigade then composed of the Thirteenth New Jersey, One Hundred and Seventh and One Hundred and Fiftieth New York Regiments. When the Thirteenth Regiment, with the Twelfth Corps, went west, he was appointed president of a military commission which held its sessions in Tullahoma, Tenn. In the Atlanta campaign the Thirteenth

Regiment was frequently engaged with the enemy, notably at Resaca, Cassville, Pumpkin Vine Creek—sometimes called Dallas and also New Hope Church—Nancy's Creek, Buffalo Creek, Peach Tree Creek, Kulp's Farm, and several times in front of Atlanta, on each occasion winning golden opinions for its gallantry and bravery. On the March to the Sea, Colonel Carman commanded the brigade, and in front of Savannah held the extreme left of the army. The brigade was ordered to the South Carolina shore, for the purpose of closing up Hardee's only avenue of escape, but that wily officer, afraid of a movement of that kind, as he had noted the crossing of the brigade to Argyle Island in the middle of the Savannah river, evacuated the city, which was entered by part of the Second Division of the Twentieth Corps, who captured a guard detail of the enemy who were unable to get away. At Savannah Colonel Carman was ordered to Nashville on special duty. He was brevetted brigadier-general of volunteers for gallant and meritorious services during the war to date from March 13, 1865.

## BREVET BRIGADIER-GENERAL FREDERICK H. HARRIS.

General Frederick Halsey Harris, of the Thirteenth Regiment. New Jersey Volunteers, was born in the city of Newark, N. J., March 7, 1830. He is descended on the maternal side from the Baldwin and Gould families, who settled in Newark over two hundred years ago. His grandfather, Robert Baldwin, was born in Orange, N. J., and was engaged in the war of 1812, on the New Jersey coast. His mother was a grand-daughter of General William Gould of Caldwell. His father's ancestors were originally of Welsh origin and the date of their settlement in this country is forgotten. Moses Harris, the grandfather of General Harris was born in Morrisania, New York, and in 1805 moved to Newark, N. J., when the father of the general was an infant. He was engaged for many years in business near the corner of Market and Broad streets in Newark as a merchant tailor. His father's mother was a Halsey and came originally from Elizabeth, N. J. William H. Harris, his father, was an architect and builder for many years in Newark, where he learned his trade.

The subject of this sketch attended private school in Newark when a boy, being one of the attendants at the Newark Academy—where the postoffice building now stands—afterward attending the select school of Reverend William R. Weeks, D. D., on Washington street. In the Fall of 1844 he was sent to the Bloomfield Academy, then under the management of Messrs. Holt & Rindler, where he remained until the Fall of 1847. A long-cherished desire to enter Princeton College, for which he was preparing, was interfered with by the serious illness of his father, who urgently requested him to leave school and temporarily abandon the proposed college course and the profession of medicine, which he then contemplated. This put an end to his schooling; until 1858 he remained in business with his father, when he began the reading of law in the office of Charles R. Waugh, Esq., afterward presiding judge of Essex county, and in the office of David A. Hayes, Esq., and was admitted to the bar in June, 1862.

The urgent call for troops after the Peninsula campaign led him to begin recruiting for the Thirteenth Regiment, both in the city of Newark and township of Bloomfield, and on the 25th of August, 1862, his company, E, was mustered into the United States service with the regiment, and on Sunday, August 31, proceeded to Washington. He participated in the Chancellorsville campaign and at the battle of Gettysburg, Company E was the color company of the regiment. During his military service Captain Harris was constantly with his regiment and on frequent important occasions commanding it, notably at the time of the advance of the army to Atlanta, where the Thirteenth under Colonel Harris was sent out to support the skirmish line then heavily engaged. Advancing his regiment to a knoll overlooking the enemy's breast works, he halted it there, and when the skirmish line was driven back, he deployed the right and left companies as skirmishers, until the skirmish line advanced and reëstablished itself. This was the nearest point to Atlanta ever reached by any command during the siege, and it was fortified by the Thirty-third Wisconsin Regiment, which relieved the Thirteenth. On the arrival of the regiment at Savannah Colonel Carman was sent to Nashville on special service, and during the whole of the Carolina campaign, Colonel Harris commanded it, participating in the battles of Averysboro and Bentonville. In the latter battle the Thirteenth Regiment particularly distinguished itself under his command, by repulsing the enemy, who were advancing in large numbers, and won the highest encomiums of praise from its superior officers. At Goldsboro, N. C., severe illness caused him to relinquish the command to Major John H. Arey, and he went to hospital at Newburn for medical treatment. He rejoined the regiment at Washington and participated in the grand review, and was mustered out with it on June 8, 1865. On July 17, 1864, he was promoted major and November 1, 1864, lieutenant-colonel of the regiment. For gallant and meritorious services during the campaign in Georgia and the Carolinas he was brevetted colonel, and subsequently brigadier-general of United States Volunteers for gallant services at Bentonville.

At the close of the war General Harris was married to Miss Elizabeth J. Torrey at Honesdale, Pa. He never held political office though frequently solicited to be a candidate for numerous important and lucrative positions. In the Summer of 1865 he resumed the practice of law, and in the Spring of 1866 became the treasurer and assistant secretary of the American Insurance Company of Newark. Being elected a director, he continued to perform the duties of secretary and treasurer until the death of President Gould in January, 1883, when he was unanimously elected to fill the position of president of that old and prominent company.

## JOHN JAMES HENRY LOVE, M. D.

Surgeon J. J. H. Love, of the Thirteenth Regiment New Jersey Volunteers, was born on April 3, 1833, in Harmony township, Warren county, New Jersey. His father was the Rev. Robert Love, a Presbyterian minister, and he was the great grandson of Lieutenant Thomas Love, aide-de-camp to General Samuel Cochrane of the Continental Army during the Revolutionary War. Doctor Love was educated at Lafayette College, Easton, Pa., and in the medical department of the University, city of New York, graduating from the former in 1851 and from the latter in 1855. When the Thirteenth Regiment was being recruited he was appointed surgeon on July 19, 1862. He had seen some service, however, previous to this. After the battle of Williamsburg and the beginning of the siege of Yorktown, May 5, 1862, he was sent out as a volunteer surgeon by Governor Olden to look after and care for the wounded of New Jersey regiments. On the 23d of March, 1863, Surgeon Love was assigned to duty as surgeon-in-chief

Third Brigade, First Division, Twelfth Army Corps, and served in that capacity during the battle of Gettysburg, doing most efficient service in the care of the wounded. On the first of August, 1863, when the Twelfth Corps had settled down for a rest at Kelly's Ford, Va., after the arduous campaign then just ended, he was appointed surgeon-in-chief First Division, Twelfth Corps, and became a member of General A. S. Williams' staff. In this capacity he served until the following January, after accompanying the corps to the west, when on the 28th of that month, 1864, he resigned his commission and was honorably discharged from the service. On his return home he at once entered upon the practice of his profession, in which he holds a high place.

## CAPTAIN AMBROSE M. MATTHEWS.

Captain Ambrose M. Matthews, of Orange, N. J., was engaged in business as a hat manufacturer when the war broke out, and leaving his business he enlisted on May 10, 1861, as a private in Company G, Second Regiment, New Jersey Volunteers. Twice he was offered a first lieutenancy in the Excelsior Brigade, but declined, and on the fifth of August, 1862, was discharged by Special Order No. 223, C. S. Headquarters Army of the Potomac, at Harrison's Landing, Va., at the request of the Governor of the State, to assist in raising a new regiment. On August 22, 1862, he was commissioned second lieutenant of Company E, Thirteenth Regiment, New Jersey Volunteers, and was mustered with it into the United States service three days later. At the battle of Antietam he was wounded, and his gallant services there were recognized in his promotion as first lieutenant of Company K. On November 1, 1862, he was promoted Captain of Company I. At Chancellorsville, where the Thirteenth Regiment did splendid and praiseworthy service, Captain Matthews was again wounded, and he received honorable mention in a regimental order, issued a few days after the return to their old camp, by Captain Beardsley, who was then in command. At Gettysburg his Company I, with that of Captain Ryerson's Company C, comprised the left flank of the regiment, they being formed almost perpendicular to the main line, creating an angle. This brought these two companies, then commanded by Captain Matthews (Captain Ryerson acting as major of the regiment) directly in front of the enemy, and when the charge by part of Steuart's rebel brigade was made upon this position, they aided in repulsing it. Captain Ryerson was wounded, and Captain Matthews had a narrow escape from death, a ball penetrating his hat just above the scalp line. At Resaca, Ga., he was again wounded. Captain Matthews accompanied his regiment through all its campaigns, the siege of Atlanta, the March to the Sea, the Carolina campaign, and in every emergency was noted for his courage and coolness. He was a strict disciplinarian and held his men to a rigid performance of duty, and always looked carefully after their interests. No man of the Thirteenth Regiment to-day is held in higher esteem by his comrades than the subject of this sketch.

## COLONEL JAMES N. DUFFY.

Colonel James N. Duffy, the President of the Gettysburg Battle-Field Commission of New Jersey, served during the battle on the staff of General H. G. Wright, commanding First Division, Sixth Army Corps, his rank being that of lieutenant-colonel and his duties those of acting assistant inspector-general. Colonel Duffy entered the service as captain of Company C, Second Regiment, New Jersey Volunteers, in May 27, 1861. On July 1, 1861, he was promoted major, and on September 14, 1862, was commissioned lieutenant-colonel of the Third New Jersey Regiment. September 29, 1863, after the battle of Gettysburg, he was commissioned colonel of the Fourth Regiment New Jersey Volunteers, but as the organization had become reduced below the minimum he could not be mustered. He served with the Third Regiment until the close of the war and was mustered out with it as lieutenant-colonel June 23, 1864. Colonel Duffy has been prominently identified with the manufacturing interests of Newark and for several years maintained a large factory for the manufacture of patent and enameled leather in that city. Subsequently he started a factory in Eldred, Pennsylvania. His appointment as a member of the State Commission for the erection of monuments at Gettysburg was received with great favor by all the survivors of the commands interested.

## BRIGADIER-GENERAL WILLIAM H. PENROSE.

William H. Penrose was born at Madison Barracks, N. Y., March 10, 1832, and his early life was spent in garrison, following his father, who was an officer in the Regular Army, to the various posts at which he was stationed. The outbreak of the Mexican war separated the father from his family, the latter finding a comfortable home with the Honorable Charles B. Penrose, of Carlisle, Pa., and William was then sent to Dickinson College. While here the death of his father occurred, and as the family were not in affluent circumstances, it became necessary for the young lad to seek employment, which he found in the machine shops at Reading, Pa. The old military instinct, imbibed when a mere boy, kept continually asserting itself within him, and the breaking out of the rebellion gave him the opportunity he sought to enter the service. Receiving an appointment in the Regular Army—the commission dating April 13, 1861—he was assigned, as second lieutenant, to the Third Infantry, but as he was then out West and his company in Texas he was ordered to report to the commanding officer of the Fourth Artillery, then stationed at Fort Randall, Dakota. From here he went to New York to join his company of the Third Infantry which had arrived from Texas, and he there ascertained that it had been surrendered by General Twiggs to the State authorities, and the men paroled. Five of the companies of the regiment were at Washington, and after considerable delay Lieutenant Penrose secured his orders and transportation to go to the Capital where he arrived two days before the first battle of Bull Run, and found his regiment encamped at Arlington, the commanding officer being Major (afterward Major-General) George Sykes. The regulars were soon after brought to Washington and put on provost duty, and Lieutenant Penrose was selected for duty in the Secret Service. Just after the battle of Ball's Bluff he was called to Philadelphia by Lieutenant-Colonel Weister of the First California Regiment (Colonel Baker's), afterward known as the Seventy-first Pennsylvania, and was tendered the colonelcy of the regiment. This was a great surprise to the young officer, but learning that he had been recommended by some of the oldest and best officers in the army, he consented to accept it. Days passed and weeks flew by until at last one Sunday, while attending church, a telegram was brought to him asking why he did not come and take command. The telegram further stated that Colonel Weister had his commission and the order from army headquarters to proceed to the regiment. This was a matter of extraordinary importance to Penrose, and going to the adjutant-general with the telegram, that officer, much confused, said he would see about it. At midnight that same night marching orders were received, and nothing more was heard of the order until the army had reached Harrison's Landing, when an investigation revealed the fact that the order had been issued but General Sykes pigeon-holed it, as he was opposed to any officer of his command leaving it. During the Peninsula campaign the colonelcy of three other regiments were offered him, but the same power intervened to prevent his taking either of them. Sometime in January, 1863, General Torbert, then commanding the First New Jersey Brigade, sent for Penrose, and asked him if he would take a regiment. He explained the difficulty of getting away from Sykes, but on Torbert's assurance that he would take care of that part of it, Penrose accepted. Some time went by and the matter had about passed from his mind when a note from General Torbert informed him that he had his commission as colonel of the Fifteenth Regiment New Jersey Volunteers, and the order for him to take command would be issued at once. Penrose received his order and was in the performance of his new duties before Sykes knew anything about it. From this time on the record of Colonel Penrose is that of the Fifteenth Regiment. Its forced march from Manchester to Gettysburg with the Sixth Corps, is recorded elsewhere in the pages of this book. Colonel Penrose's own recollections of what transpired when the column reached Rock Creek, are thus described by himself. As no record of the exploit appears in the history of the Fifteenth Regiment, it is given in full here. General Penrose says:

"We had arrived none too soon. Our troops had been repulsed at almost every point, the fate of the army trembled in the balance. Canteens had hardly been filled when the order came to cross. The bluffs on the opposite side were steep, the water deep, but nothing could stop those brave men. In we went, and up the steep ascent on the other side. I was leading the brigade with the gallant Fifteenth. Hardly had I reached the level ground beyond when Captain Whittier, personal aid-de-camp to General Sedgwick, rode up in great haste and saying to me, 'Penrose, for God's sake get to the front as quick as you can; cut loose and follow me, everything is gone to the devil!' I put the men on a dog trot. Meeting a column crossing our track I gave the order to close up and cut through it, which was promptly obeyed. I followed on and came into line just in rear of the Third Regulars, who were on the right of the Fifth Corps—our lines had been driven to the crest of the hill. The situation was everything but encouraging. Regular formation of the troops engaged there was none. Every man appeared to be fighting on his own hook, but with a determination not to yield one inch further. An incident occurred just at this time, which in my opinion had great weight in the result of that day's fight. As I went into line a man approached me having as prisoner a Confederate colonel mounted. The man asked me where headquarters were. I pointed out the corps flag in a field to the rear. The colonel then addressed me as follows: 'For God's sake, how big is this —— Catholic corps?' (having reference to our corps badge, a Greek cross.) I answered 'Why?,' He replied, 'You were thirty miles from here last night. We saw your colors (corps) coming over the hill, and the orders for our reinforcements to be pushed in were countermanded.' It will thus be seen that our timely arrival checked a movement that, had it been made, would have given them the crest of the hill, and cut our army in two. As soon as my line was formed it was moved forward. Going over the weary and worn out troops in our front, down the hill we went at a thundering pace, driving every thing before us, across the swamp at its foot, through the woods, never stopping until we reached a house just on the edge of the wheat-field, where the enemy made a decided stand. Here also stood an entire battery, every horse killed. The enemy had captured it in the afternoon, but had had no time to take it from the field. Here I halted, as night was coming on, and I could see none of our troops on my right or left. Covering these guns with our rifles, I deployed two companies to my right before I made a connection with our troops, finding them to be part of General Wheaton's command which had gone in on my right. Six companies were deployed to my left before finding any one to connect with; it was then, if I remember right, with the Twelfth Regulars. Here we lay all night, but at the first peep of day

I advanced and took the house and secured the battery. In this position we remained until about 12 m. of the third when I was relieved by the Third Regulars, and after considerable search found and joined my brigade about 3 p. m. In the last day's fight the brigade was not called into action, and the Fifteenth was the only regiment of the brigade that took part in the fighting on that memorable field. The advanced position gained on the night of the second by the Fifteenth was the same that had been occupied by the Third Corps, and from which they had been driven, speaks louder than words for their gallantry. Their steadiness under most trying circumstances, speaks volumes for the discipline for which the regiment was noted, and thus ended our share, of no insignificant value, in the turning and decisive battle of the war."

On the tenth day of May, 1864, Colonel Penrose was assigned to the command of the First Brigade by order of General Grant, approved by the President. This was a mark of distinction seldom conferred upon a junior officer, and is probably the only instance of the kind in the Army of the Potomac, except in the case of general officers to command the army. On the nineteenth of October, 1864, Colonel Penrose was brevetted brigadier-general of United States Volunteers. He is now major of the Twelfth Infantry United States Army, and is stationed at Fort Sully, Dakota Territory.

## MAJOR A. JUDSON CLARK.

A. Judson Clark, commander of Battery " B," First New Jersey Artillery, was born in Fayetteville, N. Y., October, 1838, and became a citizen of Newark in 1860, where he began the study of medicine. Enlisted April, 1861, for three months under the first call for seventy-five thousand men and was made sergeant of Company F, First Regiment New Jersey Volunteers. At the expiration of his term of service assisted in organizing and putting into the field the second battery of light artillery (Battery " B "

First New Jersey), then known as Beam's battery, being commissioned as first lieutenant. After the death of Captain John E. Beam was promoted captain and the battery was afterward known as Clark's battery. Throughout the whole period of the war the battery was prominently engaged in every important battle except that of Antietam and won a splendid reputation for its fighting and staying qualities. At Chancellorsville Captain Clark was placed in command of the First Division Artillery, Third Army Corps. When the attack on the Eleventh Corps was made by Jackson, Clark's battery was at Hazel Grove firing on the Furnace road. The enemy came through to the right of Sickles' corps, and in close pursuit of Howard's fleeing troops. The battery was immediately turned around, and began firing to the rear with canister which enabled Pleasonton to form his line. At Gettysburg Captain Clark was with his battery during all of the terrific firing of the second of July, and the gallant conduct of the battery on that occasion is well attested by the frequent mention, in the official reports, of its splendid services. At the close of the day's engagement Colonel Randolph, chief of artillery of the Third Corps, was wounded and Captain Clark was appointed to that office which he held until just before the fight at Mine Run when Randolph returned to duty. At the fight at Ream's Station in front of Petersburg Captain Clark was slightly wounded in the forehead by a minié ball. When the terms of service of the three year members of the battery who had not reënlisted expired, Captain Clark accompanied them to Trenton where they were mustered out, and immediately afterward returned to the battery remaining with it until the close of the war. At the time of the surrender the battery was in position in the line of the Second Corps, to which it then belonged. Captain Clark was specially recommended to the President for promotion by General Sickles for bravery and gallantry at Chancellorsville and Gettysburg, and in 1864, General Hunt, chief of artillery Army of the Potomac, General Birney, General Mott and others sent strong letters to the State authorities urging that the several batteries of the State be given a field officer and recommending Captain Clark for the place, and in 1865, General Mott sent the following additional appeal to the Governor, but for some reason or other was not complied with. The following is General Mott's letter :

HEADQUARTERS THIRD DIVISION, SECOND ARMY CORPS,
May 21, 1865.

*Governor :*
As New Jersey has five batteries in the service, and no field officer—four being entitled to a major—allow me to call your attention to Captain A. Judson Clark, Battery "B," as an officer justly entitled to the position. Captain Clark has served since 1861, is the senior artillery officer from the State, and has on all occasions conducted himself in an efficient and gallant manner. He is about leaving the service, as his battery is to be mustered out, and a recognition of his services by the State will be a just reward for gallant and meritorious conduct in the field.

I take great pleasure in making this recommendation as the captain has served under, with or near my command in almost all of the actions of the Army of the Potomac.

Very respectfully, your obedient servant,
G. MOTT, Brevet Major-General.

His Excellency Joel Parker, Governor, etc.

Captain Clark was brevetted major of United States Volunteers for gallant and meritorious services in front of Petersburg, by Congress, to date from April 2, 1865. Since the war Major Clark's signal abilities have been recognized by his own people who have repeatedly appointed him to responsible positions, first as chief of police of the city of Newark, then as secretary of the Board of Assessments and Revision of Taxes, and as Receiver of Taxes. He is also a prominent officer in the National Guard of the State.

## MAJOR WILLIAM W. MORRIS.

Major William Wallace Morris was born in the city of New York in 1830, and in 1832 his parents took up their residence in the city of Newark. His ancestors on his mother's side were Huguenots, who settled in Canada in the sixteenth century, after the massacre of Paris, France. His paternal ancestry were of the Morrises who immigrated from Wales, and settled in Monmouth county, New Jersey, in 1669. His great grandfathers on both sides were soldiers during the Revolutionary War from 1776 to 1783, and in the war of 1812 and 1814 both fought against the British. Many of the male members of the family had fought in every war on this continent except in the war with Mexico. Major Morris was educated in private schools, and learned the coach, harness and saddlery business and was superintendent of a large factory at the time of his enlistment. When a stripling, he joined the old Lafayette Guards as a private, and subsequently became Ensign, and afterward joined the City Battalion under Major Carter. In 1861 Major Morris raised a company and was about to offer their services to the government when a severe family affliction compelled him to defer his departure to the field. In August, 1862, under the call for ten thousand men he recruited Company A, Twenty-sixth Regiment New Jersey Volunteers, having enlisted as a private soldier, and was so mustered in September 3d. Subsequently he was elected captain of the company, and was mustered in the United States service September 18th. He left with his regiment for the front from Camp Frelinghuysen September 26, 1862, and was promoted major November 19th following, and mustered in December 6, 1862. He took part in the battle of Fredericksburg, under General Burnside December 13th and 14th, acting as colonel of the regiment a considerable part of the time, having but one staff officer to assist him—Sergeant-Major Amos J. Cummings, the regiment numbering nine hundred and seventy-five men present. Major Morris was one of the storming column at Fredericksburg Heights, and participated in the battle of Salem Church May 3d and the battle of Salem Heights or Banks' Ford May 4, 1863. At the storming of the rifle pits at "Franklin's Crossing," three miles below Fredericksburg, June 5, 1863, he was acting as lieutenant-colonel.

During the great draft riot in New York and Newark in July, 1863, when the Newark "Mercury" newspaper office owned by ex-Sheriff E. N. Miller, and his residence was attacked by a mob—Sheriff Miller being at that time provost marshal of the district—Major Morris offered his services which were gladly accepted, and Sheriff Miller commissioned him to organize a body of veterans, secure arms and make arrangements with the military district commander, General Wool, to put down the enemies of peace and good order. Major Morris organized some four hundred men, and many of his brother officers rallied around him, among whom were Captains Fordham, P. F. Rogers, John Hunkele, John McIntee, Mark Sears, Lieutenant Rochus Heinisch, and others. Before the arrangements with General Wool were fully completed the riot in New York was put down and that in Newark speedily ended.

## LIEUTENANT ROCHUS HEINISCH.

Lieutenant Rochus Heinisch was born in the city of Newark, N. J., December, 1835. He was educated in private schools, and was brought up in manufacturing and business pursuits, following the cutlery business in his father's factory. At the age of seventeen he joined the Putnam Horse Guards, a famous battalion of mounted men, commanded by Major Heinisch, the father of Rochus. Subsequently he joined Company B, Newark City Battalion, and during the war enlisted as a private soldier in Company A, Twenty-sixth New Jersey Volunteers. He was afterward elected second lieutenant and was promoted first lieutenant in the field. He participated in the several engagements of his regiment, and was a faithful and a brave soldier. At the advance of the Twenty-sixth across the Rappahannock on June 5th, Lieutenant Heinisch was one of the very first to enter the rebel earth works. At the expiration of his term of service he reëntered business life, and served two terms in the House of Assembly of the New Jersey Legislature.

## COLONEL HUGH H. JANEWAY.

Hugh H. Janeway was born in New Brunswick, N. J. He went into the service as first lieutenant of Company L, First New Jersey Cavalry, and soon became noted for his daring as well as for his other strong soldierly qualities. He was devoid of fear, and many are the incidents related of his personal encounters with the enemy, and his adventures. He had been in the service but a short time when he went on a scouting expedition and meeting with a body of the enemy he boldly charged into them. Janeway himself was wounded in seven different places, and was left for dead, but his wounds, though severe, were none of them fatal, and his reappearance among his men for duty a short time after was hailed with great joy. February 19, 1862, Janeway was promoted captain; on January 27, 1863, major; July 6, 1864, lieutenant-colonel, and on October 11, 1864, colonel of the First Cavalry. During some of the encounters with the enemy at Trevillian's Station Colonel Janeway was wounded, but he soon after returned and took command of his regiment. In the Weldon Railroad expedition in December, 1864, the First New Jersey bore a conspicuous part. Nearing Hicksford, where the road to Gaston and Raleigh branches off from the Weldon line, a force of the enemy was found in strong works, defending the crossing of the Meherin river. The works were covered by a thick wood extending for a mile along the road ; and along the skirts of a wood a body of cavalry was posted. Colonel Janeway sent forward Captain Brooks to charge these men and clear the way. Pyne, in his description of this action, says :

"Of course no Southern cavalry then in the field could stand against a charge in which Robbins, Brooks and Craig were all engaged. Along a narrow road, breaking off here and there to pursue a fugitive visible through the trees, the Fifth Squadron swept forward at the run; until the road took a sudden twist, and lost itself in an abbatis of felled trees, perfectly impassable for horses. From the rifle-pits along the front of the rebel works a heavy fire was poured into the squadron as soon as it appeared. Robbins received a bullet through the hat, which grazed his head; Craig and Johnson had their horses shot and some of the men were unhorsed in like manner; but Brooks, covering his men as well as possible, held his position until the rest of the brigade came up. Then Sargent, with the First Massachusetts, was ordered to make a charge. Nothing could be more gallantly attempted; but it was wild to hope for any success so long as the enemy were not frightened from their guns. Sargent fell dead from his horse before they took the gallop; and the regiment pulled up in confusion, with the loss of several horses and some men. Then Janeway and the rest of the New Jersey took the field. Janeway was in his element at once. There never was a quiet-mannered man who took more delight in fighting, whether mounted or on foot; and no one ever did his work more thoroughly and with more perfect management of the troops under his command. As a consequence the regiment was always ready to do what he directed with a confidence that made them irresistible. Dismounting his whole force under cover of the woods, he charged them straight into the rifle-pits, over ditches and fallen trees, under a heavy fire of musketry and artillery from the woods behind. Nothing would have been more after Janeway's heart than a charge onward into the rebel forts, a quarter of a mile beyond."

At Dinwiddie Court House Janeway was in the very thickest of the fighting and Davies, who commanded the brigade, being wounded, Janeway succeeded him only to be wounded in turn. Soon recovering Janeway was again with his regiment, and at Five Forks distinguished himself by his bravery. At Amelia Springs, the regiment again encountered the enemy, and Colonel Janeway immediately ordered a charge, in leading which he was shot through the head, and died almost instantly. This was April 5, 1865, but four days before the surrender of Lee at Appomattox. Colonel Janeway had endeared himself to every man in his command, and no braver soldier, truer patriot, or courteous gentleman ever perished on the field of battle than he.

## COLONEL PERCY WYNDHAM.

Sir Percy Wyndham, colonel of the First New Jersey Cavalry (Sixteenth Regiment New Jersey Volunteers), was a member of an ennobled English family, son of Captain Charles Wyndham, of the Fifth Light Cavalry of the English army, and born on board the ship "Arab" in "the Downs," September 22, 1833. When but fifteen years of age he entered the "Students' Corps" in Paris, and took part in the French revolution of 1848. In July of that year he was transferred, at his own request, to the navy, and given the rank of ensign of marines. He resigned his commission in the French navy, April 7, 1850, and in the following year entered the artillery branch of the English army. Resigning in October, 1852, he received the commission of a second lieutenant in the Eighth Austrian

Lancers in December following. He served a period of two years, being promoted first lieutenant on April 15 1854, and squadron commander shortly afterward.

On May 1, 1860, he resigned from the Austrian service to enter the Italian, and was commissioned a captain on the twentieth. He greatly distinguished himself by his dashing gallantry in the battles of Palermo, Nuloggo, Rager and Capua. On July 20th he was promoted to the rank of major and placed in command of his regiment, and on October 1, to that of lieutenant-colonel on the field before Capua and given command of a brigade by General Garibaldi in person. He was knighted on the field by King Victor Emanuel and appointed a chevalier of the Military Order of Savoy. Colonel Wyndham remained in command of his brigade till October 8, 1861, when he obtained a leave of absence for twelve months and came to the United States to offer his services to the Federal Government.

Early in the month of February, 1862, upon the special recommendation of General McClellan and by the appointment of the Governor, he became Colonel of the First New Jersey Cavalry. He assumed command of the regiment on the 9th, and called upon officers and men alike to aid him in securing the most efficient condition by a strict obedience to orders and thorough military discipline. The joint influence of Colonel Wyndham and Lieutenant-Colonel Kargé was felt almost immediately, and by the middle of May the regiment was performing meritorious military service. On the afternoon of June 6, the regiment drove the enemy through the village of Harrisonburgh, Va., and fell into an ambuscade in the woods, to the southeast of the town, in which Colonel Wyndham was captured and considerable loss sustained; the colonel soon afterward escaped. October 30, a skirmish took place between a detachment of cavalry under command of Colonel Wyndham and a force of rebels stationed at Thoroughfare Gap, resulting in the retirement of the latter to the almost impassable hills in the vicinity; and on February 2, 1863, Colonel Wyndham surprised Warrenton, Va. He took part in General Stahl's reconnoissance, leading the advance in the attack upon the enemy at Snicker's Ferry, and during the raid of General Stoneman through Virginia in April and May, 1863, he commanded the cavalry which took possession of Columbia.

The regiment was on almost constant duty from the day Colonel Wyndham took command, scouting, raiding and fighting; while its impetuous leader was time and again placed at the head of a brigade when services of an extraordinary character were to be attempted. He was severely wounded in the battle of Brandy Station, June 9, 1863, and was mustered out of the service on July 5, 1864, when he opened a military school in New York city at which he was doing fairly well. Wyndham, however, was an adventurer, of a roving disposition, and when war broke out in Europe—1866-1867—he gave up his school, joined the Italian army and was appointed by Garibaldi a member of his staff. At the close of this war he returned to New York and with an Italian chemist, engaged in petroleum refining. An explosion of one of the large stills ruined them, and Wyndham went to Calcutta where he started the well-known comic paper "The Indian Charivari." While in Calcutta he organized an Italian opera company, and married a rich widow. It would be natural to find him now settling down for the remainder of his days, but married life evidently possessed little attraction for him, as soon after that event he went into lumber operations, and in speculation in timber forests at Mandalay lost all he had made in Calcutta. He then attempted to induce the Burmese Government to cultivate cotton on a large scale, and while they praised his schemes and promised generous aid in putting his ideas into execution, they did not provide him with any means to carry them out. He then became a hanger-on of the court at Mandalay and suffered many indignities at their hands. He had become reduced to great poverty, and had pawned his jewels and decorations to get money enough to pay his debts. While at Mandalay he constructed an immense balloon and hoped by giving exhibition ascensions to be able to amass sufficient means to release his decorations, but his first ascension led to his death in the following tragic manner, as described in the Rangoon (India) "Gazette" of January 27, 1879:

"How little did a single soul among that vast crowd of people assembled on Saturday last in and about Dalhousie Park to witness the balloon ascension, which had been advertised for the last two months and more, imagine that they would be spectators—nay, participators—of a tragedy which resulted in the death of one of the most adventurous men of the day. Throughout the whole day one stream of human beings had flowed toward the Royal Lakes, on the margin of which Colonel Wyndham's balloon had been inflated. The balloon was about seventy feet in height and at the largest part ninety or one hundred feet in circumference, made of common white shirting with a coat of waterproof varnish and a somewhat slight network of thin ropes over it, the ends of which were tied around the edge of the wickerwork car in which the aeronaut was to take his seat. Crowds of all caste and degree, from the fashionable European lady and gentleman to the veriest cooly who could afford a few annas for entrance money, went around the baloon, examined its exterior, peered into its interior through its wide mouth and criticised it or expressed their wonder. About a quarter past six o'clock Colonel Wyndham got into his car, in which four small bags of sand and some refreshments had been previously placed. Colonel Wyndham having given the signal to those who held it down, the balloon was gently released and rose, swaying for a short while from side to side then straightening itself and rising majestically upward. When it had reached an altitude of about three hundred feet it was seen to burst—open out—and then to collapse, the whole falling into the lake about a hundred yards from the bank, the remnants of the balloon falling over the car which contained Colonel Wyndham. A lot of boats pulled as fast as possible to the spot, but owing to the vast spread of cloth presented by the fragments of the balloon, it was full ten minutes before Colonel Wyndham's body could be recovered. It was immediately conveyed ashore, where it was placed in the hands of Doctors Oswald and Johnstone, but although they exerted themselves for over an hour all efforts to restore animation proved unavailing. It is the opinion of medical men from the appearance presented by the body, the bleeding from the nose and the peculiar nature of the accident, that before reaching the water he had been asphyxiated by the rushing out of the hot air or gas from the balloon. As to the causes of the balloon's collapse there can be little question. It was made two years ago of flimsy white shirting, not improved by keeping, which when inflated showed several cracks or rents in it. These flaws, when pointed out to him, Colonel Wyndham said were nothing; he had gone up in balloons with holes the size of a man's head. Thus ended a singular and adventurous career."

www.ingramcontent.com/pod-product-compliance
Lightning Source LLC
Chambersburg PA
CBHW032142010526
44111CB00035B/898